R E C O N

S P H E R E S

Reconfigured
Spheres

FEMINIST

EXPLORATIONS

OF LITERARY

SPACE

Edited by
Margaret R. Higonnet
and
Joan Templeton

University of Massachusetts Press
Amherst

Frontispiece: As a nature within nature, Merian's Mother Earth nourishes male twins, progenitors of the Roman Empire in *Atalanta Fugiens.*

Copyright © 1994 by
The University of Massachusetts Press
All rights reserved
Printed in the United States of America
LC 94-16551
ISBN 0-87023-937-6 (cloth); 938-4 (pbk.)
Designed by Jack Harrison
Printed and bound by Thomson-Shore, Inc.

Library of Congress Cataloging-in-Publication Data
Reconfigured spheres : feminist explorations of literary space /
edited by Margaret R. Higonnet and Joan Templeton.
p.   cm.
Includes bibliographical references (p.   ).
ISBN 0-87023-937-6 (alk. paper). — ISBN 0-87023-938-4 (pbk. : alk. paper)
1. Feminist literary criticism.   2. Women in literature.
3. Space and time in literature.   4. Setting (Literature).
I. Higonnet, Margaret R.   II. Templeton, Joan, date.
PN98.W64R43   1994
809'.93352042—dc20   94-16551
CIP

British Library Cataloguing in Publication Data are available.

So, the map revives her words—THOMAS HARDY

Margaret Randolph Cardwell (1908–1991)
Alice Pomeroy Templeton (1916–1964)

CONTENTS

Contributors

DEBRA A. CASTILLO, associate professor of Romance studies and comparative literature at Cornell University, specializes in contemporary Hispanic literature, women's studies, and postcolonial literary theory. In addition to numerous essays, she has published *The Translated World: A Postmodern Tour of Libraries in Literature* (1984) and *Talking Back: Strategies for a Latin American Feminist Literary Criticism* (1992). Editor of *Diacritics* for five years, she is currently book review editor of *Letras femeninas*.

BARBARA HARLOW, associate professor of English and comparative literature at the University of Texas, Austin, has published *Resistance Literature* (1987) and *Barred: Women, Writing and Political Detention* (1992). She has also written essays on cultural politics and critical theory, with special reference to "Third World" literature.

MARGARET R. HIGONNET, professor of English at the University of Connecticut, has published *The Horn of Oberon* and articles on romantic literature and literary theory. She has edited a journal on children's literature (1985–90), as well as three volumes of essays (on Thomas Hardy, gender and the two world wars, and the representation of women in fiction). Another collection, *Borderwork: Feminist Engagements with Comparative Literature,* is in press.

INDIRA KARAMCHETI, assistant professor at Wesleyan University, writes on literary authority in postcolonial literature, the postcolonial as teacher, and translation of "Third World" texts. With a colleague, she has translated the collected plays of Aimé Césaire. Her current project is a book about the development of postcolonial studies in U.S. academia.

KATHLEEN L. KOMAR is professor of German and comparative literature and associate dean at the University of California, Los Angeles. A specialist in modern German and American literature, she has published articles on contemporary women writers, as well as *Pattern and Chaos: Multilinear Novels by Dos Passos, Faulkner, Döblin, and Koeppen* (1983) and *Transcending Angels: Rainer Maria Rilke's "Duino Elegies"* (1987). She is completing a book on contemporary women writers entitled *Re-Visions of the Women of the Trojan War*.

JANE MARCUS, distinguished professor of English at CUNY Graduate Center and the City College of New York, is author of *Virginia Woolf and the Languages of Patriarchy* and *Art and Anger*, as well as editor of three volumes of feminist criticism on Woolf. A visiting fellow at Clare Hall in 1993–94, she is working on *Britannia Rules the Waves*, a study of modernism and imperialism, supported by a Guggenheim.

CARLA L. PETERSON, associate professor of comparative literature at the University of Maryland, has published *The Determined Reader* (1986) and articles on French and American literature. *Doers of the Word*, a study of African American women travelers and activists in the nineteenth century, is forthcoming.

EVA MARIA STADLER, associate professor of comparative literature and film, directs the Media Studies Program at Fordham University. She has published articles on Diderot, Proust and fashion, avant-garde cinema, African film, and Robert Bresson and she coedited *Premiers textes littéraires*. She is completing a book on the films of Robert Bresson.

JOAN TEMPLETON is professor of English and comparative literature at the Brooklyn Center of Long Island University. Her work on Ibsen and other modern dramatists has appeared in *PMLA, Modern Drama, Scandinavian Studies, Themes in Drama*, and *Contemporary Approaches to Ibsen*. She is completing a book-length study, *Ibsen and His Women*.

ANCA VLASOPOLOS is associate professor of English at Wayne State University. She is the author of *The Symbolic Method of Coleridge, Baudelaire, and Yeats* and of articles on Mary Wollstonecraft, *Frankenstein*, Virginia Woolf, Shakespeare, Yeats, Tennessee Williams, and the "woman's" film. She has also published poems in *Interim, Seneca Review, Wascana Review*, and *Moving Out*, and a poetry chapbook, *The Evidence of Spring*.

RECONFIGURED

SPHERES

MARGARET R. HIGONNET

New Cartographies, an Introduction

You must know many lands to be at home on earth.—Novalis

In fact, as a woman, I have no country. As a woman I want no country.—Virginia Woolf

Space is a challenging topic for comparative literary analyses and for feminist analyses as well. Comparatists have underscored the importance of knowing "many lands," cultures, and literatures; they have widely assumed the possibility of being "at home on earth." By contrast, feminist thinkers have called attention to physical images such as the "angel in the house" that imply the domestic confinement of women. They have asked why women have not been able to hold property, to travel freely, to define the shape of a nation, or to enter certain social arenas outside the home. In response to Woolf one may ask how many women have historically had full citizenship in any country at all?[1] "A place on the map," as Adrienne Rich has written, "is also a place in history" where writers, women and men, stand in the fullness of their identities and create texts.[2] It is not happenstance that this volume is the brainchild of the first feminist session of the International Comparative Literature Association, whose leitmotif was "literary space."[3] That workshop drew on a comparative perspective to raise questions about the literary representation of space as a gendered phenomenon.

The implications of *space,* which intertwine physical, social, and political territories, offer particularly rich material for feminist analysis today. Recent years have witnessed the tearing down of many walls, both political and critical, in a transformation that for the makers of atlases has been dizzyingly profitable. These changes have fostered the recognition that local material arrangements carry cultural meanings, and meanings that are especially visible in the physical sites occupied by family, education, and labor. Fresh work on gender and geography in the form of atlases and demographic history has begun to record the uneven distribution of social, economic, and esthetic resources across lines of gender, race, age, and class. These variegated territorial arrangements have provoked investigations in the fields of anthropology, history, architecture, and that of primary interest here: literature.[4] The essays gathered in this volume address both the spatial symbolisms that organize prose fiction and drama and the spatial metaphors that shape critical discourses.

Feminist literary critics have begun to undertake new cartographies, to trace the ways writers inscribe gender onto the symbolic representations of space within texts, whether through images of physical confinement, of exile and exclusions, of property and territoriality, or of the body as the interface between individual and communal identities. Whereas a seventeenth-century writer might lay out sexual relations on a *carte du tendre,* twentieth-century critics have begun to examine the ways maps of gender overlap with other maps of status. In response to such new work, this volume looks at questions that thread through historical and cultural differences in literary representation.

Behind the work collected in this volume, which ranges from eighteenth-century European novels to postcolonial contemporary literatures, lies a set of premises and debates about spatial symbolism, about the "natural" assignment of men and women to physical places and social strata, assignments that may be further complicated by other marks of status. This introduction traces some of the general historical debates out of which arise the specifically literary topics studied in *Reconfigured Spheres.*

Past definitions of a gender division in symbolic and physical space have often been binary, deriving from or reconstructing anthropological oppositions between masculine and feminine aspects of culture. According to Robert Hertz, "Primitive thought attributes a sex to all beings in the universe and even to inanimate objects; all of them are divided into two immense classes according to whether they are considered as male or female." He pointed to the example of the Maori, who distinguish *tama tane,* the male side (representing virility, the east, the right hand, and aggression), from *tama wahine,* the female side (representing the west, the left hand, and self-defense). "In general, man is scared, woman is profane: excluded from ceremonies, she is admitted to them only for a function characteristic of her status . . . the two sexes correspond to the sacred and to the profane (or impure), to life and to death."[5] Mary Douglas elaborated on these observations, moving beyond an implied contrast between "primitive" and "civilized" thought in her study *Purity and Danger* (1966). She noted the complex dualisms in symbolic forms of organization, many of them anchored in images of bodily space, that may at once designate women as pure and relegate them to the polluted margins of society.[6]

This volume does not propose a reverse discourse that strikes blows with the left hand, as Walter Benjamin puts it, or simply inverts the values of center and margin. Rather, it sets out to analyze certain cultural "maps" of gender that inform texts and the corresponding "legends" or codes that guide our readings of texts. Some of the categories we ourselves use derive from the discourse of social history—for example, the distinction between public and private spheres; the sumptuary laws governing the dress of different classes, professions, and sexes; or the legal and de facto creation of segregated housing. These historical categories shape the themes and representational strategies of much modern Western literature. Other models of analysis that bring space into focus in a multiplicity of literatures derive from psychoanalysis, myth criticism, and postcolonial studies.

Historians have cast a spotlight on the ideological distinction between private and public spheres of action that was elaborated in the course of the eighteenth century in Europe, when these categories took their present gendered form.[7] The concept of the private on which the dichotomy rests arose in tandem with bourgeois concepts of individualism. By contrast, a very different spatial organization of the social order shaped medieval households or life on plantations run with slave labor. The institutional spaces within which women's creativity might flourish have also shifted through time, from religious communities and courts to the home, each with its own particular structures of confinement and communication.[8]

The Enlightenment discourse of "proper spheres" opposed an ideal of women's virtuous domestic retirement to the scandal of women's visibility in public life, a scandal of which figures like Olympe de Gouges and Mary Wollstonecraft were conspicuous instances. Writers such as Jean Jacques Rousseau in *Emile* (1762), Pierre Roussel in *Système physique et morale de la femme* (1775), Antoine Léonard Thomas in *Essai sur les caractères, les moeurs et l'esprit des femmes dans les différents siècles* (1773), Immanuel Kant in *Observations on the Feelings of the Beautiful and the Sublime,* and the Montagnard Amar (an influential misogynist member of the French revolutionary Convention) all insisted on women's "natural" weakness and maternal destiny and their concomitant maladaptation to serious study or public activity. A circumscribed woman's sphere was theorized in order to distinguish the roles of women and men and to explain their different statuses. Even women's bodies were reanatomized (using skeletons deformed by corsets and drawing on artistic models such as the Venus de Medici) in order to justify by small skulls, narrow ribs, and wide hips, as well as by menstruation and childbirth, women's consignment to a sphere of action separate from that of men.[9]

To be sure, liberal thinkers like Condorcet and Olympe de Gouges in France, Theodore Hippel and Caroline Schlegel-Schelling in Germany, and Mary Wollstonecraft and John Stuart Mill in England resisted the political and educational discriminations that flowed from the doctrine of separate spheres. Recent historians of the nineteenth century have shown that the would-be boundaries never became absolute in actual European and American education or labor practices. Although manufacture moved out of the household economy, peasant women continued to do agricultural work by the sides of men; some middle- and upper-class women left the home to become involved in public religious and political causes such as Methodism and the abolition movement.[10] While the poorest women lived in quarters so cramped that segregation by sex was scarcely possible and privacy a dream, the architecture of wealthy women's "private" domains subdivided into private and public arenas, such as dressing rooms and salons. The home had a very different configuration of private and public for a mistress or a maid, for an aristocrat or a peasant, "upstairs" and "downstairs," in a city or on the land.

Nonetheless, images of separate gender, class, and racial terrains gained great power in Europe and America: they helped to regulate the intersection of these categories in social relations and to form people's sense of their own identity in the nineteenth and twentieth centuries. A telling example of this imaginative and institutional power is offered by the imagery of Virginia Woolf's *A Room of One's Own,* in which she depicts her anger and dismay when she faces a looming patriarchal beadle and finds herself barred, first from a college lawn and then from the library. Such physical disbarment is of a piece with intellectual and political disenfranchisement, a process whose instruments may be institutional, psychological, or material.[11] The force, mutability, and buried contradictions of the spatial organization of gender since the Enlightenment have made the subject a particularly fertile one for students of the modern period.

One premise of the writers of this book, then, is the widespread symbolic gendering of certain types of physical and social space as masculine or feminine. Representations of individual identity and of presence in society often coincide in the body. We therefore begin, in Rich's phrase, "not with a continent or a country or a house, but with the geography closest in—the body" (212). Images of the body (perceived as both public and private terrain), along with codes governing dress and behavior, "correlate closely to social categories and the distribution of power."[12] The exploited body is one of the pages on which imperial maps of power, whether political, religious, or economic, are drawn. In a passage cited here by Anca Vlasopolos, Virginia Woolf refers ironically to patriarchy's passion for "converting" a "fine negress" and for laying claim to "a piece of land or a man with curly black hair" (52). Woolf's suggestive juxtaposition of terms points to the imperialist usurpation of world territory (as well as the local organization of domestic areas) on lines of sex, race, and religion; she reminds us of the enslavement and rapes that are hidden by sophistries about improving other races. As Jane Marcus argues here in response, however, Woolf is unconscious of her own complicity with a system that demarcates property, racial difference, and power through the gaze and through linguistic inflections.

The figure of the woman's body and its ability to move are regulated by the factors of race, nationality, wealth, and political power. Just as nations are powerfully "imagined communities," so too, Debra Castillo shows in this volume, the territorial fusions recorded in the racial tints of mestizas are both shaped and contested by "imaginary geographies." For the Mexican author Federico Campbell, the grace of seals can suggest the power, freedom, and elusiveness of a U.S. woman who is able to slip past or fly over border controls. Yet for Campbell as well as for the Mexican American writer Ana Castillo, the cut of the border also connects to cuts of the body: abortion and death inscribe limits to a woman's sexual freedom. Many twentieth-century writers such as Alice Walker and Christa Wolf,

Kathleen Komar argues here, depict rape as the ultimate usurpation of female space. In order to escape confinement in the body and its violation, a writer like Monique Wittig may imaginatively spin wings and webs from the female body, a use of interconnecting physical imagery symptomatic of a lesbian utopian enterprise.

One crucial marker in the system governing representation of the body is clothing. In her study here of eighteenth-century novels Eva Stadler shows how costume can function as a screen that segregates male from female or public from private, and at the same time as a locus of self-inscription and performance.[13] The grammar of dress is regulated by rules governing distinctions between classes and sexual statuses (virgin/wife/prostitute/widow). Apparel ("habits") as a semiotic system refers to character, class, history, and trade; it must be read as an instrument of social communication, action, and segregation. Clothes are both property and indicators of propriety. When women have no property at all, the only space that (however dubiously) belongs to them may be that of their own bodies, a space defined by its vestimentary envelope, strictly policed yet often violated.

The eighteenth-century role of dress may be compared to the representation of dress codes in a late twentieth-century novel, *The Mixquiahuala Letters,* discussed here by Debra Castillo. This fictional exchange of letters between two women of color from the United States explores issues of national, racial, and gender identity through a series of border crossings. While the protagonists start from a sense of displacement by their color within white American culture, to their dismay they find themselves legible as gringas in Mexico, because they are traveling in blue jeans—and unaccompanied. Apparel that seemed unmarked by class becomes marked when transplanted culturally; the universal sartorial passport becomes a label for precisely that identity they would reject. And the external label changes the meaning of their bodies, suggesting that they are not subjects but sexual objects.

If the body seems to be an obvious site of social inscription, the vaguer locus of a domestic sphere, so important to historical analysis, may seem to lack material specificity. Does the mobility of a social circle mean we cannot *locate* it? The figure may vaporize into an abstraction, but allusions to territories, margins, outsiders, or one's place should not be lightly dismissed: they "are not just metaphors, but names of actual spatial devices that maintain hierarchies of power and privilege."[14] Powerful texts by men and women alike dramatize relationships between parties of unequal power by describing sites of action. Richardson, for example, stages his narratives of seduction and resistance through images of confinement, abduction, and escape. Charlotte Brontë depicts the thirst not just for "a room of one's own" but for room itself, in the fires that break out in the heart of Jane Eyre and in the attic of her alter ego.[15]

The configuration of spatial arrangements in any particular text reflects the distinctive cultural hierarchies it records. It is a familiar observation that in one culture men may comfortably touch one another in conversation and embrace, whereas another culture may censure such spatial behaviors and encode them as gay. As readers become more attuned to such differences through comparative cultural analyses, they can begin to recognize local factors such as legal patterns of property ownership, the cultural and class control of private and public terrains, or the geographic marginalization of the poor and subaltern from metropolitan centers of power. Spatial arrangements have special economic and psychological force in narratives of bourgeois female "self-development." As Joan Templeton and Anca Vlasopolos point out here, the transgression of social norms that shapes a tragic narrative outcome is often figured as a fall or drift away from social moorings. This is not to say that symbolic meanings are fixed on a gendered map. To the contrary, protected places like Julie's closet in Rousseau's *La Nouvelle Héloïse* may become the scene of transgressive relations and escape from paternal control; the legal status of divorce or abortion can modify the symbolism of geographic and erotic detours; and in a revolutionary historic moment, the social order may be reconstructed through movements of characters within the rural estate and landscape.

In a somber instance of the historic specificity of physical segregation, some women have had to struggle against racially dictated proscriptions on their freedom of movement, as well as gender-based institutional bars to their activities. Carla Peterson in her chapter for this volume foregrounds the importance of physical displacement in enabling even a "free" or freed woman's accession to a public voice in the nineteenth century. When barred from the Philadelphia pulpits, Jarena Lee turned to preaching at camp meetings; on the circuit she found freedom from institutional constraints and a crossroads where men and women, black and white, could meet. While her spiritual mission authorized her work as a traveler of the word, like Sojourner Truth, Lee nonetheless found her black woman's body usurped attention from her words and put her sex and authority into question. This difficulty, Peterson suggests, impelled Lee and other African American women of the period to the medium of writing, where they might find a public without the hazards of physical exposure.

In the latter half of the nineteenth century, at the height of the debate over woman's sphere, new realist techniques of mise-en-scène gave concrete expression in the theater to conflicts over woman's proper role and place in society. Thematically, the landmark plays of the period took root in the tragedy of a modern woman whose allotted social position was within the family, but whose desires threatened a fall into a world of illegitimate sexual activity. Hebbel, Ibsen, and Strindberg, as Joan Templeton shows in her chapter here, all responded to what Strindberg calls the "noise" made by transgressive women.[16] Hebbel's revolutionary work about a cabinetmaker and his daughter demands that the audience reconsider the spatial-moral trope of the fallen woman. The domestic confinement of women in arranged marriages, Ibsen goes on to suggest in *Ghosts,* has the ironic power ultimately to confine and destroy men as well. For Strindberg, women who refuse their "natural" place within women's sphere represent an abhorrent species doomed to destruction.

Experimental writers such as Ibsen or those suspected of deviant behavior may respond to the binary economy of masculine and feminine space with images that blur gender boundaries. Hedda Gabler, for example, stands at the threshold of a garden door to take potshots with her father's pistol. In other plays, Ibsen exploits women's general obligation to wear a mask of conformity to the demands of their sphere; to step offstage is to close the door on the dollhouse of femininity. Oceanic fluidity offers another image of escape, not only for male poets like Byron, who flaunted his escape from the constrictions of British proprieties through an outward-bound voyage in *Childe Harold,* but for female authors as well, including Jane Austen, Virginia Woolf, and Kate Chopin. As Anca Vlasopolos reminds us in this book, historic differences and broad cultural distinctions are inscribed in the way each new generation embraces the imagery of liberation.

While early studies of the distinctions between public and private, between male and female spheres of action, concerned themselves primarily with middle-class European ideological developments, it has now become clear that such distinctions take on different configurations if we look at minority groups within Western cultures or at non-Western cultures. Segregated realms such as the harem or purdah can serve both as boundary markers that guarantee a social order and as domains for same-sex bonding and internally structured systems of labor. The domestic feminism discounted by many students of nineteenth-century America may in another cultural context offer the most powerful and effective form of women's activism. To compare domestic realism in India with that in Britain is to recognize that realist plausibility rests on historically framed social scripts.[17] In turn, to escape the confining linkage between propriety and plausibility, a woman writer may find it necessary to shift literary modes. In one culture that shift may mean a turn to tragedy, in a second a turn to magic realism—as in the writings of Simone Schwarz-Bart, studied here by Indira Karamcheti.

Not surprisingly, architectural and landscape symbolism has been of special importance for the representation of a feminine economy in the writings of both men and women (see Spain). Several contemporary women novelists analyzed here by Kathleen Komar turn to a feminized architecture in order to represent the domestic arena inhabited by their protagonists. Round houses, baskets, and even beds may signify alternatively confinement or the possibility of self-redefinition. As figures of femininity, such images offer a shorthand sexual vocabulary, but their connotations remain slippery. The arbitrariness of symbolic binarisms is wittily exposed by the contemporary German author Sarah Kirsch, when her protagonist on changing biological sex also rearranges her physical environment. Similarly, the tightly enclosed spaces that at once closet and liberate the body in Silvia Molloy's *En breve cárcel* have been read by Amy Kaminsky as "an exercise in lesbian separatism." Molloy's narrator gives "keys" to the protagonist's peregrinations that make her "personal geography" legible as a "lesbian cartography."[18] While architectural organization often neatly corresponds to the social designation of gendered territory, a wide range of spaces can acquire a gender connotation—and the subtle scale of that gendering can be finely differentiated.

The first extended comparative study of differences in the way female and male writers may use spatial metaphors was Ellen Moers's *Literary Women* (1976), in part inspired by psychoanalytic theories that the human body dominates the symbolism of dreams. Freud explains unhesitatingly that "the female genitalia are symbolically represented by all such objects as share with them the property of enclosing a space or are capable of acting as receptacles: such as *pits, hollows and caves,* and also *jars and bottles,* and *boxes* of all sorts and sizes, *chests, coffers, pockets,* and so forth. . . . Room symbolism here links up with that of houses, whilst *doors and gates* represent the genital opening." But he also found "The complicated topography of the female sexual organs accounts for their often being represented by a *landscape* with rocks, woods and water."[19] What Moers added to Freud's thesis was a focus on the sex of the writer. In *women's* texts, she found not boxes but often a heroine's search for reflective seclusion in a "hilly, high-lying, and hard" terrain, perhaps clothed with "brambles" or "faintly vibrating" shrubs.[20]

Contemporary perspectives have elaborated but also contested the simplistic gender assignment of symbolic representations. Hélène Cixous many years ago proclaimed, "The dark Continent is neither dark nor unexplorable." She suggested that women writers cast traditionally feminine spaces into symbolic disarray: "It's no accident: women take after birds and robbers. . . . They go by, fly the coop, take pleasure in jumbling the order of space, in disorienting it, in changing around the furniture, dislocating things and values, breaking them all up, emptying structures, and turning propriety upside down."[21] While the reception of a Freudian metaphorics of "pits, hollows, and caves" has undoubtedly shaped texts by writers such as Christa Wolf and Virginia Woolf, many of the same writers also deliberately subvert the notion of female interiority. Some locations, such as Christa Wolf's caves or the *hortus conclusus,* may appear to evoke the womb, as Komar shows, but other bulbous terrains may have ambisexual suggestiveness and thus undercut any simple, heterosexually binary readings.

A particularly privileged trope of femininity in women's own writings comes not from the land but the sea: Anca Vlasopolos's study in this volume of the female bildungsroman gives texture to the archetypal links among women, flux, and the ocean, represented as a world uncharted by men. She shows how the voyage out, either to a seaport or onto the sea, leads in works by Austen, Chopin, and Woolf to a new self-awareness; to escape "social moorings" now becomes possible. Thus she reexamines the metaphor that framed the female bildungsroman in *The Voyage In* (one of the first truly comparative studies of a gender-inflected genre) to locate the

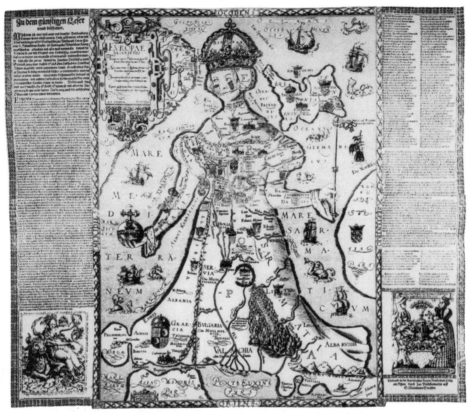

Queen Europa in the age of exploration, mapped here by Matthias Quad.

fresh specificity of each text's psychological and social fusions and part-ings.[22] The sea as a medium of connection and imperialist expansion, but also as a scene of evasion and exile, lends its own historically varied reso-nances to the marriage or death with which each text ends.

The difficulty in interpreting ambiguous landscape imagery is com-pounded by the fact that Freudian readings in which the land stands for the female sexual organs can be reversed, letting the woman stand for the land. In certain nationalist texts the female body becomes a metonymy for the nation: Renaissance maps showed England and Scotland as a skirted queen with a crowned head; Britannia represents Great Britain, Marianne post-revolutionary France, and Malinche the ambivalent heritage of the New World. The allegorical representation of one's country as female has a long history going back to anthropomorphic maps of Europa in the sixteenth century, but the propagandistic purposes of these projections have acquired special, often ironic, force in an age of nationalism.[23]

Feminist engagements in cultural critique have recently reopened this topic of national fictions. In *The Lay of the Land,* her psychoanalytical study of male writers who depict the American landscape in terms of maternal and virginal archetypes, Annette Kolodny argued the power of such metaphors to shape a national literary tradition: "the particular way in which the New World has been symbolized as feminine in American thought and writing bears out a consistent correlation between that set of linguistic images and certain psychological patterns that became codified in our literature and acted out in our history."[24] An even more sweeping approach, influenced by Foucault and Althusser, shaped Doris Sommer's *Foundational Fictions,* a study of interracial romance motifs that inscribe and mask political conflicts in Latin American postcolonial literatures. Studies like Sommer's have done the spadework for future comparative study of allegorizing modes that attribute gender to the territorial imperatives of nationhood.[25]

Under the influence of "subaltern studies" and "cultural critique," the study of national mythographies has helped to de-center comparative literature, pushing it away from the canonical, European, or North American axis of literary history and cartography.[26] Recent cultural critique has called attention to an aspect of the gendering of space that is of particular interest to comparative literature: the mapping and physical measuring of empire in sexual terms—one of the points of Jane Marcus's chapter here. Economically and militarily dominant nations, with hard currencies and military hardware, may be contrasted to colonized or dependent economies, whose peoples are cast as weak, feminized, orientalized others. All subalterns (especially those "down under") may be feminized in the discourses of empire. In such discursive economies women are doubly displaced. National myth making in the process of reaffirming a masculine, autonomous statehood tends to gender the land as feminine, to treat Woolf's negress as property.

The double displacement of subaltern women writers weighs not only on their physical depiction of place but on their general writing strategies. Space becomes a writerly problem. As Edward Said has shown in his work on orientalisms, geography is a tool of political measurement and labeling that both creates and obstructs textual meaning; in travel literature, metaphors of picturesque differences mask issues of race and sexual transgression.[27] Drawing on Said and reader-response theory, Indira Karamcheti in her chapter here explores the ways in which literary institutions register women authors from the Third World. Geopolitical hierarchies and "cognitive imperialism" collude to veil or erase the places and people they represent.[28] The material world of the subaltern may therefore collapse into the atextuality of that for which a representational vocabulary is lacking. Inevitably, the anxiety of erasure elicits responses that both resist and reinscribe codes of marginality and otherness onto the representation of geographic place.

Power, as Foucault taught us, is distributed throughout symbolic economies. Myths invite countermyths, *patria* may be paired off against *matria*. Thus some women writers in the African diaspora have sought to reimagine a feminized land in terms that would enable a transformative, "matrifocal nationalism."[29] The dominant gendering of territory or empire as female, and its proprietors or rulers as male, has significance not only for the iconographies that determine national literary traditions, but also for women writers' arrogation of citizenship and ironic reworking of their internal exile in the republic of letters. While the burden of political displacement has historically been measured in bloodshed, rape, and enslavement, the literature of diaspora can be interpreted as an extended meditation on the anxieties of influence and separation from the tradition.

As a form of politically imposed banishment, exile takes the dark form of censorship, institutionalized exclusion, imprisonment, or ghettoization, to which Barbara Harlow calls attention in her study here of "sites of struggle." The repressive force of the family for women in many societies makes (*ensilio*) a particularly endemic condition. Differentiated by culture and historic moment, internal exile figures in many of the texts discussed here, from the nineteenth-century Norwegian middle-class woman examined by Ibsen to the twentieth-century black woman trapped by rural poverty and incest in *The Color Purple*. The struggles engaged by such structures of exclusion are necessarily marked by different kinds of suffering.

As Harlow and Castillo show us, authors whose sense of national identity is not only hyphenated but contested through friction with bureaucratic institutions and border guards may make particularly dramatic use of physical description. Description serves them to expose the way physically established boundaries and barricades support political construction of the self. Harlow traces in a number of texts by minority writers the careful links between a violence in the domestic sphere that is socially framed and condoned, on the one hand, and the construction of concrete highways around ghettos and attempts to fence off rivers that mark a national boundary, on the other. Ironically, the sites of potential growth, flux, and travel become for minority women writers sites of imprisonment and exclusion. Place brands them as poor women, as women of color, as women who speak the wrong language.

Exiled within patriarchy and within the *patria,* those privileged women who have the means to leave home, especially those who are double outsiders, have done so with surprising frequency in the twentieth century. Chosen exile, unlike the homelessness of those cast out by civil war or the silence of those imprisoned within totalitarian systems, can acquire positive, liberating meaning. It can offer access to a constructed motherland, like the Nigeria of *The Color Purple* or the Africa that freed the voice of Isak Dinesen. The possibility of comparing two cultures can grant critical purchase on both. The divided national allegiances of women displaced from home within empire have made it possible for some writers like Schwarz-Bart or Sandra Cisneros to recognize and explore race, class, and gender divisions.

Yet, as Jane Marcus argues, exile can become an alibi for the writer or critic who would slip out of the confines of history and social responsibility. Feminist and other critics at times deploy the metaphorics of exile as if it could exempt us from responsibility for the operations of patriarchy. The abuse of a metaphorical margin by feminist critics masks the actual economic and physical import of political and social exclusions, whose burden of violence is borne by minority and working-class women. Marcus points here to some of these contradictions in Virginia Woolf's self-representation as an "outsider."[30]

Both Marcus's work and my own focus on the benefits and risks of metaphorization. Just as a critic can gain insight into literary structures by examining the varied ways in which cultures and classes constitute gendered spheres of action, the critic can also gain leverage on these symbolic processes by examining the way spatial metaphors function in feminist criticism. For some of the writer-critics discussed in this volume by Kathleen Komar, such as Monique Wittig and Christa Wolf, the blank page symbolizes a location of self-birth. Successful metaphors can enable writing; they can also lend pungency and point to the more abstract arguments of criticism; they may, however, box the critic into essentialist positions or into binary schematisms. The simplistic reproduction of the figure "women's sphere," itself embedded in modern Western living arrangements, masks the divergences and conflicts among women. One goal shared by my essay and that of Marcus is to attune readers to the darker implications of our own critical language.

The comparative issues raised here also concern the critical frames through which much feminist theory has recently been thought. It is important to examine not only the site of the fictional subject or the narrator but the site of the critic. What is the institutional locus occupied by the critic in the various Republics of Letters, and how is it gendered? As in many other professions, women have often been assigned to nurturing tasks—advising students and teaching composition or introductory language classes in seminar rooms rather than theory courses in lecture halls. They are likely to have chosen topics such as children's literature, personal narratives, and sexuality; they may publish in specialist journals rather than vehicles of "general" interest. These sociological and institutional issues intersect with Marcus's meditation on Woolf's Society of Outsiders; they may explain why feminist critics have selected certain spatial images through which to interpret their own roles.

This volume combines historical analysis with theory and insists on a broad, comparative perspective to frame feminist literary analysis. The collection weaves together certain recurrent strands, especially the distinctions between the private and the public, the domestic and the political, the physical body and the mythic social body. The historic line traced between private and public realms shapes the contours of eighteenth- and nineteenth-century literature. More recent literature, especially from postcolonial nations, stresses rather the formation of the social body, the interplay of nationalism and imperialism, and their figuration through the body of woman. Thus the volume moves forward and outward from eighteenth-century European figurations of private and public aspects of femininity to late twentieth-century African, Caribbean, and Indian questioning of these gendered themes, in juxtaposition to broad political issues, especially of nationalism.

The curve of such historical shifts should not obscure sharp differences in critical approach among the essays collected here. As a wide-ranging metaphor, *space* invites ideologically inflected analysis. As my own study recalls, the spatialization of our critical categories can be productive or destructive. Because space does not just record gender-based assumptions and roles but also reinforces them, it sharpens the debate between essentialist and constructionist feminisms. While the essays by Castillo, Stadler, Templeton, Vlasopolos, and Komar seek out continuities in modes of representation across cultural boundaries (continuities that may result from similar, cross-cultural structures of gender distinction), those by Peterson, Harlow, Karamcheti, and Marcus insist on heterogeneities and cultural difference. One aim of juxtaposing here a group of studies whose subjects span three centuries and many national literatures is precisely to resist the universalizing tendencies that have infected much comparative and feminist criticism alike. Some of the contributors explore spatiality as a social and psychological construction that may foster or block the expression of the gendered subject. Others challenge and deconstruct such pairings as center/margin, inside/outside, or unity/fragmentation.

The images of a feminine sphere and of feminized spatial symbolism occur, of course, in texts by men as well as in texts by women. Whether these materials are encoded differently by men and women is one of the questions the volume invites the reader to consider. For, in Joan Scott's phrase, the term *gender* suggests "that information about women is necessarily information about men." The multiple zones of cultural practice that men and women inhabit necessarily overlap and undercut sexual lines of division. To focus on representations permits us to explore the cultural fiction of separate spheres without perpetuating "the fiction that one sphere, the experience of one sex, has little or nothing to do with the other."[31] It is the intersection of spheres and the power of these metaphoric structures that *Reconfigured Spheres* addresses.

NOTES

1. Friedrich von Hardenberg, *Novalis Schriften, Die Werke Friedrich von Hardenbergs,* ed. Paul Kluckhohn and Richard Samuel, vol. 2 (Stuttgart: Kohlhammer, 1981) 646. Vir-

ginia Woolf, "Professions for Women," *The Death of the Moth and Other Essays* (1942; New York: Harcourt Brace Jovanovich, 1970) 237; *Three Guineas* (1938; San Diego: Harcourt Brace Jovanovich, 1966) 109. See also Biddy Martin and Chandra Talpade Mohanty, "Feminist Politics: What's Home Got to Do with It?" *Feminist Studies/Critical Studies,* ed. Teresa de Lauretis (Bloomington: Indiana UP) 191–212.

2. Adrienne Rich, *Blood, Bread, and Poetry: Selected Prose, 1979–1985* (New York: Norton, 1986) 212.

3. We would like to thank the organizers of the 1988 meeting of the International Comparative Literature Association at Munich, who made it possible for us to initiate this exchange of ideas.

4. See Joni Seager and Ann Olson, *Women in the World: An International Atlas* (London: Olson, 1986); Anne Gibson and Timothy Fast, *The Women's Atlas of the United States* (New York: Facts on File, 1986); Dolores Hayden, *The Grand Domestic Revolution: A History of Feminist Designs for American Homes, Neighborhoods, and Cities* (Cambridge: MIT P, 1981); Beatriz Colomina, *Sexuality and Space* (New York: Princeton Architectural, 1992); and Daphne Spain, *Gendered Spaces* (Chapel Hill: U of North Carolina P, 1992). The new serial *Gender, Place and Culture: A Journal of Feminist Geography* will address the cultural construction of gender and its intersection with race, ethnicity, class, age, and other social divisions.

5. Robert Hertz, *Death and the Right Hand,* trans. Rodney Needham and Claudia Needham (Glencoe, IL: Free, 1955) 97.

6. Mary Douglas, *Purity and Danger: An Analysis of Concepts of Pollution and Taboo* (New York: Praeger, 1966).

7. See Joan Landes, *Women and the Public Sphere in the Age of the French Revolution* (Ithaca: Cornell UP, 1988). Landes developed the neglected gender component in the earlier study of Jürgen Habermas, *The Structural Transformation of the Public Sphere,* trans. Thomas Burger (Cambridge: Harvard UP, 1989). See also Leonore Davidoff and Catherine Hall, *Family Fortunes: Men and Women of the English Middle Class, 1780–1850* (London: Hutchinson, 1987).

8. See Susanne Zantop, "Trivial Pursuits? An Introduction to German Women's Writing from the Middle Ages to 1830," *Bitter Healing: German Women Writers from 1700 to 1830, an Anthology,* ed. Jeannine Blackwell and Susanne Zantop (Lincoln: U of Nebraska P, 1990) 9–50.

9. See Londa Schiebinger, *The Mind Has No Sex* (Cambridge: Harvard UP, 1989); and Thomas Laqueur, *Making Sex: Body and Gender from the Greeks to Freud* (Cambridge: Harvard UP, 1990).

10. See Martha Vicinus, ed., *A Widening Sphere* (Bloomington: Indiana UP, 1977); Mary Kelley, *Private Woman, Public Stage: Literary Domesticity in Nineteenth-Century America* (New York: Oxford UP, 1984).

11. Virginia Woolf, *A Room of One's Own* (1929; San Diego: Harcourt Brace Jovanovich, 1957) 7. The psychological residue of such barriers may be even more lasting than their physical presence: having been barred from the libraries of men's colleges and universities in my youth, I still have difficulty crossing their thresholds today.

12. Caroll Smith-Rosenberg, "Writing History: Language, Class, and Gender," *Feminist Studies/Critical Studies,* ed. de Lauretis, 49.

13. For the complications that ensue from cross-dressing, see Marjorie Garber, *Vested Interests: Cross-Dressing and Cultural Anxiety* (New York: Routledge, 1992).

14. Joni Seager, "Blueprints for Inequality," *Women's Review of Books* 10.4 (January 1993): 1.

15. Sandra Gilbert and Susan Gubar, *The Madwoman in the Attic: The Woman Writer and the Nineteenth-Century Literary Imagination* (New Haven: Yale UP, 1979).

16. August Strindberg, *Selected Plays,* ed. and trans. Evert Sprinchorn (Minneapolis: U of Minnesota P, 1986) 1: 208.

17. See Nancy Armstrong, *Desire and Domestic Fiction: A Political History of the Novel* (New York: Oxford UP, 1987); and Meenakshi Mukherjee, *Realism and Reality: The Novel and Society in India* (Delhi: Oxford UP, 1985).

18. Amy Kaminsky, "Lesbian Cartographies: Body, Text, and Geography," *Cultural and Historical Grounding for Hispanic and Luso-brazilian Feminist Literary Criticism,* ed. Hernán Vidal (Minneapolis: Institute for the Study of Ideologies and Literature, 1989) 244.

19. Sigmund Freud, *A General Introduction to Psycho-analysis,* trans. Joan Riviere (New York: Liveright, 1963) 139.

20. Ellen Moers, *Literary Women: The Great Writers* (Garden City, NY: Doubleday, 1976) 257. Moers also traced a tradition of intertextual allusion passing sexual symbolism from one woman writer to the next, as in Gertrude Stein's citation of George Eliot's phrase, the "red deeps" (65–66). Another direction that feminist study of space has taken concerns the political import of genre rules. Patricia Parker connects the verbal display of a woman's body in the lyric *blazon* to the "narrative inventory of a feminized" landscape, whether of a "Mary-land" or of an English property that is simultaneously "laid open to view" and walled off. *Literary Fat Ladies: Rhetoric, Gender, Property* (New York: Methuen, 1987), especially chapters 2, 6–8.

21. Hélène Cixous, "The Laugh of the Medusa," *New French Feminisms,* ed. Elaine Marks and Isabelle de Courtivron (Amherst: U of Massachusetts P, 1980) 252.

22. See Elizabeth Abel, Marianne Hirsch, and Elizabeth Langland, eds., *The Voyage In: Fictions of Female Development* (Hanover: New England UP, 1983).

23. Claude Gandelman, "Le corps du roi comme 'carte du royaume,'"*Idéologie et propagande en France,* ed. Myriam Yardeni (Paris: Picard, 1987) 19–29.

24. Annette Kolodny, *The Lay of the Land: Metaphor as Experience and History in American Life and Letters* (Chapel Hill: U of North Carolina P, 1975) 156, 149. Elaine Savory Fido uses the same image of the mother's body in "Mother/lands: Self and Separation in the Work of Buchi Emecheta, Bessie Head, and Jean Rhys," *Motherlands: Black Women's Writing from Africa, the Caribbean and South Asia,* ed. Susheila Nasta (New Brunswick: Rutgers UP, 1992) 351.

25. Doris Sommer, *Foundational Fictions: The National Romances of Latin America* (Berkeley: U of California P, 1991). See also Sandra Gilbert, "From *Patria* to *Matria:* Elizabeth Barrett Browning's Risorgimento," *PMLA* 99 (1984): 194–211; and Kaminsky 247.

26. See Michael Palencia Roth, "Contrastive Literature," *ACLA Bulletin* 24.2 (1993): 47–60.

27. Edward Said, *Orientalism* (New York: Pantheon, 1978); see also Mary Louise Pratt, *Imperial Eyes: Studies in Travel Writing and Transculturation* (London: Routledge, 1992).

28. Theodore von Laue, *The World Revolution of Westernization: The Twentieth Century in Global Perspective* (Oxford: Oxford UP, 1987); see also Michael Palencia-Roth, "Comparing Literature, Comparing Civilizations," *Comparative Civilizations Review* 21 (1989): 1–19.

29. Elleke Boehmer, "Stories of Women and Mothers: Gender and Nationalism in the Early Fiction of Flora Nwapa," *Motherlands* 3–23.

30. See also Mary Lynn Broe and Angela Ingram, eds., *Women's Writing in Exile* (Chapel Hill: U of North Carolina P, 1989).

31. Joan Scott, *Gender and the Politics of History* (New York: Columbia UP, 1988) 32. See also Renate Bridenthal and Claudia Koonz, eds., *Becoming Visible: Women in European History* (Boston: Houghton Mifflin, 1977).

EVA MARIA STADLER

Addressing Social Boundaries: Dressing the Female Body in Early Realist Fiction

Costume is a language.—Fernand Braudel

As a literary topos, dress spatializes the relations between a woman's body and the social order. An encroachment of social norms upon the body's surface, dress may identify status or conceal identity and embellish or disguise corporal traits. A woman's vestments can publicize her servitude as well as cloak her private space. These varied functions of clothing figure in the realist novel from its beginnings in the eighteenth century. Daniel Defoe, Pierre Carlet de Marivaux, and Samuel Richardson all use the language of dress to construct and define a woman's social, sexual, and psychological identity by manipulating a cultural system.

Clothing has always been a sign that defines the place of its wearer, whether man or woman, within the social hierarchy; accordingly, it has also served to record irreversible cultural and historical transformations. In every period, as Daniel Roche has noted, "clothing is a good indication of the material culture of a society, for it introduces us immediately to consumer patterns, and enables us to consider the social hierarchy of appearances."[1] At any historical moment, women's specific class position as well as the restrictions on their physical mobility are revealed to a large degree through their clothing. "Differences in the rules governing the body (dress and sexual codes, freedom of movement and so forth) will demarcate social difference and positions of relative power."[2] In the sixteenth century, for example, Elizabethan proclamations of sumptuary laws regulated the relation between social status and dress. These laws that controlled aristocratic display also constituted a vehicle for surveillance of women.[3] Middle-class writers of conduct books pursued the discipline and control of women by legislating dress codes well into the nineteenth century.

Because old hierarchies began to shift during the eighteenth century, clothing became a particularly sensitive indicator of social position. Even the redefinition of social categories and roles manifested itself in sartorial language.[4] In the words of the *London Tradesman* of 1747, "Prometheus . . . was really no more than a Taylor, who, by his Art metamorphosed Mankind so, that they appeared a new species of Beings."[5] Richard Sennett in *The Fall of Public Man* discusses appearance and strictly coded costume as precise indicators of class and rank in the *public* sphere of eighteenth-century Paris and London. In mid-eighteenth-century France, especially complicated sumptuary laws distinguished all social strata and trades. Women "whose husbands were laborers were not permitted to dress like the wives of masters of a craft, and the wives of 'traders' were forbidden certain adornments allowed women of quality." In the *private* sphere of the home, however, "the body appeared as expressive in itself" in simpler loose-fitting garments.[6] These distinctions in dress also helped to define the geographic boundaries of the public and private realms during the Enlightenment.

Because clothing confers social identity as well as personal individuality, it is not surprising that a number of "realist" novels from the early eighteenth century on make complex use of references to costume, particularly to the clothing of women. Telling details of dress, or "written clothing," serve both realistic historical reference and characterization.[7] Actualized and displayed on the individual character's body as well as presented through a narrator's voice, clothing becomes at once a language of institutions and a particular speech act. Clothes mediate interpersonal and social relationships by encoding social and sexual communication. At the same time that they attract sexual attention, clothes can also stand between a woman's body and the violence threatened by the exterior world. In this way, clothes define, mediate, and even, at times, protect a woman's gendered space.

Defoe's *Moll Flanders* (1722), Marivaux's *La Vie de Marianne* (1731–41), and Richardson's *Pamela* (1740) are all feminocentric novels of apprenticeship that deal with a woman's attempt to assert herself within the patriarchal system. Not only does the heroine's name figure in each title, but a female voice gives her first-person account in letters or pseudo-memoirs that confront the ambiguities of women's position in eighteenth-century France and England. Like other novels of apprenticeship and conquest, *Moll Flanders, La Vie de Marianne,* and *Pamela* exploit three aspects of clothing that according to Roche institute a dialogue between reality and fiction: social masks, amorous strategy, and utopian dreams of power (*People of Paris* 178–180). Dress reflects and manipulates the rules of public decorum tied to wealth, class, and gender. Although dress—particularly in its public manifestations—was strictly coded, Defoe, Marivaux, and Richardson all explore ways in which clothing can also be tied to a particular female body and personalized. These vestimentary expressions may constitute an envelope that veils or reveals the erotic body. They may also assert and assure a new social position or may frame the inner, psychic space of the female character. For these male authors, the system of dress finally becomes a discourse of individualist empowerment, a tool in the (fictitious) ascendancy of women.

The first forty years or so of the eighteenth century, a "period of crucial transformation," saw the rise of the middle class and the development of capitalist ideology.[8] This period increasingly emphasized qualitative differences between the sexes, using an ideology of sexual difference to buttress a new social order. "Male and female imagery and activities became more distinct and increasingly associated with contrasting 'rational' and 'affective' styles."[9] By the end of the century, this marking of gender roles expressed itself in sartorial terms. While the dress of upper- and middle-class women continued to emphasize ornamentation and the display of finery, men's clothing, under the pressure of commercial and industrial ideals, gradually became more discreet, more uniform. In this shift away from male vestimentary display, the "great masculine renunciation" transferred exhibitionistic desire onto persons of the opposite sex.[10] This sartorial gendering of space surfaces in some of the roles assigned to clothing even in early realist novels; it is also apparent in male novelists' interest in women's attire.

Critics have often noted fundamental stylistic differences between the early novel in England and in France. According to Ian Watt, Defoe and Richardson write in a language "whose very diffuseness tends to act as a guarantee of the authenticity of their report," while in France works of fiction are "too stylish to be authentic."[11] In his study of the French novel of manners Peter Brooks argues that Marivaux and other French novelists of the period also represent individual life authentically, but that they do so within a public system of values that uses "an exact, elegant and general language of psychological and moral analysis."[12] These distinctions between a language that is detailed, accumulative, and individualized, as in the English novel, rather than succinct and universal, as in the French novel, are reflected in descriptions of women's clothing and adornment in *Moll Flanders, La Vie de Marianne,* and *Pamela.*

In *The Fortunes and Misfortunes of the Famous Moll Flanders,* Daniel Defoe depicts the life of an unprotected woman in late seventeenth-century London. Moll is a victim of society, an adventuress, and a shrewd champion of self-interest. Her adventures, which take place on the public stage of the city, revolve around securing her social and economic position. In the accumulated material details about the society in which Moll Flanders lives, cloth and clothing are indicators of wealth and worldly possessions. Moll's mother is sent to Newgate for stealing "three pieces of fine Holland."[13] The poverty and destitution of the young child born in prison constitute a state "without Friends, without Cloaths, without Help or Helper in the world" (7). When the young Moll begins to support herself, she notes that she provides her own clothes; generosity is expressed through gifts of petticoats, stockings, and gowns (13). In these topical references, clothing and linen signify the patrimony of an individual, especially a servant or wage earner (Roche, *People of Paris* 162).[14] When Moll turns to thievery, almost all her bundles contain articles of clothing and pieces of linen, lace, silk, velvet, and other fabrics. After several years, Moll is "in good Circumstances indeed . . . the richest of the Trade in England" (197). Her wealth consists of "700£ . . . in Money, besides Cloaths, Rings, some Plate, and two gold Watches, and all of them stol'n" (197). Once in America, Moll orders English goods, among them "all sorts of Cloaths," stockings, shoes, hats, and textiles for herself, her husband, and her servants. She is now a woman of "very considerable Circumstances" (267).

Although clothing in *Moll Flanders* is always viewed as property rather than fashion, its inclusion among the attributes of wealth of the older Moll points to the eighteenth-century beginnings of the "commercialization of fashion." The English middle class occupied a central position in developing consumer patterns during a century that witnessed a shift from a fashion that was "expensive, exclusive and Paris-based, to a fashion which was cheap, popular and London-based" (McKendrick 43). In *Moll Flanders* dress is a commodity for the poor, as well as for the middle class.

In his description of clothing, "much of Defoe's realism is on the elementary level of naming."[15] Objects are denoted only by their primary qualities of solidity, extension, motion, and particularly number (Watt 102). Little attention is paid to secondary qualities such as color, texture, design, or fit. Not only do cloth and clothing count as visible tokens of wealth, but in a strictly stratified society the garments identify condition and status. Defoe's descriptions also illustrate the self-consciously public mode of an era that deployed the body as a "mannequin" to carry markers of social condition (Sennett 87). Even moral integrity could be measured in dress and adornment. In her most desperate moments Moll did not "stoop" to "painting" her face (100); in choosing a home for one of her children, she recognized the honorable character of a country woman by her wholesome look as well as her "very good Cloaths and Linnen" (138). Yet where status is codified, it can also be mimed: since a gentlewoman can be identified by her dress and her gold watch, clothing can transform a thief into the likeness of a duchess.

During her early years, the poor and abandoned Moll prostitutes her body to survive and then to secure her social and economic position. Clothing enhances her natural beauty, and although she admits that she was vain as a young woman and "lov'd nothing in the World better than fine Clothes" (89), few descriptions of her clothed appearance occur in the first part of the novel. Her "conquests"—the series of lovers and husbands— testify sufficiently to her success in a society that measures achievement by the accumulation and accounting of material goods.

When Moll can no longer use her body to seduce, once "it was past the flourishing time with [her]" (148), she reshapes her appearance through costume to prepare for a new career as a thief. Cross-dressing, by blurring the lines of gender and class, acts as a protective screen enabling her to move with ease in crowds among the wealthy and powerful. New appearances correspond to new names, new identities, and new social positions. Indeed, when Moll plays the role of a gentlewoman wearing a "good" dress and a gold watch or disguises herself as a man, dress signifies power and sends a deceptive sartorial message of integration within the privileged social hierarchy. Transgressive dress, however, has its limits. When Moll dresses in men's clothing, she comments afterward that she did things clumsily "in a Dress so contrary to Nature" (167) and elaborates the dangers that she ran. While class-based dress codes are socially or culturally determined, gender-based dress codes seem to her and perhaps to Defoe "natural." The only other transgression that appears to worry Moll (unlike theft, confidence games, bigamy, prostitution, or abandoning children) is incest, again presented as a crime "against Nature."[16] Moll's retrospective fears reflect an anxiety about the "unnatural" confusion of the sexes, which manifests itself in conduct books and other writings throughout the century.[17] The moral meaning of masquerade remains uncertain: a gap opens up between the moralizing older woman who tells the story of her life and the younger Moll she remembers, who used her body and her wits to assert herself. While the older woman seems to evoke the biblical prohibition against gender-based cross-dressing, another, seemingly younger voice recalls with pleasure that she was "Tall and Personable but a little too smooth Fac'd" in this costume (167).[18]

Formal masquerade, that social arena of performance in the eighteenth century where one could violate class- and gender-based codes, does not appear in *Moll Flanders*.[19] However, dressing that crosses the full range of class lines allows an acceptable, efficacious, and credible transmutation during Moll's long and successful career as a thief. Through skillful disguise, Moll transforms herself into a servant, a beggar woman, a widow, a gentlewoman. Moll's adventures point to the anonymity and fluidity of an urban world in transition, where people can assume any identity and go any place their appearances allow. Her costumes and her careers also underscore the roles permitted to women, while her disguises show both the dangers and advantages of transgressing class and gender. Through the freedoms of dress, sexual persona, and class mobility that Moll claims, Defoe unsettles social stratification and the accepted avenues to empowerment open to women.

By contrast, in *La Vie de Marianne* Marivaux questions neither conventional gender roles nor social mores and manners. If Defoe focuses on an urban, lower-class milieu, whose drama of modernization is paced by changes of wardrobe and of scene, Marivaux focuses instead on the aristocratic world of the salon, the milieu of most seventeenth- and eighteenth-century French novels. Here too clothing is tied to the seductions, the dangers, and the opportunities of city life.

In *Marianne* clothes are first of all signs of social position. We know the heroine through a vestimentary token that automatically points to her status. The infant Marianne, found after an accident among the bodies of several adults, has nothing to identify her except "the small costume which indicated that she was of gentle birth" ("la petite parure (qui) marquait une enfant de condition").[20] This general comment on the garment's meaning typifies the lack of specific detail in the novel's many references to clothing. Marianne is given new outfits (*des habits*); she covers her head with a "headdress" (*une cornette*); when she is ill she appears in a *négligé*. Items of clothing are neither counted nor described. As Béatrice Didier suggests, generic designations suffice, because Marivaux's readers participate in the same culture, know its codes, and therefore are easily able to visualize the garment and understand its message.[21]

Marianne's adopted mother, Mme de Miran, transmits a benevolent and clearly understood social message when, before a dinner party, she tells Marianne, "I want you to put on all your finery" ("Je veux que tu te pares" [244]), while M. de Climal sends an equally clear though dangerous and compromising message when he buys the young woman a full wardrobe that includes beautiful linen. In the French eighteenth-century novel the verb *se parer* and its related noun *la parure* confer an almost autonomous life to clothing by metonymically relating elegant dress and finery to the will to impress and attract recognition. The motif of linen (*linge*), by contrast, alludes to the possibility of licentious adventure.[22] These strictly encoded literary, social, and sartorial conventions enable clothing to distinguish public from private occasions, proper from improper relations, as well as degrees of birth.

Despite the lack of descriptive detail regarding color, fabric, and shape, clothing plays multiple referential and narrative roles in *La Vie de Marianne*, by contrast to the works of other French novelists of the period such as Abbé Prévost and Mme de Graffigny, who make only cursory mention of the apparel worn by their female protagonists. Because Marianne is convinced that the *parure* with which she was found as an infant spoke symbolically of the person it covered, she deploys clothing in subsequent scenes to achieve the status that befits her. Arriving poor in Paris, she can acquire fashionable finery only by accepting gifts from an admirer or patron. She sees these as instruments allowing her to (re)gain a place obscured and disguised by the circumstances that made her an orphan.

When she meets her future benefactress, Mme de Miran, she is happy that she is well-dressed:

> My affliction, which seemed to her extreme, touched her; my youth, my good behavior, and perhaps also my dress [ma parure], made her sympathize with me; I speak about fine dress [parure] for that never does any harm. It is good on such occasions to please the eye because it recommends you to the heart. If you are unfortunate and badly dressed, the most generous persons will either overlook you or only take a mild interest in you since you lack the attractiveness which flatters their vanity. (194)

This cynicism reflects on the society, manners, and values of Marivaux's Paris. As the elderly Marianne recalls this incident from her youth, she also gives the reader a double perspective on her own character: the young girl's calculating shrewdness and the mature woman's cool view of the place of women and the avenues of domination open to them.

Beautiful dress is an envelope that makes the body socially visible, presentable, and powerful, not only a tool of social advance but a "weapon" in an encoded seduction game between men and women. "Dress evokes seduction, sexual display, [and] the dangers to which the city exposes a young girl's virtue" (Roche, *Culture* 394). In eighteenth-century fashion, frilly fichus that covered the deep décolletages of fashionable dresses, delicate sleeve ruffles, and fine petticoats worn under the paniers of heavy overgowns evoked the body that they veiled. These sheer accessories worn close to a woman's body hint at an intimacy that novelists frequently linked to lascivious prospects. Although the young Marianne suspects the elderly M. de Climal's offers to buy her linen, she accepts, out of vanity and expediency. She subsequently resists Climal's further attempts to transgress the line between public and private, but the elegant costume that he buys serves to launch her in the social world.

The arrival in the French capital and the meeting with Climal and his rhetoric of seduction, in effect, introduce the ambiguous social and moral codes of contemporary Paris. We are told that Marianne's intuitive sense of her own worth intensifies the innate feminine desire to adorn herself. In front of a small mirror she masters the "science" of placing a ribbon and choosing a dress, and, as she prepares herself to go to church, she is overwhelmed by her reflection's charm (119). The scene at the church has often been read to emblematize Marianne's social ascendancy in Paris. Upon entering the church, her costume allows her to go to the elevated choir where the elegant people gather. Once there, through studied and provocative gestures, she manipulates clothing to conceal and reveal her seductive body. She looks up at paintings to make her eyes seem more attractive and adjusts her hair in order to expose a naked hand. In describing these actions in the public space of the church and, after Marianne's minor accident, in the more vulnerable private space of Valville's house, where the surgeon forces her to remove her shoe and expose a part of the body that should remain hidden in the presence of the young man, Marivaux tests the constraints permissible to nonlicentious literature.[23]

At such moments, although Marianne continues to tell her own story, she seems to be a woman observed through a masculine eye. The underlying eroticism of her body framed by her clothing reflects a man's sensual imagination. These scenes also relate the novel to the provocative emphasis on legs, feet, and their clothing so often seen in the works of eighteenth-century painters: fleeting moments depicted in the paintings and particularly the drawings of Greuze, Gainsborough, Fragonard, and Watteau, where an undercurrent of desire is suggested by a lifted skirt, a décolletage, a slightly turned back sleeve.[24] In emphasizing the seduction of elegant dress, Marivaux's novel both reflects the imaginary world of painters and underscores the social codes that govern every human encounter. *La Vie de Marianne* is a novel of manners in which the heroine's clothing tells us less about her as an individual than about the customs (and perhaps also the fantasies) of the period when it was written. In her studied attempt to rise to her "rightful" position, she uses the conventionally accepted dress codes to captivate, to seduce, and to dominate. Barely fifteen when her Paris experiences begin, she is also herself seduced by fashionably elegant clothing and its appeal to her vanity. Marivaux thus dramatizes the social function of dress by showing Marianne's rise through a theater of clothing and gesture, and, in a reverse dynamic, her capitulation to the social values she manipulates.

A more individualist irony emerges in Samuel Richardson's *Pamela*, where the language of dress with its accepted meanings in eighteenth-century society is often challenged by the young heroine, who exploits prevailing dress codes to gain recognition of her person on her own terms. In Pamela's earliest letters describing her life as a servant in a manor house, clothing is tied, quite conventionally, to social position and wealth. Richardson also describes a system of hand-me-downs that conflicts with clothing as a fixed grammar of class or moral status. Clothes can be transferred, conveying wealth, either to reward the honest labor of a woman servant or to seduce a young servant.

The transgression of social and sexual boundaries inherent in this transfer becomes apparent early in the novel. Soon after her mistress's death, Pamela informs her parents that Mr. B. has given her clothing from his mother, which she calls "too rich and too good for me."[25] She lists all the items in careful detail, including ribbons, topknots, and shoes, and then she notes: "I was inwardly asham'd to take the Stockens . . . he smil'd at my Awkwardness and said, Don't blush, Pamela: dost think I don't know pretty Maids wear Shoes and Stockens?" (32). Pamela's father senses the dangers of items of clothing as tools of seduction and cautions her particularly "about his free Expression . . . about the Stockens." She should reflect on "the Delights that arise from a few paltry fine Cloathes, in Comparison with a good Conscience" (32). Evidently, these gifts, like the clothing and linen Climal gives to Marianne, represent a sexual encroachment upon the young girl's space and endanger her physical and moral integrity. When her new master tries to kiss Pamela, she tells him, "I am honest, tho' poor," a declaration of probity that translates immediately into nostalgia for the rough homespun dress she used to wear. "O how I wished for my grey Russet again," she writes to her parents, "and my poor honest Dress with which you fitted me out" (36).

Moral probity and vestimentary proprieties conform in Pamela's mind to a rigid class stratification. She studies the elegant dresses she has "inherited" from her lady, musing on the inappropriateness of the clothes to her condition. If she were to return home wearing them, would not she as well as her elegant clothes look like "old cast-offs" (52)? Her shocking realization affixes the secondhand quality of the clothes to her very body. Conduct books would approve Pamela's decision to create a wardrobe more appropriate to the simple daughter of "Goody" Andrews. In 1740, Wetenhall Wilkes warns in *A Letter of Genteel and Moral Advice to a Young Lady:* "Be not industrious to set out the beauty of your person; . . . let your dress always resemble the plainness and simplicity of your heart."[26] The stress on simplicity of dress in *Pamela* suggests to Nancy Armstrong that the "production of female subjectivity entails the dismantling of the aristocratic body," while the refusal of sartorial display enhances the domestic woman's "value as a subject."[27]

But Pamela has acquired her lady's taste for quality, and as she re-makes herself in the image of her own class, she does so with a difference. She specifies the rough, dull fabrics that she buys—"good sad-colour'd stuff, of their own spinning" from a farmer's wife, printed calico, "pretty good Scots Cloth" (52)—from which she herself, in secret, makes gowns, petticoats, and shifts. From a peddlar she buys two "round ear'd Caps," a straw hat, a pair of knit mittens and "two pair of ordinary blue Worsted Hose . . . with white Clocks" (52–53). Even as she enumerates these rough fabrics and dull hues, she notes their "smartish" appearance and is pleased with herself "trick'd up" in her new garb.

> [I] . . . put on my round ear'd ordinary Cap; but with a green Knot however, and my homespun Gown and Petticoat, and plain leather Shoes; but yet they are what they call *Spanish* Leather, and my ordinary Hose, ordinary I mean to what I have been lately used to; tho' I shall think good Yarn may do very well for every Day, when I come home. A plain Muslin Tucker I put on, and my black Silk Necklace, instead of the *French* Necklace my Lady gave me, and put the Earrings out of my Ears; and when I was quite 'quip'd, I took my new Straw Hat in my Hand, with its two blue Strings, and look'd about me in the Glass, as proud as anything—To say Truth, I never lik'd myself so well in my Life. (60)

Gazing at her framed image in the mirror, she is proud of the virtue her appearance reflects. The many details of color, texture, and quality constitute a sharp contrast to the generalized descriptions of Marivaux or Defoe. Caren Chaden notes the odd combination of clothing, both humble and ornamental, that Pamela assembles in her rustic outfit: the green knot on the ordinary cap, the black silk necklace on the plain muslin tucker. This mingling of simplicity and seductive adornment in truly individual costume appears to "mix class markings" and reflects the ambiguity of Pamela's position even in her own eyes.[28]

Her new style of dress both redefines and disguises her; even her good friend Mrs. Jervis is astonished at the "Metamorphosis" (60). Like her diaries, Pamela's clothing inscribes as well as circumscribes her intermediate and shifting social position. Angered when he mistakes her for an attractive farmer's daughter, Squire B. calls her a hypocrite. Pamela herself raises the issue of clothes conferring class identity by insisting that in the elegant castoffs of her lady she had actually been "in Disguise."

In the erotic struggle between Pamela and B., which occupies more than half the novel, danger and violence lurk in the concealment of identity by dress. The dark power of clothing to dissimulate violence is dramatized when B. cross-dresses as a serving girl to penetrate Pamela's bedroom and rape her. Undressed in bed she can defend herself only through a "Fit" of fainting (175–176). Throughout the many months that follow, however, Pamela's calico shift and straw hat with blue strings become emblematic of the determined virtue that awaits its reward. When she hopes to leave the house at Lincolnshire and return to her parents, she divides her clothing into three bundles: the first containing items received from her lady, the fruit of her legitimate work; the second, presents from her master, which could have been "the Price of [her] Shame"; and the third, "poor Pamela's Bundle," which is "the Companion of [her] Poverty, and the Witness of [her] Honesty" (79–80).

This tripartite division of her clothing has symbolic bearing throughout the novel, both for her relationship to the squire and for her social position. Although similar, the first two bundles signal ways in which a woman can move up or down the social scale; the third, Pamela's greatest source of pride during her captivity, implies static class hierarchy. Yet she wears none of these clothes during her captivity. As Carey McIntosh has noted, "Pamela plays the whole central part of the drama in costume" when she wears the rustic garb she has specifically devised to define and protect her virtue.[29]

The social meanings conveyed by the three bundles shift when Pamela moves from prison to liberty, from servants' quarters to the place of legitimate mistress, beside Mr. B as his wife. She then chooses for her wedding dress "a rich white Sattin Night-gown, that had been [her] good Lady's" (287). Already on the day before the wedding, Mr. B. tells her "to dress as [she] used to do," adding "for now, at least you may call your other two Bundles your own" (256). With delight, Pamela puts on the fine clothes from the two bundles. Once married, she has a duty to adhere to the dress codes of her new condition, to wear, in B.'s words, "such Ornaments as are fit for my beloved Wife to appear in" (296).

Most brilliantly, in Richardson's novel, clothing not only serves as a visible emblem of social standing and an item in sexual barter but is also directly tied to Pamela's person, her body, and her writing. Her power of resistance depends on a peculiar combination of language and dress. "I love Writing," Pamela declares as she begins her letters to her parents (30).

Squire B. objects to her "scribbling" as unsuitable and inappropriate to her sex. "You mind your Pen more than your Needle," he complains (55). When a letter disappears, she is forced to protect her writings by hiding them "under the Toilet" in her late lady's dressing room (37). The next time she fears B.'s coming, she thrusts a letter in her bosom (40). Beginning with this conventional gesture, Richardson develops intimate relationships among Pamela's writing, her clothing, and her body. Once imprisoned, she makes provisions to continue writing by hiding pens, ink, "and a sheet of Paper here and there among [her] Linen" (105). From her linen closet, the writing moves closer to Pamela's body. "But I begin to be afraid my Writings may be discover'd: for they grow large! I stitch them hitherto in my Under-coat, next my Linen. But if this Brute should search me!" (120). As Mr. B. becomes more assiduous, she places the papers closer to her most private parts, "sew'd in my Under-coat, about my Hips" (198). In Mr. B.'s demands for the papers and threats to undress Pamela to possess them, Pamela's writings and her body merge.

When she agrees to relinquish the papers to retain her virtue, she retires to the privacy of her closet and begins an elaborate process of separating the papers from her body. Detailed references here to undergarments and the private role of clothing contrast sharply with Marivaux's vague references to *linge* and *négligé*. "I must all undress me in a manner to untack them. . . . So I took off my Under-coat, and, with great Trouble of Mind, unsew'd them from it. And there is a vast Quantity of it" (204).

During her isolation her letters become a diary in which she delineates the boundaries of her interiority; her "scribblings," like the petticoat made of "good, sad-colour'd stuff," become extensions of her person as well as layers of protection against the intrusions of the outside world. Initially sewn into the folds of her petticoat to protect her body as well as her precious diaries, once unsewn from her garments and surrendered to B., the papers become the instruments that lead to the final triumph of virtue and its reward. As Pamela has established a private space of her own by means of clothing that visibly frames her person, she now achieves a place in the world by means of the writing that enclosed and defined her body and person. Her simple clothing, symbolizing her virtuous person to the gentry who are her future husband's friends and relations, becomes a source of curiosity and interest; one of the elegant young ladies "begg'd it as a Favour" to see Pamela in her rustic garb (243).

From B.'s early attempts on her virtue until her marriage, Pamela connects her struggle for honor and integrity with the appropriateness of her clothing to her condition. In three scenes before a mirror she studies how her clothing defines and describes her moral position. Pamela takes pride in the costume that reflects her humble parentage and her will to resist B.'s advances (60). When she later rejects the rich squire's proposals, she imagines herself standing in front of a glass ashamed of wearing the diamonds that would be "the Price of [her] honesty" (166). Finally, on the day before her wedding, when she again puts on some of the clothes inherited from her lady, she "looked in the Glass and saw [herself] a Gentlewoman again" (256). Evaluating her position, she thanks God that she can wear these elegant clothes "with so much Comfort." In this last image, clothing embodies the solace, the satisfaction, and the opulence of her triumph.

As Pamela plans her married life as a "domestic woman," she seems to echo the warnings of conduct literature about the dangers of excessive elegance, modestly begging B. not to let her "go very fine in Dress" lest she "excite the Envy of [her] own Sex [by seeing a person set above them in Appearance" (227). And yet one of the novel's last scenes shows Pamela and Squire B., dressed in full regalia, accompanied by liveried servants in a newly refurbished chariot, as they set out to meet the Lincolnshire gentry.

> I was dress'd in the Suit I mention'd, of White flower'd with Gold, and a rich Head-dress, and the Diamond Necklace, Ear-rings, etc. . . . I said, I was too fine, and would have laid aside some of the Jewels; but he said, It would be thought a Slight to me from him, as his Wife; and tho', as I apprehended, it might be, that People would talk as it was, yet he had rather they would say any thing, than that I was not put upon as equal Foot, as his Wife, with any Lady he might have marry'd. (399–400)

The visit to their neighbors becomes a triumphal procession in which elegant clothing and other trappings of wealth exhibit Pamela's social position and give new meaning to her person. In contrast to her earlier use of clothing to assert and protect her personal identity, once she has become the squire's wife, Pamela, like Moll Flanders and Marianne, allows dress to proclaim her new public persona.

In these early realist novels dress carries moral and social significance and marks differences of class origin and psychology. Moll Flanders, Pamela, and Marianne must define and shape their social position. In each case of self-fabrication, clothing plays a central role. During this time of social fluctuation, sartorial language labels individual class and economic position and marks the boundaries of social hierarchy; yet dress can also, through gifts, purchase, or barter, become a "most public manifestation of the blurring of class divisions" (McKendrick 53). While each of the novels indicates the important extent to which clothing demarcated a woman's place in the public realm during the first half of the eighteenth century, the three also trace variants in the relation of clothing to the female body. In *Moll Flanders* the body acts as a mannequin to exhibit clothing from which it assumes a momentary societal meaning. In *La Vie de Marianne* clothing both conceals and reveals the erotic body and, like a mask, can be manipulated to impose respect for the heroine's person. In *Pamela* clothing most dramatically moves into the private realm, becoming almost interchangeable with the young woman's body it shields; it bespeaks not only the social space she occupies but the determined limits of her inner self.

In each of the works under consideration, the novelist uses the language of dress as a rhetorical frame for the construction of female characters. Moll Flanders and Marianne use the avenues provided by society to define their space. While Moll moves in a world measured by commercial values and Marianne manipulates the social and aristocratic conventions of a strictly stratified society to her own advantage, Pamela challenges accepted dress codes to assert her individuality and to defend her virtue. The symbolic role she assigns to her clothing becomes a sartorial reflection of her self-image whether she dresses as "Goody" Andrews's daughter or as the wife of Squire B. Clothing in the three novels, then, participates in multiple referential systems that identify a woman's place and delimit her physical and social mobility. Like a shell, clothing can protect from destructive encroachment, but even more important in these texts is its function as an instrument for change. Through her creative selection, composition, and disposal of attire on her own person, the heroine may succeed in crossing class and gender boundaries, asserting her own individuality and sense of personal value, and gaining entry into reserved arenas where she can find security and power.

NOTES

1. Daniel Roche, *The People of Paris: An Essay in Popular Culture in the Eighteenth Century,* trans. Marie Evans and Gwynne Lewis (Berkeley: U of California P, 1987) 160.

2. Carroll Smith-Rosenberg, "Writing History: Language, Class, and Gender," *Feminist Studies/Critical Studies*, ed. Teresa de Lauretis (Bloomington: Indiana UP, 1986) 49.

3. See Peter Stallybrass, "Patriarchal Territories: The Body Enclosed," *Rewriting the Renaissance: The Discourse of Sexual Difference in Early Modern Europe*, ed. Margaret W. Ferguson, Maureen Quilligan, Nancy Vickers (Chicago: U of Chicago P, 1986) 123–142.

4. See Fernand Braudel, *The Structures of Everyday Life: The Limits of the Possible*, trans. Sian Reynolds, rev. ed. (New York: Harper, 1981) 321–325.

5. Quoted in Neil McKendrick, "The Commercialization of Fashion," *The Birth of a Consumer Society: The Commercialization of Eighteenth-Century England*, ed. McKendrick, John Brewer, and J. H. Plumb (Bloomington: Indiana UP, 1982) 49.

6. Richard Sennett, *The Fall of Public Man* (New York: Random House, 1978) 65–66, 66–67.

7. See Roland Barthes, *Système de la mode* (Paris: Seuil, 1967) 23–28.

8. See Michael McKeon, "Generic Transformation and Social Change: Rethinking the Rise of the Novel," *Modern Essays on Eighteenth-Century Literature*, ed. Leopold Damrosch, Jr. (New York: Oxford UP, 1988) 160.

9. Ruth H. Block, "Untangling the Roots of Modern Sex Roles: A Survey of Four Centuries of Change," *Signs* 4.2 (1978): 245. See also Thomas Laqueur, *Making Sex: Body and Gender from the Greeks to Freud* (Cambridge: Harvard UP, 1990).

10. J. C. Flugel, *The Psychology of Clothes* (London: Hogarth, 1950) 110–118. See also Eugénie Lemoine-Luccioni, *La Robe: Essai psychanalytique sur le vêtement* (Paris: Seuil, 1983); and Kaja Silverman, "Fragments of a Fashionable Discourse," *Studies in Entertainment*, ed. Tania Modleski (Bloomington: Indiana UP, 1986) 139–152.

11. Ian Watt, *The Rise of the Novel* (Berkeley: U of California P, 1957) 30.

12. Peter Brooks, *The Novel of Worldliness: Crébillon, Marivaux, Laclos, Stendhal* (Princeton: Princeton UP, 1969) 92.

13. Daniel Defoe, *Moll Flanders*, ed. Edward Kelly (New York: Norton, 1973) 8.

14. Aileen Ribeiro also notes that for "all wage earners, clothing took a considerable proportion of their income." In the 1740s, for example, the lowest domestic servant could earn as little as 3 shillings per week while a common stuff gown cost 6s. 6d. and a linsey-woolsey petticoat 4s 6d. The poor wore several layers "to keep warm and to keep their hard-earned wardrobe together." *Dress in Eighteenth-Century Europe, 1715–1789* (London: Batsford, 1984) 64.

15. G. A. Starr, "Defoe's Prose Style: The Language of Interpretation," *Modern Essays on Eighteenth-Century Literature* 248.

16. I would like to thank Elizabeth Harries of Smith College for calling my attention to Defoe's apparent separation of gender-based and class-based dress codes.

17. On the fear of one sex encroaching upon the other, see Tassie Gwilliam, "Pamela and the Duplicitous Body of Femininity," *Representations* 34 (1991): 104–133.

18. "The woman shall not wear that which pertaineth unto a man, neither shall a man put on a woman's garment: for all that do so are abomination unto the Lord thy God" (Deut. 22:5). According to Marjorie Garber, this injunction functioned since Elizabethan times as a "kind of sumptuary law, divinely ordained," especially among Puritans. *Vested Interests: Cross-Dressing and Cultural Anxiety* (New York: Routledge, 1992) 28.

19. See Terry Castle, *Masquerade and Civilization: The Carnivalesque in Eighteenth-Century English Culture and Fiction* (Stanford: Stanford UP, 1986).

20. Pierre Carlet de Chamblain de Marivaux, *La Vie de Marianne* in *Romans de Marivaux*, ed. Marcel Arland (Paris: Gallimard, 1949) 345; my translation. The complete

text of *La Vie de Marianne* has not been translated into English since the eighteenth century; a 1743 translation, which modified the title and made other textual changes, was reissued in 1965: *The Virtuous Orphan, or The Life of Marianne Countess of ****: An Eighteenth-Century English Translation by Mrs. Mary Mitchell Collyer of Marivaux's "La Vie de Marianne,"* ed. William Harley McBurney and Michael Francis Shugrue (Carbondale: Southern Illinois UP, 1965).

21. Béatrice Didier, *La Voix de Marianne—Essai sur Marivaux* (Paris: José Corti, 1987) 88.

22. Daniel Roche, *La Culture des apparences: Une histoire du vêtement (XVIIè-XVIIIè siècle)* (Paris: Fayard, 1989) 394–396.

23. Béatrice Didier has shown that signifiers of the female body are strictly codified and limited in the French eighteenth-century novel: description of the face is most often limited to the eyes, for anything below the throat points to debauchery; the hand can suggest the existence of the arm, but the foot must not allude to any suggestion of the leg (*La Voix de Marianne* 89). To heighten the moral tone of her work, Mary Collyer, the eighteenth-century translator of *La Vie de Marianne,* abridges the foot scene and deletes much of the church scene.

24. See Jean Starobinski, *The Invention of Liberty, 1700–1789,* trans. Bernard C. Swift (Geneva: Skira, 1964) 119–126; and Anne Hollander, *Seeing through Clothes* (New York: Avon, 1980) 214.

25. Samuel Richardson, *Pamela, or Virtue Rewarded,* ed. T. C. Duncan Eaves and Ben D. Gimpel (Boston: Houghton Mifflin, 1971) 30.

26. Wetenhall Wilkes, *A Letter of Genteel and Moral Advice to a Young Lady,* reprinted in *Women in the Eighteenth Century—Constructions of Femininity,* ed. Vivien Jones (London: Routledge, 1990) 30. In 1774, John Gregory, in *A Father's Legacy to his Daughters,* also affirms "how much we consider your dress expressive of your characters. Vanity, levity, slovenliness, folly appear through it. An elegant simplicity is an equal proof of taste and delicacy" (Jones 48).

27. Nancy Armstrong, *Desire and Domestic Fiction: A Political History of the Novel* (New York: Oxford UP, 1987) 77.

28. Caren Chaden, "Pamela's Identity Sewn in Clothes," *Eighteenth-Century Women and the Arts,* ed. Frederick M. Keener and Susan E. Lorsch (New York: Greenwood, 1988) 112–113.

29. Carey McIntosh, "Pamela's Clothes," reprinted in *Twentieth-Century Interpretations of "Pamela,"* ed. Rosemary Cowler (Englewood Cliffs, NJ: Prentice-Hall, 1969) 90–91.

CARLA L. PETERSON

Secular and Sacred Space in the Spiritual Autobiographies of Jarena Lee

Feminist scholarship concerning nineteenth-century U.S. women's culture written over the last several decades has emphasized the centrality of the concept of "spheres" as an important means of understanding the lives of women during this period. Initially focusing on middle-class white women in the Northeast and the ideology of private and public spheres that claimed to define them, this research soon broadened to investigate and compare the activities of other groups of women—working-class, non-white, geographically diverse, et cetera—to whom the notion of separate spheres did not apply. Such comparative study of the lives and writings of nineteenth-century U.S. women underscores the extent to which social spheres and the ideologies that attend them are never fixed and stable but are constantly subject to reconfiguration. It also points to the need for contemporary feminists to engage in forms of scholarship that repeatedly insist on reconceptualizing fixed ideologies of social spheres. Such scholarship must remain thoroughly interdisciplinary, grounding itself in methodologies drawn from history (contextualizing women's lives and writings in their proper sociohistorical framework), anthropology (recreating the cultural perspectives from which women worked and wrote), and literary criticism (analyzing the different narrative and rhetorical strategies used by women writers and speakers as they addressed multiple audiences).

Although never fully articulated, an ideology of social spheres delimiting the arena of African American women's cultural work in the antebellum period did in fact exist. Like their white counterparts, many black women came to challenge these limits and to demand a reconfiguration of spheres. In particular, the female evangelists Sojourner Truth and the lesser-known Jarena Lee mounted their challenge through their preaching activities. An illiterate, Truth was never able to express her concerns and convictions in writing, but for Lee literary production became a vehicle through which she could further explore and test a reconfiguration of spheres. In Lee's writings the result is the creation of a hybrid space—both secular and spiritual—that deconstructs traditional notions of social spheres. And it is rendered in a hybrid discourse that, in allowing the penetration of elements derived from African and African American folklore into the dominant language, points to yet another possible avenue of comparative study, one that emphasizes the presence of a broad African diasporic culture in the early nineteenth century.

Starting in the late eighteenth century, leaders of the free black population in the urban North began the slow process of creating a set of social institutions that would provide intellectual and political direction to all African Americans and help restore that sense of "local place" disrupted by the experience of the Middle Passage. Within local communities, the most important of these institutions were benevolent and reform associations, antislavery organizations, and literary societies. On a broader level, or what might be called the ethnic public sphere, they were the Masonic lodges, the church, the press, and the annual conventions.[1] Most importantly, it is out of these institutions, conceptualized as "national" because dedicated to the national interests of the black American population, that much early African American narrative writing originated. Indeed, these institutions may be seen as part of what Michel Foucault has called "discursive formations," considered central to the production and dissemination of social and cultural knowledge. In essence, discursive formations are social practices that consist not only of a "corpus of statements" referring to the same objects of knowledge, but also of "the status of the statement's production, . . . the question of its institutional site."[2]

As arenas established to debate public civic issues and to determine public policy nationally, these organizations remained closed to black women, who were expected to confine their activities to the more domestic spheres of home and local community. For example, in the first several years of its existence women were denied membership in the American

Moral Reform Society; moreover, women were neither allowed to attain leadership positions in the A.M.E. church nor permitted to voice their opinions at the annual national conventions. In thus restricting the role of black women in the articulation of racial uplift ideologies, black men of the elite strove, in what they believed were the best interests of the community, to contain heterogeneity, silence difference, and gender blackness as male.

How, then, could black women enter the arena of public civic debate? I would contend that they were able to do so by "achieving" an additional "oppression," by consciously adopting a self-marginalization that became superimposed upon the already ascribed oppressions of race and gender and that paradoxically allowed empowerment.[3] In so doing, these women reconfigured spheres to enter states of liminality defined, following Victor Turner, as that moment and place in which an individual, separated from society, comes to be "betwixt and between the positions assigned and arrayed by law, custom, convention and ceremonial," and in which the creation of *communitas* becomes possible: "*Communitas* emerges where social structure is not. . . . [I]t transgresses or dissolves the norms that govern structured and institutionalized relationships and is accompanied by experiences of unprecedented potency."[4] From the perspective of many antebellum black women, these liminal spaces came to function, however temporarily, as their "center," offering them greater possibilities of self-expression as well as the potential to effect social change.

Yet, even in their marginal positions these women cannot be seen as purely "outside of," but must also be viewed as being "a part of"; as such, they were never fully free from, but remained in tension with, the fixed social and economic male-dominated hierarchies that structured Northern urban life. Finally, we may note that these women most often entered the space of *communitas* alone and remained isolated within it despite the fact that their activities were designed to enhance community welfare. Indeed, they rarely became part of the *communitas* but rather maintained an ambiguous insider/outsider status to it.

For the older generation of women born in the last decades of the eighteenth century, Sojourner Truth and Jarena Lee, for example, the marginal space they chose to enter was that of religious evangelical activities that had been unleashed by the Second Great Awakening. Historians such as Alice Rossi and Carroll Smith-Rosenberg have described how the industrial advances of the early nineteenth century represented improvement in the lives of certain Americans but marked a further loss in social and economic stability for many, particularly women, blacks, and rural folk. They have argued that these marginalized groups consequently turned to evangelicism as an outlet for their frustrations, participating in what Smith-Rosenberg has called the socially and geographically liminal spaces and experiences of the Second Great Awakening in which the carnivalesque flourished. In this space hierarchies of class, race, and gender are over-turned and deconstructed, and the individual self loses its boundaries to merge with the other congregants and with the Godhead.[5] In her 1846 *Memoirs*, the evangelist Zilpha Elaw described a camp meeting:

> [The congregants] repair to the destined spot, which is generally some wildly rural and wooded retreat in the back grounds of the interior: hundreds of families, and thousands of persons, are seen pressing to the place from all quarters. . . . Many precious souls are on these occasions introduced into the liberty of the children of God; at the close of the prayer meeting the grove is teeming with life and activity; the numberless private conferences, the saluta-tions of old friends again meeting in the flesh, the earnest inquiries of sinners, the pressing exhortations of anxious saints, the concourse of pedes-trians, the arrival of horses and carriages of all descriptions render the scene portentously interesting and intensely surprising.[6]

In addition, for these women as well as others who belonged to a younger generation, liminality was located on the public platform from which they lectured to "promiscuous assemblies," an activity deemed by the dominant culture to be proper only for men and to unsex women through its unseemly exposure of the female body. Finally, marginality was also engendered by the act of travel, in which mere geographic displace-ment or the journey away from "home" to another location could open up new sites of empowerment.

If such marginal spaces functioned as centers of empowerment, how-ever, they also remained sites of oppression, separating the women from their "homes" and "native" communities, forcing an unfeminine exposure of the body, and thus further reminding them of their difference. Indeed, nineteenth-century black women were conceptualized by the dominant culture chiefly in bodily terms, in contrast to middle-class white women whose femininity, as defined by the cult of true womanhood, cohered around notions of the self-effacing body. Such women were absconded into the privacy of the domestic sphere, where they were encouraged to develop purity of mind and soul, to impose complete emotional restraint on their physical movements through stringent rules of etiquette, and to veil their already pale and delicate bodies in clothes that, following the sentimental ideal of transparency, would translate inner purity into outward form.[7] In contrast, the black woman's body was always envisioned as public and exposed. If in Europe this exposed body was caged and subjected to minute scientific inquiry, in the United States it was perceived, at least initially, as an uninhibited laboring body that is masculinized.[8]

Intimately linked in the white imagination to the masculine work of slave women were those more feminine forms of labor—the reproductive labor of childbirth, the fruits of which were of economic benefit to the slaveholding class, the obligation to fulfill the sexual pleasure of slave masters, and the duty to nurture the latters' children. Feminine attributes and functions of the black female body were thus commonly represented in degraded terms as abnormal excessive sexual activity; and, when superimposed on masculine ones, they led to the creation of a complexly ambiguous portrait of the nineteenth-century black woman. As a result, the public exposure of black women cultural workers on the margins could only be perceived by the dominant culture, and by a segment of the black male elite as well, as a form of social disorder that confirmed notions of the black female body as unruly, grotesque, carnivalesque.[9]

Such cultural constructions could quite possibly result in the transformation of the black female subject into an "abject creature" who internalizes the images of herself as dirty, disorderly, and grotesque.[10] While the writings by, and about, many antebellum black women may at times suggest racial insecurity, they are much more frequently pervaded by portraits of a sick and debilitated body. Indeed, almost all these women were plagued throughout their lives by illnesses that often remained undiagnosed but whose symptoms were headaches, fevers, coughs, chills, cramps, or simply extreme fatigue. In such instances, illness may quite possibly have occurred as a consequence of the bodily degradation to which these women were subjected or as a psychosomatic strategy for negotiating such degradation.

In either scenario, the black female body might well have functioned as what Elaine Scarry has called the "body in pain," whereby the powerless are voiceless bodies subject to pain and dominated by the bodiless voices of those in power. In her book, Scarry enumerates different mechanisms through which the voiceless body in pain can be transformed into a bodiless voice of power: most generally, the human subject seeks to alleviate pain by giving it a place in the world through verbal articulation; in the Judeo-Christian tradition, God authorizes humans to divest themselves of their bodies and seek power through the making of material artifacts, including language; in Christian interpretations of death, finally, the resurrection of the soul privileges the verbal category over the material by endowing humankind with an immortal voice.[11] Similarly, for Julia Kristeva, abjection may be spiritualized by means of the Christian ritual of communion in which "all corporeality is elevated, spiritualized, and sublimated"; but, most importantly, it is "the Word . . . [that] purifies from the abject" (120, 23).

How, then, did nineteenth-century black women cultural workers conciliate these differing interpretations of the black female body as empowered on the one hand, and disordered on the other? The need to negotiate between these two extremes was particularly urgent for black women public speakers and preachers, who offered themselves so vulnerably to the public gaze. In her *Memoirs,* for example, Zilpha Elaw recollected with pain how "the people were collecting from every quarter, to gaze at the unexampled prodigy of a coloured female preacher. . . . I observed, with very painful emotions, the crowd outside, pointing with their fingers at me, and saying, 'that's her,' 'that's her' " (91).

Ultimately, I would argue that from their position of liminality and isolation, these black women turned to the *literary representation* of self-marginalization in a final effort to veil the body and legitimate their activities on behalf of racial uplift, community building, and saving souls. In particular, they turned to writing in reaction to, and in tension with, their exclusion from black national institutions; through writing they hoped both to challenge the power of those institutions to which they had been barred access and to seek legitimation through them.

In 1836 Jarena Lee, an African American woman evangelist who traveled throughout the northeastern and mid-Atlantic states during the antebellum period to preach the gospel, published her first autobiographical narrative, *The Life and Religious Experience of Jarena Lee,* which she reprinted in 1839. She then brought out an expanded version, *Religious Experience and Journal of Mrs. Jarena Lee,* in 1849. The titles of these two narratives suggest Lee's intent to record her religious experiences in accordance with the conventions of the spiritual autobiography. The focal points of the narratives are indeed Lee's religious experiences—her conversion to Christ in 1804, followed several years later by her sanctification, defined as a rebirth to a life free of sin and an aspiration to spiritual perfection, and finally her career as an itinerant exhorter preaching the gospel.[12] Yet Lee's autobiographies consist of much more than the record of the spiritual progress of an individual soul. They are also the poignant account of an African American woman struggling to survive the harsh conditions of black poverty in the early nineteenth century, who, in the process, transgresses the social spheres to which she had been confined, risks repeated exposure of her bodily self, and turns finally to writing as an act of both self-assertion and institutional legitimation.

In the first sentence of her narratives Lee informs us that she was born in Cape May, New Jersey, in 1783 but tells us nothing about her parents, refusing even to divulge their names; it is quite possible that they, like Sojourner Truth's parents, were firmly rooted in African cultural traditions. Much like the poet and public lecturer Frances Ellen Watkins (Harper), Lee was obliged to leave her family while still a young girl to become a "servant maid" to a white family and consequently was never able to obtain "more than three months schooling." Her journal and two narratives constitute, then, remarkable literary accomplishments.[13]

In 1811, several years after her conversion, Lee married and was thus obliged to leave her own religious society and move with her husband to Snow Hill outside of Philadelphia where he served as pastor of a "Coloured Society." Lee's account of her married life is highly interesting, as it suggests that opposition to her preaching was to come not only from the official church hierarchy but also from the domestic sphere. Joseph Lee's refusal to acquiesce to her wish to relocate illustrates the degree to which marriage obliged her to subserve her own spiritual needs to those of her husband and to which such subservience resulted in a loss of community, in loneliness, in feelings of discontent, and ultimately in ill health.

Joseph Lee's death six years into the marriage enabled Lee to devote herself fully to her religious concerns, but it by no means resolved her feelings of loneliness or her ill health, both of which recur as constant tropes throughout the narratives. Yet, if Lee could describe her situation in 1831 as one in which "my money was gone, my health was gone, and I measurably without home. But I rested on the promises of God," she was invariably able to fall back on the support of African American familial and community structures (61).

To fulfill God's command that she preach the gospel by becoming an itinerant minister, Lee was obliged to separate herself from her family and leave her son in her mother's care for a period of time. Even after lengthy absences, however, she always managed to reunite with her mother and sister and throughout her life maintained close parental ties with her son, taking joy in his religious conversion and grieving with him in later years over the untimely deaths of his children. Moreover, Lee was also able to rely on nonkin domestic networks within the African American community, boarding with strangers in her travels and allowing her son to live for several years with Richard Allen, the founder of the A.M.E. church, who "with unwearied interest" provided for the young man's education and endeavored to set him up in a trade (61). Finally, Lee also became involved with some of the broader public institutions, joining in 1840 the New York Anti-Slavery Society, a regional affiliate of the interracial American Anti-Slavery Society, and working closely with Richard Allen in A.M.E. church activities, both at Mother Bethel and the annual conferences of the discipline.

Lee's relationship to the A.M.E. church is of particular interest, for it illustrates the ambiguous, if not inferior, status accorded women by black male institutions in the ethnic public sphere. From its inception under Richard Allen in 1816, the A.M.E. church had strictly prohibited the licensing and ordination of women preachers; thus, Lee could never become an integral and authoritative member of its organizational structure but was obliged to remain on the periphery. Yet her official relationship to the church was doubled, and at times superseded, by an unofficial personal friendship with Allen. If Allen had initially refused Lee the permission to preach in 1811, maintaining that "as to women preaching . . . our Discipline knew nothing at all about it—that it did not call for women preachers," by 1819 he had reversed his position after witnessing a spontaneous exhortation by Lee at Bethel in which "God made manifest his power in a manner sufficient to show the world that I was called to labor . . . in the vineyard of the good husbandman" (11, 17). Thereafter, Allen appears to have frequently called upon Lee to labor with him "in the vineyard of the good husbandman," inviting her on several occasions in the early 1820s to preach at Bethel, requesting her to accompany him to several discipline conferences, and interceding on her behalf with ministers opposed to female preachers.

Indeed, while Allen exhibited a remarkable liberality insofar as female preaching was concerned, many other clergymen both on the circuit and in Philadelphia mounted a fierce opposition to Lee's attempts to preach. Lee keenly felt the contradiction in the stance of these black ministers, who themselves were subject to racial prejudice but in turn discriminated against one of their own race on the basis of gender. A passage in Lee's 1849 narrative gives an especially vivid account of the negative attitudes of black men toward her itinerant ministry. Attempting to preach in Reading, Pennsylvania, in 1824, Lee was refused by the local black minister, a Presbyterian, "with his over-ruling prejudice, which he manifested by saying no woman should stand in his pulpit." To overcome his opposition, "the men of color, with no spirit of christianity remained idle in the enterprize"; and it was left to a "sister . . . to open the way" (44).

Conditions for women preachers in the A.M.E. church deteriorated further after Allen's death in 1831 and following the ascendancy of Daniel Payne in the church hierarchy; by the late 1830s Lee found her access to the pulpits of Philadelphia's A.M.E. churches severely curtailed.[14] A strong advocate for an educated ministry and opposed to any displays of religious fervor or African or folk survivals in church services, Payne decried those who believed that preaching consists "in loud declamation and vociferous talking; . . . in whooping stamping and beating the bible or desk with their fists, and in cutting as many odd capers as a wild imagination can suggest; . . . that he who hallooes the loudest and speaks the longest is the best preacher." Given such an attitude, Payne could only have opposed those uneducated women preachers like Lee whose only authority to preach was direct inspiration from God. And indeed, in 1850 Payne voiced explicit disapproval of a group of "women members of the A.M.E. Church, who believed themselves divinely commissioned to preach by formal licenses" and consequently organized themselves into an association; he was greatly relieved when "they . . . fell to pieces like a rope of sand."[15]

Excluded from the organizational structure of the A.M.E. church, where then could Jarena Lee locate her sources and sites of power? As other scholars have noted, Lee grounded her authority in her firm belief that it was God himself who had singled her out, sanctified her, and appointed her to preach the gospel (Andrews 14–15; Foster 58). Such a source of empowerment led Lee to adopt forms of self-marginalization that were both psychological and geographical (see Andrews 12). Indeed, Lee's conviction that she was a humble instrument of God allowed her to resist full privatization in the domestic sphere, to set herself apart from others in the community, and to construe God as the enabling force behind both her mystical experiences and her preaching. Safeguarded by his divine protection and favor, Lee was emboldened to place herself before the public, expose herself to its gaze, and risk its perception of her bodily self as disorderly and grotesque; as would later happen to Sojourner Truth, Lee's public appearances occasioned the charge that " 'I was not a woman, but a man dressed in female clothes' " (23). Finally, Lee sought to legitimate her preaching, which betrayed forms of religious knowledge "illegitimate" for women to possess, by insisting that it was God who had endowed her with the ability to speak: "The Lord again cut loose the stammering tongue, and opened the Scriptures to my mind, so that, glory to God's dear name, we had a most melting, sin-killing, and soul-reviving time" (22).

To maintain such a stance of authority Lee, like Truth, also adopted a geographical self-marginalization, whose power lay both in constant mobility and in the habitation of those liminal spaces opened up by the Second Great Awakening. Thus, Lee sought to turn her expulsion from the pulpits of Philadelphia's churches to her advantage, deriving strength, as Sue Houchins has noted, from the very fact of travel, which itself becomes a form of home (xl–xli). In her 1849 narrative Lee insisted on her obligation constantly to travel: "I felt it my duty to travel up and down in the world, and promulgate the gospel of Christ. . . . I have travelled, in four years, sixteen hundred miles . . . and preached the kingdom of God" (30, 36). In so doing, Lee was able to forestall the possibility of any sustained local opposition to her preaching activity and to take advantage of the novelty occasioned by her presence: "They all marvelled at a woman taking such a deep subject, but the Lord assisted the organ of clay, and we had the victory" (95).

Lee's travels, like Sojourner Truth's, were undertaken within the context of the evangelical movement of the Second Great Awakening. In 1824, for example, Lee attended a camp meeting in Delaware which she described in the following terms: "The people came from all parts, without distinction of sex, size, or color, and the display of God's power commenced from singing; I recollect a brother Camell standing under a tree singing, and the people drew nigh to hear him, and a large number were struck to the ground before preaching began, and signs and wonders followed" (45). This space of the clearing is structured, not according to a capitalist economy of exchange, but rather following what Luce Irigaray has called an alternative economy of mysticism—a transgressive libidinal economy that exists outside the labor market and its symbolic linguistic order and is characterized by the nonrational, the sensual, the oral, the carnivalesque.[16] Lee's awareness of the dominant culture's perceived threat of this transgressive power is evident in her comment that, despite "the good done at Camp meetings," they are "much persecuted" (39).

Discouraged from preaching in Philadelphia's churches and turning to such a space free of commodification, exchange, and profit systems, why would Lee choose to memorialize her religious experiences in writing? Quite clearly, she believed that by writing for publication she could narrate the story of her conversion, sanctification, and call to preach the gospel to a wider audience and thereby gain more converts to the evangelical cause. Furthermore, the act of composition itself allowed Lee both to deflect a curious public's gaze away from her bodily self and to discourage invidious speculations about her gender as well as to assert her possession of a narrative authority and power of interpretation sanctioned by God. Finally, by selling her life story in "camp-meetings, quarterly meetings, in the public streets, etc.," much as Sojourner Truth would later do with her biography and photographs, Lee hoped to find a means of becoming financially self-sufficient (77).

Yet Lee was also well aware that in so doing she was reentering the dominant system of commodity exchange where value is no longer purely spiritual but is measured in terms of profits and losses, where the economy of mysticism comes into conflict with that of writing. Indeed, having financed the publication of the 1836 narrative at her own expense, Lee remained reluctant to make money from its sale—"to sell them appears too much like merchandize"—yet admitted that the profit, which was used to pay printing expenses, gave her "great tranquility of mind" (77). In striking contrast, a later passage laments the fact that the second printing of the narrative in 1839 "had caused me to be very scarce of money," obliging her to rely on the help of others (86).

Just as importantly, I would argue that Lee envisioned literary self-representation—writing and publication—as tools of legitimation that would permit her to forge an entrance into the dominant economy and, in particular, gain acceptance into the all-male hierarchy of the A.M.E. church.[17] In this sense writing became for Lee a necessary supplement. Indeed, the 1849 narrative indicates that, although Lee had kept a private journal for many years, she did not contemplate literary publication until after 1831, when Richard Allen's death signaled the loss of her most powerful protector within the A.M.E. church. The first sign of Lee's interest in publication occurs in her account of her life in 1833 when, impelled by "a great anxiety to publish my religious experience and exercise to a dying world," she paid five dollars to an unknown editor to have a portion of her journal corrected for publication (66). In so doing, Lee was perhaps seeking to emulate the example of Richard Allen, whose *Life of Richard Allen* had been published posthumously in 1833. Book writing and publication are not mentioned again until several pages later, however, when Lee records that with the encouragement of friends she was finally able to publish her book in 1836. Although Lee's rhetoric here and elsewhere emphatically insists on the positive reception of the narrative—"my pamphlets went off as by a wind" (85)—it also delineates the much more discouraging institutional context within which her efforts to publish took place, her increasing exclusion from the pulpits of Philadelphia's A.M.E. churches: "I seemed much troubled, as being measurably debarred from my own Church as regards this privilege I had been so much used to; I could scarcely tell where to go or stay in my own house" (77).

As a consequence of such "debarment" Lee turned to literary composition as a supplement to her evangelical activities in the Second Great Awakening in an effort to erase her "public" bodily self and silence the "private" voice of religious ecstasy in favor of a more "public" language that she hoped would legitimate her preaching in the eyes of institutionalized religion.[18] That she did not accomplish her purpose and that her narratives remained a marginal hybrid discourse are signaled by the refusal of the A.M.E. church's book committee in 1845 to help finance the publication of Lee's second narrative, insisting that it was "written in such a manner that it is impossible to decipher much of the meaning contained in it" (Payne 190).

In her narratives Lee at the outset acknowledged her need explicitly to validate the authority of women preachers in the aftermath of Richard Allen's initial refusal to allow her to preach. She did so by harkening back to biblical times, but she shifted the basis of her argument from one of gender to one of class, in response perhaps not only to Allen's specific rejection of women preachers but also to those like Payne who emphatically insisted on the need for an educated ministry. Indeed, I would concur with Jualynne Dodson's suggestion that Lee's assertion of her right to preach was not carried out within a larger theoretical framework of women's rights but was founded on her conviction that all those who felt a special call should be enabled to preach.[19] Following Lee's exegesis, in biblical times the act of preaching was permitted to all individuals who were divinely inspired, including those of the lower classes; indeed, it is perhaps the uneducated who are the most willing to watch "the more closely, the operations of the Spirit" (97). Thus, even "the unlearned fishermen" may tell the "simple story . . . of our Lord," and the issue of gender is thereby rendered secondary (12). It is not surprising, then, that as she overcame her initial reluctance to preach, Lee should have invoked the authority of the poor villager Jonah, who had likewise resisted the Lord's order to prophesy.

In both of her narratives Lee directly addressed the twin issues of the power and problematics of verbal representation, spoken and written. Not only are Lee's acts of preaching portrayed as a coming to voice but so is the moment of conversion itself as it loosens Lee's tongue, enabling her to utter words and tell of God's glory in the presence of a silenced minister (5). Lee's narratives further indicate her awareness that the act of narration itself must carefully negotiate between the extremes of hyberbolic and understated language. In attempting to account for a moment of intense spiritual despair in which she came to fear eternal damnation, Lee acknowledged the potential excessiveness of biblical rhetoric when applied to human rather than eternal time: "This language is too strong and expressive to be applied to any state of suffering in *time.* Were it to be thus applied, the reality could no where be found in human life; the consequence would be, that *this* scripture would be found a false testimony. But when made to apply to an endless state of perdition, in eternity, beyond the bounds of human life, then this language is found not to exceed our views of a state of eternal damnation" (7).

Although Lee continued to rely on such hyperbolic language to record her inner mystical visions and dreams, she turned increasingly to "the plain language of the Friends" (20), particularly in the added sections of her 1849 edition, to record her religious activities in the public sphere. The result is a hybrid discourse, informed by both silences and denied knowledges, that, while seeking to gain the approval of the established church, counters the conventions of spiritual autobiography and constitutes itself as a site of resistance to the commodification of Lee's religious activities in the public sphere.

A close reading of both the 1836 and 1849 autobiographies suggests that at certain narrative junctures Lee deliberately resorted to silence, rejecting any gesture toward narration. Indeed, at times Lee claimed that her religious experience was so intense that words could not compass it: "So great was the joy, that it is past description. There is no language that can describe it" (10). Moreover, although Lee's stated goal in publishing was to offer an account of her "religious experience and exercise" for the edification of a "dying world," she steadfastly refused to record her sermons in writing. Willing on every occasion to quote the biblical text from which she preached and to describe the effect of her preaching on her congregation, she remained reluctant to represent either the form or substance of her sermons to her reading public. To do so would have perhaps signaled a fall back into the excessive language of religious ecstasy characteristic of the Second Great Awakening but unacceptable to the ministers of the established church and would have only served further to delegitimate her. The only sermons available to her readers are, then, the autobiographical narratives themselves, in which Lee strove carefully to negotiate between the private language of mysticism and the public language of the institutional church.

Lee likewise refused to specularize herself in the bodily act of preaching but sought instead to deflect the gaze of her reading public away from her body. The body is presented only once—at the moment of conversion—and this perception is one of self-revelation rather than of vision by others: "That instant, it appeared to me as if a garment, which had entirely enveloped my whole person, even to my fingers' ends, split at the crown of my head, and was stripped away from me, passing like a shadow from my sight—when the glory of God seemed to cover me in its stead" (5). Sue Houchins has argued that such bodily images are evocative of "incarnational theology, which asserts that 'the Word was made flesh,'" and Houchins warns against any attempts to "'secularize'" them (xxxvii–xxxviii).

Yet other references by Lee to her physical self illustrate the "body in pain" that manifested itself during periods of intense spiritual oppression, when Lee found herself struggling with demonic temptations such as the impulse to commit suicide, fears of damnation, or unacknowledged feelings of anger. Thus, Lee's apparent acquiescence to the primacy of her husband's pastorate over her own preaching ambitions resulted in her fall into "an ill state of health, so much so, that I could not sit up; but a desire to warn sinners to flee the wrath to come, burned vehemently in my heart" (14). In such instances Lee is indeed a voiceless body in pain who can alleviate suffering, overcome abjection, and transform herself into a bodiless voice of power only by means of the workings of spirituality and its languages: "From this sickness I did not expect to recover. . . . [But the Lord] condescended to hear my prayer, and to give me a token in a dream, that in due time I should recover my health. . . . From that very time I began to gain strength of body and mind, glory to God in the highest, until my health was fully recovered" (14).

In both her 1836 and 1849 autobiographies, Lee attempted to adhere to a chronological patterning of events in order to produce an intelligible narrative, one whose meaning A.M.E. church members, and readers generally, would find possible to decipher. A careful reading of both texts, however, suggests the degree to which the temporal architecture of spiritual autobiography dissolves here into a more spatialized organizational form. Lee's—or the unknown editor's—effort to provide a chronological structure to her 1836 autobiography is evident in the meticulousness with which the opening pages of her narrative record the distinct stages of her spiritual journey—ignorance, conversion, backsliding, sanctification—as well as in the later provision of chapter headings that chronicle subsequent important events in her life—"My Call to Preach the Gospel," "My Marriage," "The Subject of My Call to Preach Renewed" (10, 13, 15).

In fact, the linearity of chronological time is disrupted from the beginning, as the very first pages of the narrative repeatedly circle back around Lee's moment of conversion, so that, although the autobiography progresses by means of a metonymic accumulation of words, sentences, and paragraphs, it also insistently looks back to that single conversionary moment. The first account—"The man who was to speak in the afternoon of that day, was the Rev. Richard Allen, since bishop of the African Episcopal Methodists in America. . . . Three weeks from that day, my soul was gloriously converted to God, under preaching, at the very outset of the sermon"—is supplemented by two subsequent ones: "From this state of terror and dismay [fear of Satan], I was happily delivered under the preaching of the Gospel as before related"; and "Through this means [of prayer and supplication] I had learned much, so as to be able in some degree to comprehend the spiritual meaning of the text, which the minister took on the Sabbath morning, as before related. . . . This text, as already related, became the power of God unto salvation to me, because I believed" (5, 6, 8). Following Mircea Eliade, we may view such a representation of time as the configuring of a "sacred time" that reactualizes the past sacred event and "appears under the paradoxical aspect of a circular time," "indefinitely recoverable, indefinitely repeatable . . . that does not 'pass,' that . . . does not constitute an irreversible duration."[20]

Such a reactualization of past sacred events creates, according to Eliade, a break in profane temporal duration, which, I would argue, appears in Lee's narratives as a spatialization of certain temporal experiences. Thus, Lee's earlier comments on the appropriate application of expressive language to "suffering in time, . . . in human life," as opposed to suffering in "an endless state of perdition, in eternity," transmute the category of time into that of space, invoking in fact both this world and the next. Once again, Lee's reconceptualizations of time and space become comprehensible in the context of Eliade's theological speculations, in which the sacred world is defined as a heterogeneous space that "does not only project a fixed point into the formless fluidity of profane space, a center into chaos; it also effects a break in plane, that is, it opens communication between the cosmic planes (between earth and heaven) and makes possible ontological passage from one mode of being to another" (63). Such a capacity to facilitate communication between cosmic planes is, we may note, applicable to sacred space not only in Christianity but in African and African American religions as well, in which life and death are perceived as a continuum, death often being envisioned as a door between two worlds or the crossing of a river.[21]

Lee's 1836 autobiography is structured around this concept of a heterogeneous sacred space that enables the ontological passage from one cosmic plane to another. As a result, the narrative is invaded by representations of the "illegitimate" visions of the female mystic, several of which in turn invoke, much as Sojourner Truth's speeches would, denied knowledges of the native—African and African American—culture. Heterogeneity of sacred space in Lee's narrative is marked first of all by those "fixed points" or "centers"—represented by the "secret place" or "closet" and analogous to Truth's rural sanctuary—to which Lee repeatedly retired to pray for divine guidance (9, 10, 12). More significantly, it is represented by the mystical realm of Lee's visions and dreams that signals her ontological passage from the natural to the supernatural world. As Irigaray has suggested, the function of such a sacred space is to offer the female mystic an alternative local place that would nullify the inequities of a capitalist economy and of male institutions.

To articulate her visions, Lee resorted to the traditional Christian iconography of the New Testament: her representation of hell as a bottomless pit derives from Revelations, her dream of the need to keep the sheep away from the devouring wolf echoes a verse from Matthew, that of the sun obscured by a dense black cloud for a portion of the day is reminiscent of the apostles' description of the day of crucifixion (6–7, 13, 14; see also Braxton 54). Yet several of Lee's other visions, like Sojourner Truth's, point to the lingering presence of elements of African and African American folklore, underscoring both the hybridity of Lee's religious discourse and the complexity of her attempts to recreate local place spiritually in the New World.[22] Lee's description of her conversion experience, for example, is reminiscent of Truth's in its evocation of spirit possession. Her repeated fantasies of suicide by drowning, although represented from a Christian point of view as satanic temptation, may also express the conviction of newly arrived Africans that death by drowning would ensure a return to one's original local place in Africa.[23] Even more tellingly, Lee's vision of Satan "in the form of a monstrous dog, and in a rage, as if in pursuit, his tongue protruding from his mouth to a great length, and his eyes . . . like two balls of fire" not only reflects the low status of the dog in African folklore but relates more specifically to African American popular beliefs about animals (6). Many of these beliefs, according to Newbell Puckett, were African in origin. An omen of death, the dog—particularly when howling or lying on its back pawing the air—was often viewed as the devil himself in disguise. The vision also recalls descriptions of the African American evil spirit called the Jack-o'-lantern—"a hideous creature, five feet in height, with goggle-eyes and huge mouth, its body covered with long hair, which goes leaping and bounding through the air like a gigantic grasshopper"—whose task it is to lure unsuspecting travelers to their death.[24] Finally, Lee's concept of hell "covered only, as it were, by a spider's web on which I stood" (16), is suggestive of yet another African American folk belief, in which the death process is conceptualized as a spider's web that gradually envelops the dying individual from the feet up to the mouth, or, perhaps even more pertinently, in which the claim of conversion is authenticated only for those who have "hung over hell on a spider web" (Jackson 247–248; Puckett 542).

To some A.M.E. church members and other readers as well, such visions and dreams might indeed be replete with meanings "impossible to decipher." Tacitly acknowledging that these might be perceived as "fiction[s], the mere ravings of a disordered mind" (9), Lee sought to render her private visions intelligible to her reading public through acts of narration and interpretation. Her aspirations toward intelligibility are evidenced in her decision to have portions of her private journal narrativized for publication. Moreover, in the published narrative itself Lee took great pains to interpret her two recorded dreams not only for herself but for her readers as well. Lee's interpretations of these dreams, both of which occurred during her married life—the one of a flock of sheep threatened by a devouring wolf and the other of the sun temporarily obscured by a black cloud—strike the reader as fundamentally conservative, designed to conciliate the contradictory demands of patriarchal marriage and God's call to preach the gospel. In the first dream, Joseph Lee becomes the shepherd chosen by God to protect his flock; in the second, the eventual return of the sun becomes God's promise to Lee of future preaching.

In her 1849 narrative, which adds a significant amount of new material to the 1836 edition, Lee turned increasingly away from a narration of inner mystical experience in order to record in detail her extensive travels as an itinerant exhorter, which took her as far north as the black townships of Canada West, as far west as Ohio, where Truth was likewise lecturing and testifying to the nation, and south to Baltimore. The act of travel itself functioned for Lee as an empowering marginalization, as the novelty and skill of her preaching enabled her to attract the faithful while her transience kept her relatively immune to protracted conflicts over the authority of female preachers. Yet travel also came to complicate the process of the recreation of an African American local place and to raise the question of whether "home" is ever possible for the African in the New World.

Lee's longer 1849 narrative also differs from the 1836 version in its expansion beyond purely spiritual concerns to a broader consideration of social issues. Thus, on several occasions Lee's religious goals are conflated with abolitionist ones, as, for example, when she attended an antislavery society meeting in Buffalo in 1834 and the annual antislavery convention in New York in 1840: "I felt that the spirit of God was in the work, and also felt it my duty to unite with this Society. Doubtless the cause is good, and I pray God to forward on the work of abolition until it fills the world, and then the gospel will have free course to every nation, and in every clime" (90).

The greater length of the 1849 autobiography created, however, certain problems of narration for Lee, revealing, in the absence of a helpful editor, the limitations of her literacy skills as well as her continuing ties to oral culture. The latter are intimated, for example, in Lee's account of her activities for the year 1821, in which she reproduced verbatim a passage from letter 11 of Lydia Maria Child's *Letters From New York*. In this passage, Child had suggested that male objections to female preaching may be answered with the question, "If an ass reproved Balaam, and a barn-door fowl reproved Peter, why should not a woman reprove sin?"[25] As Lee's insertion of this comment occurs in a portion of the narrative in which she attempts to respond to the church's opposition to female preachers, it may well be that Lee deliberately turned here to a form of "voice merging," a technique through which African American writers sought to enhance their own narrative authority by incorporating passages from well-known authorities into their texts without explicit reference. Indeed, in Child's text the question itself is presented as one derived from oral culture—"I have heard that as far back as . . ." (23)—suggesting that the proverbial comment in fact belongs to no one but may be appropriated by any writer and used both to enhance one's authority and to impress its message on readers' memories by means of repetition.

In addition, Lee's 1849 autobiography preserves the journal format, characterized by the serialization of dated entries, to a much greater extent than did the 1836 version. Here again, however, time is rendered non-chronologically, as the years, and the experiences contained in them, are often recorded not consecutively, but haphazardly. The events of July 1824 are narrated after those of 1825, and the events of 1832 and 1833 after those of 1834, for example. Such random chronicling points to Lee's profound indifference to the workings of profane chronology and suggests instead the extent to which her text is structured around another narrative pattern—

that of repetition. On the level of language this pattern consists of the repetition of certain key phrases, many of which are derived from the Bible—"the stammering tongue was loosed," "he caused a shaking of dry bones," "signs and wonders followed the preaching," "backsliders reclaimed, sinners converted, and believers strengthened"—designed to emphasize the narrator's religious authority as well as her primary goal, the conversion of her readership.

A still more significant form of repetition, however, structures Lee's 1849 autobiography—her iteration of each of her returns to Philadelphia at the end of her preaching tours. Here again the temporal organization of spiritual autobiography is transmuted into a spatial one. Resisting the impulse further to narrate her mystical visions or dreams and seeking instead to emphasize the importance of her religious activities in the world, Lee chose in the latter portions of this narrative to depict in great detail her travels as an itinerant exhorter. In this account Philadelphia, home to her cherished son, to the revered Richard Allen, and to Mother Bethel Church, figures as the temporal resting place—and narrative center—to which Lee repeatedly insisted on returning. Here too the homogeneous space of the profane world is transformed into a heterogeneous sacred space in which the city of Philadelphia, rather than the secluded secret places of her youth, comes to function as its fixed theological center, as a sacred site around which the formless fluidity of profane space may be organized and an African American local place finally constructed. Yet even this spatial narrative pattern, which foregrounds this world over the next, proved to be incomprehensible to the A.M.E. church's book committee, who, in 1845, found the autobiography "written in such a manner that it is impossible to decipher much of the meaning contained in it." Thus, to the end, Lee's texts remain permeated by that tension between the heterogeneous sacred spaces of mystical vision and of the Second Great Awakening and the institutional space of the A.M.E. hierarchy that not even the act of writing could reconcile.

Jarena Lee constitutes one example of African American women in the antebellum period who sought to attain leadership positions within the black community and in the process insisted on a reconfiguration of the ideology of social spheres that attempted to regulate their behavior. Called by God to the task of saving souls, Lee moved from the domestic sphere into public spaces whose access was generally prohibited to women of the period—the pulpit and, more broadly, an itinerant ministry that took her up and down the eastern coast and into the Midwest. Given her intense religious fervor, however, Lee transcended geographical place in order to inhabit the spiritual realm of mystical ecstasy. Turning to writing, finally, both to subvert the hierarchies established by institutionalized religion and to seek legitimation from them, Lee reinscribed these experiences in, and of, heterogeneous sacred space in her two spiritual autobiographies. In the process, she allowed her imagination to reach back—however unconsciously—across the rupture of the Middle Passage to traditions of her African homeland and create a hybrid discourse that attests to the presence of a vital African diasporic culture in the early nineteenth century.

NOTES

Revised from *Doers of the Word: African-American Women Reformers in the North (1830–1880)* by Carla L. Peterson. Copyright © 1995 by Carla L. Peterson. Reprinted by permission of Oxford University Press, Inc. Some portions of this chapter appeared first in " 'Doers of the Word': Theorizing African-American Writers in the Antebellum North," in *The (Other) American Traditions: Nineteenth-Century Women Writers,* ed. Joyce Warren. Copyright 1993 by Rutgers, the State University.

1. My use of the term *ethnic public sphere* is an amplification of the vocabulary employed by Margaret S. Boone, "The Uses of Traditional Concepts in the Development of New Urban Roles," *A World of Women,* ed. Erika Bourguignon (New York: Praeger, 1980) 235–269.

2. Mark Cousins and Athar Hussain, *Michel Foucault* (New York: St. Martin's, 1984) 84, 92.

3. See Michelle Zimbalist Rosaldo, "Woman, Culture, and Society: A Theoretical Overview," *Woman, Culture, and Society,* ed. Michelle Zimbalist Rosaldo and Louise Lamphere (Stanford: Stanford UP, 1974) 28–30, for the use of the terms *ascribed* and *achieved* in anthropological discourse.

4. Victor Turner, *The Ritual Process: Structure and Antistructure* (Ithaca: Cornell UP, 1977) 44–45, 126, 128.

5. Carroll Smith-Rosenberg, "The Cross and the Pedestal," *Disorderly Conduct* (New York: Oxford UP, 1985) 129–164; Alice Rossi, ed., *The Feminist Papers from Adams to de Beauvoir* (New York: Columbia UP, 1973) 241–274. Frances Smith Foster has noted, however, that "even camp meetings carefully adhered to certain protocol. For example, physical accommodations were usually racially segregated and certain activities or services were dominated by whites and others by blacks." *Written by Herself: Literary Production by African American Women, 1746–1892* (Bloomington: Indiana UP, 1993) 67.

6. Zilpha Elaw, *Memoirs of the Life, Religious Experience, Ministerial Travels, and Labours of Mrs. Elaw,* in *Sisters of the Spirit,* ed. William L. Andrews (Bloomington: Indiana UP, 1986) 65.

7. I paraphrase here the discussions of Barbara Welter, "The Cult of True Womanhood: 1820–1860," *American Quarterly* 18 (Summer 1966): 152, and Karen Halttunen, *Confidence Men and Painted Women* (New Haven: Yale UP, 1982) 71–91, 97.

8. For a discussion of European perceptions of the black female body, see Sander L. Gilman, "Black Bodies, White Bodies: Toward an Iconography of Female Sexuality in Late Nineteenth-Century Art, Medicine, and Literature," *Critical Inquiry* 12 (Autumn 1985: 204–242.

9. For a discussion of the female grotesque, see Mary Russo, "Female Grotesques: Carnival and Theory," *Feminist Studies/Critical Studies,* ed. Teresa de Lauretis (Bloomington: Indiana UP, 1986) 213–229.

10. Julia Kristeva, *Powers of Horror: An Essay on Abjection,* trans. Leon S. Roudiez (New York: Columbia UP, 1982) 10–11.

11. Elaine Scarry, *The Body in Pain: The Making and Unmaking of the World* (New York: Oxford UP, 1985) 233–234, 219.

12. For discussions of sanctification, see William L. Andrews, introduction, *Sisters of the Spirit* 15; Sue E. Houchins, "Introduction," to *Spiritual Narratives,* ed. Houchins (New York: Oxford UP, 1988) xxxiv; and Foster 61–62.

13. Jarena Lee, *Religious Experience and Journal of Mrs. Jarena Lee* (Philadelphia: Printed and Published for the Author, 1849) 3, 97. Because this 1849 edition of Lee's autobiography reproduces with no significant changes the 1836 edition (pages 3–20 and 97–98), all references will be to the 1849 edition.

14. See also David W. Wills, "Womanhood and Domesticity in the A.M.E. Tradition: The Influence of Daniel Alexander Payne," *Black Apostles at Home and Abroad,* ed. David W. Wills and Richard Newman (Boston: Hall, 1982) 138.

15. Daniel A. Payne, *History of the African Methodist Episcopal Church* (Nashville: A.M.E. Sunday School Union, 1891) 269, 237. See also Wills 138.

16. Luce Irigaray, *Speculum of the Other Woman,* trans. Gillian C. Gill (Ithaca: Cornell UP, 1985) 191–202.

17. Nellie Y. McKay notes that Lee wrote to give "herself voice and authority within the established religious community." "Nineteenth-Century Black Women's Spiritual Autobiographies: Religious Faith and Self-Empowerment," *Interpreting Women's Lives: Feminist Theory and Personal Narratives,* ed. Personal Narratives Group (Bloomington: Indiana UP, 1989) 145.

18. Joanne Braxton notes that "Lee's inner voice sets up a tension between her inner self and external religious authority." *Black Women Writing Autobiography: A Tradition within a Tradition* (Temple UP, 1989) 58.

19. Jualynne Dodson, "Nineteenth-Century A.M.E. Preaching Women," *Women in New Worlds,* ed. Hilah F. Thomas and Rosemary Skinner Keller (Nashville: Abingdon, 1981) 277.

20. Mircea Eliade, *The Sacred and the Profane: The Nature of Religion* (New York: Harcourt Brace & World, 1959) 68, 70, 69.

21. Margaret Washington Creel, *"A Peculiar People": Slave Religion and Community-Culture among the Gullahs* (New York: New York UP, 1988) 82, 86.

22. Foster suggests that Lee's narrative has affinities with the African tradition of the praise song as well as with the Western genre of spiritual autobiography (63).

23. William D. Piersen, *Black Yankees: The Development of an Afro-American Subculture in Eighteenth-Century New England* (Amherst: U of Massachusetts P, 1988) 75.

24. For the African origins of animalisms, see Niles Newbell Puckett, *Folk Beliefs of the Southern Negro* (New York: Dover, 1926) 35; for the dog as an omen of death, see Puckett 478–479, and Bruce Jackson, ed., "Superstitions of the Negro," *The Negro and His Folklore in Nineteenth-Century Periodicals* (Austin: U of Texas P, 1967) 248; for the description of the Jack-o'-lantern, see Puckett 135.

25. Lydia Maria Child, *Letters from New York* (New York: C. S. Francis, 1845) 73–82.

JOAN TEMPLETON

Fallen Women and Upright Wives: "Woman's Place" in Early Modern Tragedy

In one of the least recognized examples of what genre owes to gender, the derogatory notion of "woman's place," both in its nineteenth-century manifestation and in its status as one of history's "true universals," occupies a crucial role in the development of modern tragedy.[1] The genre's first important theoretician, Friedrich Hebbel, chose woman's social and sexual oppression as the subject of the bourgeois tragedy he was inventing in *Maria Magdalena* (1844), for the subject was both "timely," a contemporaneous preoccupation, and "eternal."[2] Hebbel's successor, Ibsen, in the greatest and most influential of the early modern tragedies, *Ghosts* (1881), crafted a drama whose power springs from its female protagonist's poisonous submission to the ideals of "woman's place." Strindberg seized on the contemporary feminist debate to write his own Darwinian brand of modern tragedy; Miss Julie, the woman who would defy the social and sexual constraints placed upon her by class and gender, represents an aberrant species doomed to destruction.

In Hebbel's Hegelian poetics, great drama occurs only in periods of great historical change and takes as its natural subject the dialectical struggle between the old and new epochs. The "world-wide historical process" bringing to birth the modern world makes possible the third great period of world drama, after Greek and Shakespearean; the former, which "gave form to Fate," was called forth by the waning of paganism, and the latter, which "emancipated the individual," resulted from the rise of Protestantism (75, 77). Reflecting its epoch, modern tragedy of necessity will be "bourgeois tragedy" and will show how the warring elements of the new age "are begetting a new form of humanity in which all things will return to place, in which woman will once again stand face to face with man, as man stands face to face with society, and society with the Idea" (77).

As an avid student of history, Hebbel knew well that "woman" had never stood "face to face with man," and thus his "once again" is a curiously wishful modifier; it is nevertheless striking that in 1844 the visionary young playwright saw the relegation of women to a status inferior to that of men as incompatible with modern life. In Hebbel's German Idealist conception of drama as a mediating force between the universal Idea and the actual condition of the world, the "only basis" for dramatic action must be a current "problem" (78); in *Maria Magdalena*, Hebbel ushered in bourgeois tragedy with a dramatization of patriarchy's most important mechanism for maintaining woman in her powerless place: male control of female sexuality.

The play's title announces its subject as one of patriarchy's oldest continuing obsessions—female sexual purity—and at the same time links the play to the contemporaneous figure of the "fallen woman." A spatial trope for sexually sinful womanhood, the "fallen woman" was fast becoming the most popular stock character on the nineteenth-century European stage. Although in France she was almost always an adulterous courtesan, in Germany she was usually a "ruined maiden," long a favorite figure of folktales and ballads.[3] By the end of the seventeenth century, seduction dramas already constituted a genre, and when the greatest German poet took a ruined maiden from Alsatian folk balladry and made her the heroine of his greatest work, the legitimacy of the figure as a serious dramatic subject was firmly established. Goethe's "ruined" Gretchen is the prototype of a host of fallen heroines, including those of Germany's greatest early modern dramatists: Hebbel's Klara (*Maria Magdalena*), Frank Wedekind's Wendla (*Spring's Awakening*, 1891), and Gerhart Hauptmann's Rose (*Rose Bernd*, 1903).

In *Faust,* the ruined maiden's downward trajectory is conventional; seduced, then abandoned, she kills her illegitimate infant, is thrown into prison, and dies. Goethe's innovation was to transform a ruined maiden into his famous "Ewig Weibliche," who leads Faust, and, symbolically, all men, toward their spiritual destiny. Gretchen is saved because her sin was unintentional, Faust because he strove for truth, and both are reunited in heaven in the poem's mystical ending. But whereas Goethe builds on Gretchen's "fall," seeking to achieve pathos in her suffering and death, Hebbel (followed by Wedekind and Hauptmann) critically examines the sexual morality that Goethe's pathos depends on, exposing how sexual woman is marginalized through the imposition of the double standard.[4]

The sex of Hebbel's protagonist, and, more precisely, what we now call her "gender," wholly determines her life.[5] Klara, the play's magdalene, the loving and dutiful daughter of Anton, an upright and tyrannical cabinet maker, has been deserted by Frederick, whom she loves; pressured by her mother, she agrees to a marriage of convenience with Leonard and, in an effort to forget her former sweetheart, gives in to Leonard's insistent sexual demands. She becomes pregnant, but when Leonard learns that her dowry will be less than expected and that her brother is a suspected thief, he abandons her. The ruling passion of Klara's father, one of Hebbel's greatest obsessional portraits, is the family honor; he swears that he will cut his throat if Klara shames him further. Desperate at the idea of causing her beloved father's death, Klara frantically begs Leonard, whom she now loathes, to marry her. Hebbel dramatizes Klara's internalization of her father's sexual morality in a masochistic tour de force:

> My father will cut his own throat if I—marry me. . . . Marry me, you can kill me afterwards! I'll be more grateful to you for the one than for the other! . . . Marry me—my life can't go on for too long. And if it does and you don't want to put out the costs for separation to rid yourself of me, then buy poison from the pharmacist and place it somewhere as though it were for the rats, and without your even looking in its direction I will take it, and in dying I will say to the neighbor women that I thought it was crushed sugar. (118–119)

The womanizing opportunist Leonard, one of drama's meanest villains, has seduced a more interesting prey—the mayor's niece, whose hunchback does not deter him—and refuses Klara's plea. Thinking of her father with his throat slit and murmuring, "Our Father, Which art in Heaven," Klara throws herself into the village well, literally falling to her death as she reinscribes her sin.

In the terms of traditional Aristotelian theory, the tragic action, the praxis of *Maria Magdalena,* is a woman's conflict with the sexual ethos of patriarchy. The underlying motion of the tragedy can thus be properly described as "gender as fate." Klara's status as unmarried pregnant woman clashes with the two colluding bastions of male power over women, the church and the family, which confirm her badness and sanction her destruction. She must kill herself to conform to a monstrously narrow notion of woman's honor, grounded on the basic misogynist principle that woman is sexually evil and must therefore be controlled and confined. "What a fool our grandfather Adam was," Klara's father says to Leonard, "to take Eve so naked and unprotected, without even a fig leaf. You and I would have whipped her from Paradise for a tramp" (97). If Christ healed Mary Magdalene of her "evil spirits," Klara must purify herself in the water at the bottom of a well. When the family patriarch hears of his daughter's death, he responds, "It was all for the best" (129).[6]

Hebbel provides a *raisonneur* for his drama in Klara's former sweetheart, Frederick (to whom, interestingly, Hebbel gave his own first name). When he learns from Klara of her pregnancy and Leonard's desertion, Frederick thinks only of avenging her honor and his own, which he accomplishes by killing Leonard in a duel. After Klara's suicide, he accuses Master Anton and himself: "You were the one who pointed out to her the way to her death, and I'm the one to blame for her not turning back. When you suspected her all you thought about was the tongues that would hiss, but not about the worthless snakes they belonged to. . . . And I, instead of taking her in my arms when she opened her heart to me, I could only think of the scoundrel who could mock at me" (129). Male "honor"—the father's and the lover's—depends on the daughter's and the potential wife's "unfallen" state.

Hermann Hettner, in his influential critical work *Das moderne Drama* (1852), claimed that Hebbel's bourgeois tragedy was as worthy an example of the tragedy of ideas as Sophocles' *Electra* or Goethe's *Faust*. Ibsen, who probably first heard of Hebbel's play through Hettner's book, was profoundly stirred by *Maria Magdalena*. It was one of the few literary works he liked to refer to; he relished giving oral summaries of the plot, and could recite parts of the dialogue by heart. For Ibsen, Hebbel's play stood as an example of a powerful modern tragedy, written in prose, about ordinary people. As Martin Lamm has noted, the principle at stake in Hebbel's play "is precisely the same as that in Ibsen's social plays, namely the immorality of conventional morals."[7] That the "conventional morals" were those applied to women by men undoubtedly interested Ibsen further. *Maria Magdalena* is the forerunner of both *A Doll House* (1879), in which the trapped woman frees herself, and its successor, *Ghosts* (1881), in which Ibsen answered the outraged critics of Nora Helmer by writing one of the most sinister studies in literature of a woman's submission to her "place." "After Nora," Ibsen wrote to the Swedish feminist Sophie Adlersparre, "I had to create Mrs. Alving."[8]

Under pressure from her family, Helene Alving dutifully married for money; after a year of sexual and emotional misery, during which time she discovered that her husband was a frequenter of brothels, she ran away to Pastor Manders, whom she loved and who loved her. Although he later characterized it as "the hardest battle of my life" (136), the good churchman sent her home because it was a "wife's duty" to remain with her husband.[9] Obediently returning to her place, Mrs. Alving sexually submitted to her husband as a "good wife," and decided to have a child in order to strengthen the wretched marriage. The remedy naturally failed, and when her husband began sleeping with the housemaid, Helene Alving sent her son Oswald away to school. Forced to perform more and more ludicrous efforts to hide the truth, she bought a husband for the maid her husband impregnated and took the resulting child into her home, eventually making her the housemaid. While she pretended to the world that the Alving household was a model of gendered propriety, it was not her sodden husband, who in periods of sobriety spent his time reading old government periodicals, who ran the Alving estate, but herself, a closet businesswoman who rescued the property from her husband's incompetence and expertly managed both capital and money. Alving eventually dies, and the twenty-six-year-old Oswald, a free-thinking painter who has been living in Paris and who is stricken with a mysterious sickness, has come home for the dedication of the Captain Alving Memorial Orphanage, the final step in Helene Alving's thirty-year campaign to hide the truth. Pastor Manders, also present for the ceremony and shocked at Oswald's modern notions and Mrs. Alving's defense of them, provokes her into a long recounting of the reality of her sordid marriage: in order to keep the scandal inside the house, she had become her husband's drinking companion and audience for his dirty jokes, and, while he lay "prostrate in sniveling misery," she had managed the money (131). She explains to the horrified pastor the personal little revolutionary gesture she has plotted, a secret poetic justice for her years of good behavior. She has calculated both the money she earned and her "purchase price," the money that made Alving such a *bon parti;* the latter is the exact amount she has paid for the orphanage. Now, she and her son will live only on *her* money, and later, "My son will inherit everything from me" (132). She compares herself to the man who got a paltry sum for marrying the maid, "a fallen woman," while she got an "entire fortune for marrying a fallen man," and she explains how her mother and aunts "did my arithmetic for me," adding ruefully, "If only Mother could see me now" (135).

Helene Alving's years of married wretchedness have taught her the evil of the hypocrisy she agreed to live, and her enlightenment causes her to berate herself for her collusion: "What a coward I was! . . . That's what a coward I am! . . . If only I weren't such a miserable coward! . . . If only I weren't such a miserable coward!" (135–136). It is this recognition of her frailty that leads her to the celebrated epiphany of the "ghosts":

> It's not just what we actually inherit from our fathers and mothers that lives on in us. It's all kinds of things—old, dead ideas, dead beliefs. They seem to come back from the dead, somehow, and we can't get rid of them. All I have to do is pick up a newspaper, and I seem to see ghosts creeping between the lines. There must be ghosts all over the whole country, as thick as sand. And here we are, all of us, so miserably afraid of the light. (137)

Mrs. Alving is speaking far better than she knows. When she finally tells Oswald the truth, the disclosure of the ruined father reveals to the ghost-son the nature and origin of the sickness that is destroying him, and in the tragedy's reversal he announces the syphilis "I got as my inheritance, the illness [points to his forehead and speaks very low] sitting here inside" (154). Helene Alving's efforts to save her son from the truth are not only vain but ludicrously irrevelant, for had she told him—or, for that matter, told the world—the truth years ago, it would not have mattered a whit; the *fatum* was already there, present in the son's conception. It is only now that the dutiful daughter, parishioner, and wife can feel the full potency of the powers she has so eloquently defined as "ghosts"; she must bear the terrible knowledge that having obeyed the pastor's dictates of church and family, having lived "rightly," she lived wrongly, that her Herculean effort to bury herself in the confinement of respectable wifehood was deadly pernicious, not only to herself but to her beloved child. Oswald, the fruit of her womanly submission, appropriately blighted with sexual disease, confronts her with her error in the perverse pietà that ends the play, as he demands of the woman who gave him life that she help him to destroy himself: "I never asked you for life. And what kind of life did you give me? I don't want it. Take it back again!" (155).[10]

Like Hebbel's Klara, Helene Alving is abused by her family and by the man she is pressured into marrying and is abandoned by the man who claims to love her. Conforming to society's ideal of proper womanly behavior, doing their duty, both women perform enormous self-sacrifices that in their destructiveness and futility can only be called grotesque. But if the tragic action of *Maria Magdalena* is one of necessity, "gender as fate," in *Ghosts* necessity and choice operate like even weights on the scale of conduct. For while both plays are grounded in the vision of the human condition that we now call naturalism, whose basic credo, to quote Rainer Friedrich, is that "human freedom is an illusion and the quest for it tragically doomed," Hebbel makes Klara little more than a victim, noble and unlucky, while Ibsen gives Mrs. Alving a choice.[11] When Helene Alving ran away from the unhappiness of her arranged marriage, the man she loved, weak and terrified of scandal, preached her a sermon on woman's place: "Woman, go home to your lawful husband!" (137). Remembering his admonishments, the pastor now repeats: "Your duty was to keep to the man you had married and to whom you were linked by holy bonds. . . . A wife isn't required to be her husband's judge. It was your proper role to bear with a humble heart that cross that a higher will saw fit to lay upon you" (129). Helene Alving could return to her proper place or live penniless and in scandal alone—a choice so difficult that it qualifies as impossible. And yet, although we do not blame Helene Alving for her cowardice, and although we pity her, we hold her, as she herself does, and as her son does, responsible. It is the presence of this paradox that puts *Ghosts* firmly in the tradition of classical tragedy; like Oedipus and Lear, Mrs. Alving dooms herself and others by her own acts.

In 1888, seven years after the publication of *Ghosts,* Strindberg defended the notion of "woman's place" in the famous preface and manifesto to his domestic tragedy *Miss Julie,* whose protagonist is the most literarily respectable fallen woman on the nineteenth-century stage. In one of the canonical documents of the modern theater, Strindberg claims that his subject, his aristocratic heroine's fall and suicide, the result of her having made love with her father's valet, "may be said to lie outside current party strife, since the question of being on the way up or on the way down the social ladder, of being on the top or on the bottom, superior or inferior, man or woman, is, had been, and will be of perennial interest."[12]

In fact, however, the universality Strindberg is claiming for his "natural" spatial topos of rising and falling explodes when he lists the circumstances of Julie's "tragic fate"; his animus against emancipated women becomes not only the determining factor in the play's action, but its very raison d'être: (1) "her mother's basic instincts": Julie's mother was a feminist and a man hater who passed on her nefarious principles to her daughter; (2) "her father's improper upbringing of the girl": in deference to his wife's wishes, the count allowed Julie to be brought up as a boy; (3) "her own inborn nature" (Strindberg does not feel the need to explain this popular naturalistic tenet); and (4) "her fiancé's sway over her weak and degenerate mind" (the fiancé was a liberal thinker; Julie inherited her degeneracy from her mother) (206).

If Julie sleeps with her father's valet, loses her honor, and subsequently kills herself because she has been brought up as a feminist, a man hater, and a boy, and because she has inherited her mother's "defective constitution" (209), then Strindberg's "naturalistic tragedy" cannot be, as he maintains, a modern version of a timeless and universal truth, but is rather precisely what he claims it is not: a personal treatment of a topical and controversial issue. Miss Julie "falls" because she tries to be a "new woman," whom Strindberg renames in his preface, in a clear allusion to Ibsen's Nora, "the manhating half-woman," who, now that she "has been brought out into the open [and] has taken the stage," is "making a noise about herself" (208). Claiming that his play is no "moral lesson," Strindberg delivers a moralistic tirade:

> The half-woman is a type that forces itself on others, selling itself for power, medals, recognition, diplomas, as formerly it sold itself for money. It represents degeneration. It is not a strong species for it does not maintain itself, but unfortunately it propagates its misery in the following generation. Degenerate men unconsciously select their mates from among these half-women, so that they breed and spread, producing creatures of indeterminate sex to whom life is a torture, but who fortunately are overcome eventually either by hostile reality, or by the uncontrolled breaking loose of their repressed instincts, or else by their frustration in not being able to compete with the male sex. It is a tragic type, offering us the spectacle of a desperate fight against nature. (206)[13]

The main flaw in Strindberg's argument is that if one does not agree that a woman who refuses to stay in her place is an unnatural phenomenon inevitably doomed, Strindberg's claims for her as a tragic subject break down. And although Strindberg boasts of having achieved scientific detachment and "complex" character motivation in his treatment of Julie's fall, both his analysis in the preface and his dramatization in the play exhibit illogical thinking and idiosyncratic judgments masquerading as universal truth. Determined to connect feminism with sexual permissiveness, Strindberg gives Julie's mother a lover, and thus she cannot, as he claims, have "hated all men"; moreover, that she wanted Julie to be brought up as a boy hardly suggests that she was a man hater (249). More importantly, one cannot accept Strindberg's moral phallicism; Jean "is superior to Miss Julie in that he is a man. In the sexual sphere he is the aristocrat" (211). And to assume that Julie *alone* is guilty, that it is the woman who is shamed and loses honor, is, of course, to accept the double standard as both psychological and moral truth.

Strindberg's arguments aside, the psychology of his heroine's suicide is dubious. From its first performances, *Miss Julie* has continued to inspire debate about what is agreed is an extremely problematic ending.[14] Edvard Brandes wrote to Strindberg, "You do not kill yourself when there is no danger in sight, and here there is no danger. . . . The ending is Romanticism, determined by the need to end the play impressively"; recently, Strindberg scholar and translator Evert Sprinchorn noted: "Although I have seen five productions of *Miss Julie*—Tidbald, Kavli, Lindfors, Bergner (in English) and a very skilful amateur [production]—I have never seen the ending of the play carried off convincingly" (Törnqvist and Jacobs 99–100). Strindberg would have it that Julie goes to her death because while the male thrall Jean can live without honor, the female aristocrat Julie cannot. Her crime is a sociosexual transgression that must be redeemed. She has dirtied herself as a woman (good women do not give in to their sexual appetites), and as an aristocrat (one doesn't sleep with the servants). Class, sex, and gender merge in Jean's accusation: "An aristocrat, a woman,—and fallen" (264). Jean explains "what difference" it makes that Julie kill herself as a woman when he is not required to do so as a man: "just the difference that there is—between a man and a woman" (265). Strindberg has made Julie "fall" to her own cook's lover in the cook's own bed, site of the domestics' regular couplings, and Julie dutifully judges herself in the terms of her creator's spatial/moral trope: "I'm one of the last. I am the very last!" (267).

But in fact the play could just as well have ended differently. In one of Strindberg's more spectacular diatribes, Julie, *post coitum*, declares to Jean:

Oh, how I'd love to see your blood, your brains on that chopping block. . . . I could drink blood out of your skull. Use your chest as a foot bath, dip my toes in your guts! I could eat your heart roasted whole!—You think I'm weak! You think I loved you because my womb hungered for your semen. You think I want to carry your brood under my heart and feed it with my blood? Bear your child and take your name?—Come to think of it, what is your name? I've never ever heard your last name. I'll bet you don't have one. . . . Do you think I'm going to share you with my cook and fight over you with my maid? Ohh!—You think I'm a coward who's going to run away! No, I'm going to stay—come hell or high water. (259–260)

Why should the woman who speaks these lines to this man hurt a hair of her head because of him? After all, she now hates him "like I hate rats"; "I'd like to see you killed like an animal" (247, 250). Julie's aristocratic reaction to having slept with this vulgar and dishonest menial, instead of "O God in heaven, put an end to my worthless life! Lift me out of this awful filth I'm sinking in! Save me! Save me!" (244) could just as well have been, "When my father returns, never let him know by so much as a hint that his daughter had a moment of folly with his lackey!" Strindberg would have it that Julie's death is both necessary and noble, but sleeping with Jean seems a paltry, unconvincing motive for Julie to end her life; moreover, just before her final exit, Julie speaks with dignity of her pride and her intelligence as Jean grovels before her father's boots. Her suicide thus seems both foolish and forced, and the play itself less dramatic than melodramatic.

In *Miss Julie*, Strindberg defends woman's internalization of patriarchy's sexual morality, as Hebbel had dramatized its horror and waste. Julie's nobility lies in the expiation of her "fall." For Ibsen, like Hebbel, male control of female sexuality was one of history's tyrannical ghosts, but unlike Klara, Helene Alving is agent as well as victim. Ibsen burdens his protagonist both with choice and with self-recognition. In making Mrs. Alving question the pernicious system she is too cowardly to resist, and in making her acknowledge her error, Ibsen accords to his female tragic protagonist the intelligence and dignity of spirit—the moral stature—of the male heroes who dominate the history of tragedy.

Miss Julie is essentially nontragic both because its protagonist's suicide seems more contrived than inevitable and because her death signifies that justice has been served. Julie redeems herself through the ultimate reinscription of patriarchy's sexual ethos: she removes herself as an offense. But the essence of tragedy is injustice, not justice; the heart of what we call the "tragic view of life" is that life is unfair and "irreparable."[15] In *Maria Magdalena,* Hebbel insists on the senselessness of Klara's death; the play's last irony is that a passerby witnessed her jump, and thus the family honor is not saved: "She spared me *nothing!* They *saw* her!" cries the outraged father (129). Not only has Klara sacrificed herself for a cruel and foolish principle, but she has done it utterly in vain. The ending of *Ghosts,* one of the grimmest in tragedy, dramatizes a mother forced to choose between death or imbecility for her beloved child, whose terrible illness is the result of her own cowardice. Either choice leads to a hell she cannot bear to contemplate: "No; no; no!—Yes! No; No!" (156). While Strindberg used the debate over "woman's place" to write a personal morality play, Hebbel and Ibsen made it the stuff of tragedy.

NOTES

1. The phrase "true universals" is Sherry Ortner's, in the groundbreaking essay "Is Female to Male as Nature Is to Culture?" *Woman, Culture, and Society,* ed. Michelle Zimbalist Rosaldo and Louise Lamphere (Stanford: Stanford UP, 1974) 67.

2. I quote from Hebbel's manifesto on bourgeois tragedy, his preface to *Maria Magdalena* (1844). References to Hebbel's works, translated by Carl Richard Mueller, are to *Masterpieces of the Modern German Theatre,* ed. Robert W. Corrigan (New York: Collier, 1967).

3. See Audrey Foote, *Beyond Respectability: From the Fallen Woman to the Free Spirit in Nineteenth-Century Drama,* diss., Columbia University, 1987, 16–20.

4. Hebbel's precedent was the Sturm und Drang genre the infanticide drama, which attacked the criminal code's treatment of unmarried mothers and infanticides, who could be tortured, drowned, or buried alive. See Georg Pilz, *Deutsche Kindesmord-Tragödien: Wagner, Goethe, Hebbel, Hauptmann* (Munich: Oldenbourg, 1982) 11. For an excellent discussion of Wedekind's and Hauptmann's treatment of women, see Gail Finney, *Women in Modern Drama: Freud, Feminism, and European Theater at the Turn of the Century* (Ithaca: Cornell UP, 1989) 123–144.

5. A widely used definition is Gayle Rubin's; she defines the "sex/gender system" as the "set of arrangements by which a society transforms biological sexuality into products of human activity, and in which these transformed sexual needs are met." See "The Traffic in Women," *Toward an Anthropology of Women,* ed. Rayna Reiter Rapp (New York: Monthly Review, 1975) 159.

6. The sexist moral principle Hebbel is exposing here—that the only good fallen woman is a dead one—controls the heroine's fate in the sentimental "fallen-woman plays" of the French second empire. The first and most famous example is *La Dame aux camélias* (1849) by Dumas fils; both in this drama and the many imitations that followed it, the fallen

heroine redeems herself through unselfish love for a man but dies in the process, thus satisfying both the French taste for stories of illicit love and French bourgeois morality.

7. Martin Lamm, *Modern Drama*, trans. Karin Elliott (1948; New York: Philosophical Library, 1953) 14.

8. Henrik Ibsen, *Letters and Speeches*, ed. Evert Sprinchorn (New York: Hill, 1964) 208. Benjamin Bennett connects Nora and Mrs. Alving with the protagonist of Hebbel's first play, *Judith* (1841), who is "deeply conscious of the difference between her personal identity and the role assigned her sex by convention"; Bennett believes that, "given what we know about Ibsen's admiration of *Maria Magdalena*, it is hard to imagine that Nora and Mrs. Alving have nothing in them of Hebbel's Klara, who is also the victim of unthinkingly conventional responses from the men in her life, her lovers and her father." *Modern Drama and German Classicism* (Ithaca: Cornell UP, 1979) 173–174.

9. Henrik Ibsen, *Ibsens Samlede Verker* (Oslo: Gyldendal, 1978) 3: 136; subsequent references to *Ghosts* are to this volume; translations are mine.

10. My reading of *Ghosts* parts from the conventional, virtually ubiquitous interpretation in which Mrs. Alving is blamed for Oswald's syphilis because she was not sexually warm to her husband; the captain, it is explained, was forced to frequent diseased prostitutes because his wife rebuffed him sexually. That this argument contradicts Ibsen's careful exposition, makes nonsense of his claim that Mrs. Alving was his answer to the critics of Nora Helmer, and violates his whole notion of the relation of love to duty are some of the points I make in " 'Of This Time, of *This* Place': Mrs. Alving's Ghosts and the Shape of the Tragedy," *PMLA* 101 (January 1986): 57–68.

11. Rainer Friedrich, "Drama and Ritual," *Themes in Drama: Drama and Religion* (Cambridge: Cambridge UP, 1981) 195.

12. August Strindberg, *Selected Plays*, ed. and trans. Evert Sprinchorn, vol. 1 (Minneapolis: U of Minnesota P, 1986) 205; subsequent references to Strindberg's play and preface are to this volume. Sprinchorn's translation of Strindberg's preface is the only English version I have found that does not expurgate the most violently misogynist passage: "Victim of a superstition (one that has seized even stronger minds) that woman, that stunted form of human being, standing with man, the lord of creation, the creator of culture, is meant to be the equal of man or could ever possibly be, [Julie] involves herself in an absurd struggle with him in which she falls. Absurd because a stunted form, subject to the laws of propagation, will always be born stunted and can never catch up with the one who has the lead. As follows: A (the man) and B (the woman) start from the same point C, A with a speed of let us say 100 and B with a speed of 60. When will B overtake A? Answer: never. Neither with the help of equal education or equal voting rights—nor by universal disarmament and temperance societies—any more than two parallel lines can ever meet" (209).

13. The theoretical sexist Strindberg chose to ignore his own taste for career women; when he wrote *Miss Julie*, his current wife, Siri von Essen, was an actress. The subsequent two Mrs. Strindbergs were a journalist, Frida Uhl, and an actress, Harriet Bosse.

14. For a full discussion, see Egil Törnqvist and Barry Jacobs, *Strindberg's "Miss Julie": A Play and Its Transpositions* (Norwich: Norvik, 1988) 99–113.

15. George Steiner, *The Death of Tragedy* (1961; New York: Hill, 1963) 8.

ANCA VLASOPOLOS

Staking Claims for No Territory: The Sea as Woman's Space

In *The Creation of Patriarchy*, Gerda Lerner persuasively identifies the historical moment of territoriality—the seizure of land—with the fall into patriarchy, thus confirming Virginia Woolf's earlier speculations about gender difference and spatial boundaries in *A Room of One's Own*.[1] The territorial imperative, Woolf writes, expresses the male impulse for personal or global conquest:

> [Women] are not even now as concerned about the health of their fame as men are, and, speaking generally, will pass a tombstone or a signpost without feeling an irresistible desire to cut their names on it, as Alf, Bert or Chas. must do in obedience to their instinct, which murmurs if it sees a fine woman go by, or even a dog, Ce chien est à moi. And, of course, it may not be a dog . . . it may be a piece of land or a man with curly black hair. It is one of the great advantages of being a woman that one can pass even a very fine negress without wanting to make an Englishwoman of her. (52)

By inextricably linking the "health" of a man's fame with the impulse not only to mark and inscribe with his name but to colonize and appropriate, Woolf attributes desire for territory to the male's—specifically the white Western male's—sexual instinct. In this version of male desire, woman's very being becomes property potential. Contrary to Stimpson's assertion that while Woolf grants "woman" subjectivity, she reduces "negress" to "mere objecthood," the point Woolf is making is that the categories "negress" and "woman," as well as land, animals, and even other men, appear as the object of the male's appraising gaze.[2] Woolf avoids essentializing even the white Western male territorial instinct, for she places her reflections, as Lerner does, within a historical framework, "not even now" suggesting that sexual difference is a historical construct.

To historicize in turn, we must acknowledge that before the twentieth century Western history records infrequent instances of women's rights to real estate of their own, and those in contexts of male systems of socioeconomic power. It is therefore not surprising that feminist theoreticians at the present time claim as territory that which is no territory, often by means of spatial tropes. Myra Jehlen's definition, for instance, informs us that "The female territory might well be envisioned as one long border, and independence for women, not as a separate country, but as open access to the sea."[3] Teresa de Lauretis, who theorizes about gender and its production in film, provides an insight into the movement, which she takes to be the very subject of feminist theory, "between the (represented) discursive space of the positions made available by hegemonic discourses and the space-off, the elsewhere, of those discourses": "To inhabit both kinds of spaces at once is to live the contradiction which . . . is the condition of feminism here and now: the tension of a twofold pull in contrary directions . . . is both the historical condition of existence of feminism and its theoretical condition of possibility. The subject of feminism is en-gendered there. That is to say, elsewhere."[4] A construction of gender outside feminism, de Lauretis argues, remains a "map of the terrain between sociality and subjectivity" that "leaves the female subject hopelessly caught in patriarchal swamps or stranded somewhere between the devil and the deep blue sea" (19).

De Lauretis's description of a movement between discursive spaces traditionally inhabited by male representation and the "elsewhere" of those discourses may be applied to the fictional practices of Jane Austen, Woolf, and Kate Chopin in their novels *Persuasion, The Voyage Out,* and *The Awakening.* While all three novels, and particularly Woolf's and Chopin's, may seem to leave their heroes caught or stranded, the refusal of closure and the metaphoric openings to the sea are attempts at representing that "view from 'elsewhere' " that de Lauretis situates precisely "in the margins of hegemonic discourses, . . . in the interstices of institutions and in the chinks and cracks of the power-knowledge apparatus" (25). These three novels are powerfully connected in their challenges of male territorial imperatives both on the geopolitical and on the genderpolitical levels and in their strategies of representing female space as a resistance to generic as well as metaphoric boundaries.

Since the definition and hierarchy of literary genres valorize patriarchal concepts of heroism, women writers' resistance to patriarchy can often be detected in their strategies of subverting generic conventions. By blurring both tragic and comic closures in ambiguity and indeterminacy, these writers leave open the possibility of revisionary readings. Critics such as Nancy Miller and Annis Pratt have examined women's plots in fiction in order to uncover and to emphasize departures from generic expectations, from "plausibility," that is, from the discursive practices of traditional male texts.[5] The insights of feminist psychoanalysis allow us to make certain generalizations about the topography of genre and its connection with the gender of the hero. Traditionally, the male hero's journey depends on successful separation from the mother and triumph over the father (comedy) or failed separation from the mother and defeat by the father (tragedy). Feminist psychoanalytic theory, which posits that a woman's survival is much more dependent on social connectedness than a man's, seems to find validation, if not in women's lives, at least in the models of women's lives created by women authors: the female hero's success or failure rests on her ability to acknowledge, or create, and sustain relations with other women, who function as sister/mother figures. In other words, exceptionality, singularity, and isolation, which mark the male hero and authenticate his quest to set the boundaries of his autonomy—whether successful or no—become for women the markers not of heroism but of victimization and loss of autonomy.

What determines the comic or tragic genres of the three novels, then, is the female hero's success at maintaining a continuing vital connection to other women, so that her plunge into the deep water of a new life proves either auspicious or fatal, depending on her recourse to that connecting lifeline. Austen's *Persuasion,* in which the protagonist remains deeply committed to her "mothers," even as she joins the less rigid and less codified society of her husband's friends and family, can triumph in the genre of comedy, whereas *The Voyage Out* and *The Awakening,* in which the heroes cannot form a similar commitment to a female tradition, are ostensibly presented as realistic; hence they end, as do so many men's nineteenth-century novels, with a female hero who dies. And yet, as is generally the case with genre in women's writing, the demise of the hero in these "realistic" novels, provided the proper emphasis is added, represents an opening to the unknown, just as the darker side of *Persuasion*'s conclusion, the persuasion on the side of risk rather than of safety—its quick alarms—represents that novel's awakening into the unknown. One reason for the ambiguous resolutions of *The Voyage Out* and *The Awakening* might be their similar cultural climates, which enforce compulsory heterosexism, in Adrienne Rich's phrase, and thus make close relationships between women suspect. Unlike the orphaned and isolated heroines of earlier women's novels who had no occasion to learn how to relate to women in mutually sustaining ways, or unlike the heroines of men's novels who had to be punished for trespassing into the male territory of sexual initiative and power, Edna in *The Awakening* and Rachel in *The Voyage Out* live in a time when it is dangerous not only to break the heterosexual taboos but to explore alternatives to heterosexuality. Both protagonists feel an attraction toward other women, which, though mostly confined to an aesthetic level (Edna revels in Madame Ratignolle's beauty, as Rachel does in Clarissa's refinement), treads on dangerous ground. Similarly, both find themselves subject to the desires of older or more experienced women to initiate them into an understanding of heterosexual practices. Because both Edna and Rachel are unwilling to understand their sexual attraction to other women or their own attractiveness for them, in their fear they choose to misread their own impulses as well as the cautions with which the older women try to arm them. Hence, their isolation from other women is as much a given of their cultural milieu as is the skepticism about empire that governs the topography of their explorations. Metaphorically, however, both heroes in their deaths turn toward the sea, which, as we shall see, represents not only the amniotic fluid of their origin but the promise of unfettered possibilities outside patriarchy.

As for the way in which nonterritory—the sea—functions as metaphor in these novels, the unconquered sea world in Jane Austen's day represents the liminal space that allows for the formation of what Victor Turner has termed *communitas,* a spontaneously consensual, antistructural community, in Austen's case the gender-blurred society of sailors.[6] The much diminished scope of Chopin's southern postbellum society and especially the shrunken and chopped-up globe of Virginia Woolf's time permit the door of discovery to open only downward, toward the depths, not the breadth, of the sea. Whereas Austen's novel moves forward toward an undefined but promising social future, Chopin's and Woolf's novels in a sense retreat into a personal crisis. At the same time, the personal, absorbed as it becomes into the largest global mass, the oceans, is symbolically transformed into an uncontrollable force of nature, mocking the constraints of the social arrangements that would seem to have defeated it.

In a deliberate gesture toward intertextuality, Woolf in *The Voyage Out* invites us to recognize a female literary tradition, one that significantly her unfledged hero cannot understand. Immensely attracted by the wealthy, upper-class couple of Richard and Clarissa Dalloway, Rachel Vinrace follows them on deck. They are all now beyond sight of land, but the Dalloways bring English terra firma with them along with their leather bags "of a rich brown hue."[7] They present for Rachel a center of adult normality that neither her Victorian aunts and father nor her Edwardian bohemian uncle and aunt have been able to show her. Finding that Rachel dislikes Jane Austen, the Dalloways attempt to convert her to the worship of a national treasure: "She is incomparably the greatest *female* writer we *possess*" (emphasis added, 62). The text Clarissa takes out because it is "less threadbare" than the others is none other than *Persuasion*. What is *Persuasion* doing on board the *Euphrosyne*? Why does Clarissa get no further than Austen's description of Sir Walter's "book of books," the *Baronetage*? We know that Austen's novel serves to put Richard Dalloway, the supreme patriarch, to sleep so that Rachel may observe him in all his human weakness, but Rachel is not prepared to make use of the moment in the same way in which Anne Elliot was armed to resist the seduction of the *Baronetage*. A century later, Rachel knows less of the world than Austen's heroine. At the same age as Rachel, Anne Elliot not only knew from experience about the desire of men for women (something that Helen has to explain to Rachel) but felt the pangs of her own frustrated desire for the man she loved, and she understood the class snobbery that had dictated the breaking of her engagement.

Rachel's Victorian upbringing makes her succumb easily to the worldly mastery of Clarissa and Richard, who seem to have the "habitable globe" at their disposal (47, 51). The Dalloways, however, are distinctly out of their element when at large, for the two of them exhibit the greatest symptoms of seasickness of anyone on board during a storm; Clarissa even wants to improve the monotony of the sea by having fields of violets growing on it. Rachel, however, hypnotized as she is by the Dalloways' glamour, fails to notice their ignominious defeat by the elements. Only after Richard's sexual attack on her and the Dalloways' departure, as she sits facing the sea and converses with Helen, does Rachel begin to see the imprisonment that her life has been, "a creeping hedged-in thing . . . the only chance she had—the short season between two silences" (82). *Persua-*

sion thus remains a pointer in a direction no longer open to Rachel because, unlike Anne Elliot, Rachel at twenty-four is just beginning to discover relations between men and women, discoveries that will be mediated by her aunt and by reading rather than acquired by experience.

Like Anne, Rachel must learn to escape being inscribed in the book of patrimony, whether the Bible or the baronetage, and like Anne, though less fortunately, she remains at large only by taking refuge in the limitless element of the sea, an escape variously interpreted by critics as a refusal to grow up as a social being, as a woman, or both; as a refusal to compromise; and as her greatest imaginative achievement.[8] It is, like Edna's in *The Awakening*, an escape "elsewhere" out of this life. Would Rachel have understood Anne's despairing resignation, voiced only to herself throughout the first part of Austen's last novel? Probably not, for despite Woolf's later injunctions against texts distorted by anger and resentment (*Room* 71), Rachel, her first hero, is many times consumed by bitterness over her own fate. And this point about the relative development of the female heroes of these three novels brings us to the difference in plot structure between Austen's novel and those of her two successors. Although critics are divided about the level of Anne Elliot's moral development, few would deny that Anne, unlike Edna and Rachel, has already experienced her awakening. Susan Rosowski might caution us that the novel of awakening begins after the marriage, when its happy-ever-after expectations prove to be delusions, and, in that respect, none of Austen's novels qualifies as a novel of awakening; but if we take the female bildungsroman to be more diffuse in its phases and to comprise a more extended time frame in which the moments of enlightenment represent not phases in the hero's climactic struggle against society but discoveries of her difference from the patterned female self delineated by patriarchy, then all three novels are indeed novels of awakening.[9]

Persuasion may be "less threadbare" than either Austen's other novels or Woolf's first and Chopin's first and only novel, because the process of defining a female space reaches beyond disillusionment not to fulfillment, for this might imply a closed-up space, but toward the happy uncertainty of a life at least metaphorically at sea. Austen's last novel, *Persuasion,* leaves us with neither a protagonist perfectly at ease going no farther than "round the Park" (*Pride and Prejudice,* as well as *Mansfield Park*) nor one who must await her father's death in order perhaps to catch a glimpse of the sea from which her seemingly free condition has kept her (*Emma*); nor are we left to contemplate the irony of the line given to one of Austen's minor ladies of misrule, Lydia Bennet: "A little sea-bathing would set me up for ever."[10] By having Anne Elliot, at the very beginning of the novel, turn from her father's favorite reading, the *Baronetage,* to navy lists and newspapers, Austen places her hero in the very midst of British empire building when Britain's maritime power still represents extraordinary possibilities for the intrepid man. In addition to disrupting established rules of upward mobility inscribed in the *Baronetage,* the sailor's family life breaks the pattern of settled domesticity upon which the rest of middle- and upper-class society depends. Austen, who minutely describes this pattern in her previous novels, here explicitly satirizes it, as she has Sir Walter add his handwritten annotations about family events on the margin of his favorite book. I do not wish to go over the well-explored and still-debated terrain of class differences in the novel except to summarize the two sides of the argument, both of which leave the issue of women's position untouched: in one camp are those who find the opposition between the landed gentry and the naval men in *Persuasion* indicative of Austen's incorporation in her last finished novel of the breakdown of British class structure; in the other camp are those who argue that the novel remains faithful to the conservative class ethos embodied in Austen's other novels.[11] What seems to have escaped this struggle over the class territory of *Persuasion* is the female space that considerably expands in this last novel, in ways that go beyond Anne's symbolic acquirement of a "very pretty landaulette."[12]

Persuasion opens in the direction of new, although still uncharted, territory for women, a direction embodied in the character of Mrs. Croft. Although Mrs. Croft attempts to give a reassuring description of life at sea, she nevertheless presents the reader with a glimpse of the unknown, the unfathomable. How did women who accompanied their husbands at sea live? We still remain in the dark, but we see the effect of such a sea change on Mrs. Croft's character. Mrs. Croft provides us with an acute analysis of the female nervous ailments from which she suffered while imprisoned in the patriarchally prescribed role of a patient Griselda: "The only time that I ever really suffered in body or mind, the only time that I ever fancied myself unwell, or had any ideas of danger, was the winter that I passed by myself. . . . I lived in perpetual fright . . . and had all manner of imaginary complaints from not knowing what to do with myself."[13] Her suffering as the inactive wife bears a striking resemblance to Anne's sister Mary's hypochondriac behavior, a constant attempt to recapture her sporting husband's straying attention.

Once she experiences firsthand the dangers and adventure of a life at sea, Mrs. Croft becomes a vigorous type of New Woman—the kind of woman envisioned by Mary Wollstonecraft as a rational human being, a partner with her chosen mate—a woman who despite her unfashionable suntan and weathered look remains attractive to men as an intelligent equal. Nor does she abjure the society of women in favor of her husband's naval comrades; she remains sympathetic to women because she need not compete for men's attention, as does Mary; her common sense and decisiveness earn her the men's respect, even in matters of contracts and leases: "a very well-spoken, genteel, shrewd lady . . . asked more questions about the house, and terms, and taxes, than the admiral himself, and seemed more conversant with business" (22). Mrs. Croft's life opens Anne's eyes to possibilities undreamed of in her own upbringing, especially as Austen blurs gendered pronouns in a passage describing Anne's reaction to the driving style of the Croft couple: "By coolly giving the reins a better direction herself, they passed the danger; and by once afterwards judiciously putting out her hand, they neither fell into a rut, nor fell foul of a dung-cart; and Anne, with some amusement at their style of driving, which she imagined no bad representation of the general guidance of their affairs, found herself safely deposited by them at the cottage" (92).

Most importantly, however, Mrs. Croft's full participation in "the general guidance of . . . affairs," which meets with Anne's admiration, encourages a wider distribution of power, not a coup, so that Anne in the end bonds with her husband and his friends. More importantly, she continues her relationship with her surrogate mother, Lady Russell, who, as the early enemy of her beloved and as the primary cause of her breaking her engagement, could have been excluded from Anne's newfound happiness. She also continues to associate with her social inferior, Mrs. Smith, who in Anne's youth functioned briefly as a surrogate mother or as the tender older sister Anne never had in Elizabeth. Through Mrs. Smith, Anne has had access to the underground world and female subversive power of boudoir and sickroom gossip that fortuitously gives her knowledge of Mr. Elliot's true character and makes her even more determined to repel his advances and encourage those of the man she loves.[14]

Although haggard rather than weathered, Anne possesses something of Mrs. Croft's ability to take charge. What makes her desirable to Wentworth is not the mediated admiration he feels for her after the sea breeze has restored her bloom and after Mr. Elliot stopped to gaze on her, but her capacity to move with ease into the unknown, borderline space of the crisis created by Louisa's fall. Anne keeps her head at a time when Louisa literally and figuratively injures hers, and everyone else including the men lose theirs. In this climactic moment, on the edge that opens to the sea, Anne commands the others, giving orders that everyone is happy to obey, acting as a rational being righting a disastrous course. In this sense, Anne does take us to the border of a yet unconquered sea. Other Austen heroes may be the moral centers of their novels, but Anne, presented to us initially as the resigned, melancholy, and fragile woman of twenty-seven, becomes transformed under the reader's eyes into a commander. With her newfound authority she is able to challenge historiography in the celebrated exchange with Captain Harville on gender constancy: "If you please, no reference to examples in books. Men have had every advantage of us in telling their own story. Education has been theirs in so much higher a degree; the pen has been in their hands. I will not allow books to prove any thing" (234). Almost immediately, Anne is rewarded by receiving from Wentworth a textual account of their courtship that has incorporated her revisions. Most importantly, she moves with an aggression characteristic in previous Austen novels of only the most consummate flirts toward securing the affection of the man she has so long loved.

The Awakening and The Voyage Out, published, respectively, at the end of the nineteenth century and at the beginning of our own, turn more resolutely toward the sea, but the direction of personal change moves from the limitless seascapes glimpsed in Persuasion toward the unexplored depths of the ocean. This downward rather than outward movement reflects the changed political climate in which Woolf and Chopin wrote. After all, the age of empire proved as limiting, if not more so, to women than Georgian and Regency societies, and the postbellum South, even in its creole version, clung more tenaciously to the ideal of southern womanhood as its other values were being undermined.[15] Thus, the opening toward the sea that seemed to offer possibilities of renewal in Austen becomes for Woolf and Chopin merely another man-shaped vista.

Instead of presenting the reader with a liminal society like the sailors' community in *Persuasion,* Woolf and Chopin as realistic writers resist the temptation to create the extratemporal dimension of exoticism or of holiday time. In *The Voyage Out,* the Santa Marina community in South America duplicates British society, and in *The Awakening* the summer community of Grand Isle subtly reinforces the kept status of the women and children. In these late nineteenth- and early twentieth-century novels, the only world into which a woman can escape from patriarchally prescribed roles is the unseen world under the sea, a world that makes its appearance hypnotically and obsessively in *The Voyage Out,* and with which Rachel identifies herself and is identified by the others, especially by Terence, the man who loves her. He describes her as "a creature who'd lived all its life among pearls and old bones" and as a mermaid who would hurl him into the sea and have no scruples about his destruction (293, 298). As it turns out, Rachel senses that her newly discovered capacity for love will trap her in the conventions of married life when she desires "many more things than the love of one human being—the sea, the sky" (302). This realization leaves her prey to nightmares, intensified by high fever, of sexual pursuit, which begin after Richard Dalloway forces a kiss on her and which characterize her death dreams.

As Rachel begins to identify herself with the sea and the sky, the indomitable elements surrounding the foreign continent, her explorations of possibilities for women's lives end in horrendous epiphanies. At the hotel for British tourists, she moves in the course of a single Sunday from rejecting Christianity to rejecting all the modes of life embodied by the British women guests who want to befriend her. During the oppressive service, Rachel notices the hospital nurse, who, while "adoring something shallow and smug," looks as if "nothing would tear her from her demure belief in her own virtue and the virtues of her religion." Rachel's reaction intensifies: "The face of this single worshipper became printed on Rachel's mind with an impression of keen horror" (229). Later, after having in turn refused Evelyn's self-deluded call to social duty and Miss Allan's generalized kindness, Rachel finds herself weeping: "Her own body was the source of all the life in the world, which tried to burst forth here—there—and was repressed now by Mr. Bax [the minister], now by Evelyn, now by the imposition of ponderous stupidity—the weight of the entire world. Thus tormented, she would twist her hands together, for all things were wrong, all people stupid" (258).

Finally, during tea, she listens to the newly engaged Susan listing her daily duties: "Her voice mounted too, in a mild ecstasy of satisfaction with her life and her own nature. Rachel suddenly took a violent dislike to Susan, ignoring all that was kindly, modest, and even pathetic about her. She appeared insincere and cruel" (261). Neither the matrons, nor the young women, nor the single elderly ladies offer Rachel the model of a life that would allow for the vitality of the body to "burst forth," to express itself. Her sensing the similarity of a stultifying self-satisfaction in the hospital nurse worshipping God and Susan worshipping her betrothed and her household duties prepares us for Rachel's ultimate rejection of sanctioned heterosexual love as a viable outlet for the freedom she seeks. Indeed, we see Rachel after her engagement, which occurs in the middle of a primeval jungle reminiscent of the sea bottom, returning to a life in society in which Terence has already decided the number and sex of their children-to-be. While Terence is to spend his afternoons at the Ambroses' villa contemplating his novel-to-be, she is dismissed to write thank-you notes to well-wishers on their engagement. Not surprisingly, it is on the afternoon when Rachel for the first time fulfills her social duties as an engaged woman that she falls ill.

Unlike Anne Elliot, who stakes her claim for the constancy of woman's affections against the inscriptions of patriarchy, Rachel is unable to resist the authority of patriarchal inscription and classification; consequently, since she cannot rewrite the script of her life, her refusal to accept her social role can only lead to death. For instance, despite her lack of romantic interest in St. John Hirst, who, as even her unworldly uncle observes, does not interest himself "in young women's education without a motive," Rachel feels that her value as a human being is lessened because she has failed to appreciate the Gibbon he recommended (201). Her illness first manifests itself as she sits listening to Terence reading *Comus,* a poem in which the Lady escapes passion by drowning, only to be deified thereafter. The passion resisted in *Comus* is "natural," that is, illicit passion, whereas Rachel is fashioning an escape from the prison of authorized love. Despite her sense that "it was painful to listen" to the Miltonian version of passion and virtue, that the "words . . . brought unpleasant sights before her eyes" (327), she waits for Terence to reach the end of the stanza before she interrupts to tell him she is unwell. In her fever "her chief occupation . . . was to try to remember how the lines went . . . and the effort worried her because the adjectives persisted in getting into the wrong places" (329). The patriarchal text read at rather than to her by Terence overwhelms her, imposing itself as the verbal pattern of her fevered nightmares. As Christine Froula observes, Rachel "finds no language in which to live" except in her "initiatory death" (85).[16]

While Rachel rapidly sinks into death, prefigured by repeated dreams of "escape," the language in which Woolf represents Rachel's dreams changes from the convolutions of Miltonian verse to the simplicity of a child's narrative: "While her tormentors thought that she was dead, she was not dead, but curled up at the bottom of the sea. There she lay, sometimes seeing darkness, sometimes light, while every now and then some one turned her over at the bottom of the sea" (341). The simplicity and repetition of the language suggest a return to an almost fetal existence, but a return rather than a regression. Rachel's inability to forge an identity for herself is clearly related to her being cut off from a female line or female community; her Aunt Helen, who identifies strongly with men and has no ties to other women, cannot become a second mother for her, and she flees from the companionship of the other women at the hotel because they embody the stereotypes of British womanhood. Only in her delirium does Rachel feel protected, camouflaged, by the amniotic element with which she identifies so strongly. Her metaphoric transformation into the storm at the conclusion of *The Voyage Out* suggests that her death represents an escape from the patriarchal patterns offered by the lives of the other women in the novel. She is as uncontained, as indomitable as the sea and the sky, the elements with which she identified earlier and with which she becomes merged.[17]

This merging of a realistic plot with symbolic imagery in *The Voyage Out* and, as we shall see, in *The Awakening* has led a number of critics to regard them as failures, or at least seriously flawed.[18] Even *Persuasion* has been read as "dislocated" and "directionless."[19] The plots in which the female hero finds satisfaction even when letting go of social moorings, as Anne Elliot does, or in which she is destined for or attached to those same moorings, as are Rachel Vinrace and Edna Pontellier, but breaks loose even if she ends up in deep water, fail to fulfill the dominant culture's expectations of "realism" or "truth," as well as normative expectations of genre. As Nancy Miller notes about women's fiction in general, "a world outside love proves to be out of the world altogether. The protest against that topographical imperative is more or less muted from novel to novel. Still, the emphasis is always there to be read" (357).

Like Anne, Edna Pontellier in Chopin's *The Awakening* finds it possible to challenge the veracity or relevance of male plots and male spiritual histories. However, like Rachel, Edna finds no socially acceptable role corresponding to her consciousness of self following her awakening, first to the love of one man, but ultimately to an understanding that the love of no one man would satisfy her. Critics have been quick to note the deficiency of Edna's spiritual awakening, pointing to the incident in which she experiences deep sensual satisfaction at being left alone first by her father, then by her husband and two small sons, and takes up a volume of Emerson, only to grow sleepy, not, one would think, an entirely anomalous reaction. However, the resistance Edna practices is almost always passive: she does not confront her husband about not keeping reception days but merely absents herself; she does not inform him that she desires a separation but announces matter-of-factly that she will move into the Pigeon house. Characteristically, Emerson's vision of self-reliance receives the same passive, almost unconscious resistance from a woman to whom the doctrine of isolation and exceptionality remains inapplicable. Edna is equally unwilling to place herself in the hands of another male interpreter of the spirit, Doctor Mandelet, who offers himself as an authority on the psyche but who infantilizes her by calling her, repeatedly, "my child" (Culley 110).

That Edna's sexual awakening is merely a prelude to her awakening to her *condition féminine* becomes clear in her attempts at revising patriarchal plots. At the dinner given by her husband ostensibly in honor of her visiting father but actually in order to have her observed by Doctor Mandelet, the three men tell after-dinner stories: Léonce reminisces about his typical plantation owner's childhood with its "mischievous idleness"; Edna's father tells stories of the Civil War, with himself "a central figure"; the doctor, who has been observing Edna and thinks he has diagnosed her, tells a case history of a woman whose love has strayed, "only to return to its legitimate source after days of fierce unrest." But Edna "had one of her own to tell," one to which she ascribes a female source, Madame Antoine, but that was really "an invention," the story of the woman who paddled away with her lover "and never came back," lost without a trace. Edna's narrative authority is such that her audience "could see the faces of the lovers, pale, close together, rapt in oblivious forgetfulness, drifting into the unknown" (70).

And how important is the lover to Edna's revisionary plot? Edna walks into the sea having determined the insufficiency of her universe: "There was no one thing in the world that she desired" (113). Although Edna has sexually awakened under the influence of Robert Lebrun, she is "a solitary soul," like Rachel, yet both alternately seek and fail to sustain ties with other women (see Culley 118–134). It is when Edna learns to swim that she awakens to the desires of her body, and swimming is a skill that Robert significantly could not teach her. It is the physical pleasure and power of swimming that liberate her, first from constraining clothes and the necessities of social intercourse as well as from her husband's physical demands, then even from the bathing costume, and, ultimately, from all human ties.

The conclusion of *The Awakening* represents both the culmination of Edna's rebellion and Chopin's own refusal to let her story be bound within the perimeters of male inscription. Edna and Chopin both reject several plot possibilities: Doctor Mandelet's plot of the straying but forgiven wife; Adele Ratignolle's plot of the sacrificing mother; Mademoiselle Reisz's plot of the *artiste maudit(e);* finally, Flaubert's plot of the fallen woman's frenzied suicide and gruesome death throes. To the respective contemporary readers of the novels I have been discussing, *The Awakening* appeared as the most threatening in its challenge to the norms of bourgeois womanhood. In 1899, a review carried the following commendation of its ending: "The waters of the gulf appropriately close over one who has drifted from all right moorings, and has not the grace to repent" (Culley 151–152). Contemporary recognition of *The Awakening* as a dangerous text led to its suppression for over fifty years. Critics even now attempt to domesticate unrepentant female heroes whose authoritative and authentic vision, unlike that of an Emma Bovary, menaces the status quo and must therefore be submerged in the critical discourse. As the 1899 critic observed, Edna goes into the ocean as one "who has not the grace to repent"; she removes herself as commodity from the orderly exchange when she declares, "I give myself where I choose." Thus, as she drifts into the final unknown, to be lost, for all we know, without a trace, she revises her own ending—the woman goes off without the lover who "would never understand" (114).

If Nina Auerbach can so insistently focus on the dark side of *Persuasion,* can we not with Gilbert and Froula see the brighter side of *The Voyage Out* and *The Awakening?*[20] I have argued elsewhere for the Shelleyan vindication of Rachel in *The Voyage Out;* her metamorphosis after death into the storm that shatters the comforts of the world of British travelers at the South American hotel constitutes an apocalyptic transformation into those elements of sea and sky to which she had connected herself when she felt most free. Edna's suicide also marks a passage to a "better" world, not of childhood, as Wolff argues, but, as Gilbert suggests, of fulfilled sexuality—a last voyage to Cythera, the island where Aphrodite can be reborn as the mother-love goddess that precedes patriarchy.[21] Just as Rachel in her fatal illness becomes a sort of chrysalis at the bottom of the sea and bursts forth as the apocalyptic storm, Edna, who ventures out to sea with the image of the broken-winged fledgling before her, ends her life in a mythic sea that combines the most benign aspects of earth and water—the blue-green of the water and Kentucky grass of Edna's childhood, along with, synesthetically, the hum of bees and the fragrance of flowers.

All three novelists resolutely turn away from traditional closures, requiring us not merely to read "beyond the ending" but to recognize the dead end for women of customary generic conclusions. Thus, just as Austen refuses to end her comedy in the happy-ever-after of marriage, both Chopin and Woolf subvert the realistic ending of their novels by implicitly denying finality to their heroes' fates. Can we claim that these writers point us in the direction of the postmodern valorization of literary indeterminacy? Particularly in regard to Austen, we should perhaps be cautious about such sweeping retrogressive appropriations. Yet the uncharted nonterritory—the open sea—toward which these three novels turn looks forward to women writers' attraction to the similarly experimental spaces of science fiction and fantasy in the last decades of the twentieth century, as well as to women writers' increasingly successful demolition of boundaries that separate autobiographical, fictional, poetic, and analytic writing within the academy and without.

NOTES

1. Gerda Lerner, *The Creation of Patriarchy* (New York: Oxford UP, 1986); Virginia Woolf, *A Room of One's Own* (1929; New York: Harcourt Brace & World, 1957).

2. Whereas Catharine Stimpson sees a "rupture" between "woman" and "very fine negress" in the last sentence of the quoted passage from *A Room of One's Own*, I see a connection between the category of the appropriating gaze (male) and the appropriated,

namely, "a fine woman," "a dog," "a piece of land," "a man with curly black hair," "a very fine negress." See Stimpson, "Woolf's Room, Our Project: The Building of Feminist Criticism," *The Future of Literary Theory*, ed. Ralph Cohen (London: Routledge, 1989) 136.

3. Myra Jehlen, "Archimedes and the Paradox of Feminist Criticism," *Signs* 6 (Fall 1981): 582.

4. Teresa de Lauretis, *Technologies of Gender: Essays on Theory, Film, and Fiction* (Bloomington: Indiana UP, 1987) 26.

5. Nancy K. Miller, "Emphasis Added: Plots and Plausibilities in Women's Fiction," *The New Feminist Criticism: Essays on Women, Literature, and Theory*, ed. Elaine Showalter (New York: Pantheon, 1985) 339–360; Annis Pratt, *Archetypal Patterns in Women's Fiction* (Bloomington: Indiana UP, 1981).

6. Victor Turner, *Dramas, Fields, and Metaphors: Symbolic Action in Human Society* (Ithaca: Cornell UP, 1974).

7. Virginia Woolf, *The Voyage Out* (1920; New York: Harcourt Brace & World, 1948) 40.

8. See, respectively, E. L. Bishop, "Toward the Far Side of Language: Virginia Woolf's *The Voyage Out*," *Twentieth Century Literature* 27 (1981): 343; Michael Rosenthal, *Virginia Woolf* (New York: Columbia UP, 1979) 61; Madeline Moore, *The Short Season between Two Silences* (Boston: Allen & Unwin, 1984) 56; Elizabeth Abel, Marianne Hirsch, and Elizabeth Langland, eds., *The Voyage In: Fictions of Female Development* (Hanover: UP of New England, 1983) 11–13; James Naremore, *The World without a Self: Virginia Woolf and the Novel* (New Haven: Yale UP, 1973) 53–55; Avrom Fleishman, *Virginia Woolf: A Critical Reading* (Baltimore: Johns Hopkins UP, 1975) 14.

9. Susan Rosowski, "The Novel of Awakening," *The Voyage In* 49–50.

10. Jane Austen, *The Novels of Jane Austen: Pride and Prejudice*, ed. R. W. Chapman, 3rd. ed. (Oxford: Clarendon, 1940) 2: 229.

11. Examples of the first camp include Alistair M. Duckworth, *The Improvement of the Estate: A Study of Jane Austen's Novels* (Baltimore: Johns Hopkins UP, 1971) 182–183, 202; for the second, see Michael Williams, *Jane Austen: Six Novels and Their Methods* (London: Macmillan, 1986) 157–162.

12. Williams 163. Discussion of female space in *Persuasion* has been mostly in terms of Austen's new landscape, her new romanticism, her new sensitivity to nature; see Walton A. Litz, *Jane Austen: A Study of Her Artistic Development* (London: Chatto & Windus, 1965) 150–153; and Virginia Woolf, "Jane Austen," *The Common Reader* (1925; New York: Harcourt Brace & World, 1953) 147.

13. Jane Austen, *The Novels of Jane Austen: Northanger Abbey and Persuasion*, ed. R. W. Chapman, 3rd. ed. (London: Oxford UP, 1933) 5: 71.

14. On the underground network of women's gossip, see Margaret Kirkham, *Jane Austen: Feminism and Fiction* (London: Harvester, 1983) 150–151.

15. See Margaret Culley, ed., *The Awakening: An Authoritative Text, Contexts, Criticism* (New York: Norton, 1976) 118–134. Quotations from Kate Chopin's text are cited here by page number; quotations from Culley's commentary include Culley's name.

16. Christine Froula, "Out of the Chrysalis: Female Initiation and Female Authority in Virginia Woolf's *The Voyage Out*," *Tulsa Studies in Women's Literature* 5 (1986): 85.

17. For a discussion of the symbolic imagery of sea, sky, and storm in *The Voyage Out*, see Anca Vlasopolos, "Shelley's Triumph of Death in Virginia Woolf's *The Voyage Out*," *Modern Language Quarterly* 47 (1986): 130–153.

18. See Carole O. Brown, "The Art of the Novel: Virginia Woolf's *The Voyage Out*," *Virginia Woolf Quarterly* 3 (1977): 67–84; Fleishman 14; and Rosenthal 49. On *The Awakening*, see George M. Spangler, "Kate Chopin's *The Awakening:* A Partial Dissent," *Novel* 3 (1970): 244–255; and Elizabeth Fox-Genovese, "Kate Chopin's *Awakening*," *Southern Studies* 18 (1979): 263–266.

19. See Julia Prewitt Brown, *Jane Austen's Novels: Social Change and Literary Form* (Cambridge: Harvard UP, 1979) 147.

20. Nina Auerbach, "Jane Austen and Romantic Imprisonment," *Jane Austen in a Social Context,* ed. David Monaghan (Totowa, NJ: Barnes & Noble, 1981) 9–27; Froula 63–90; Sandra M. Gilbert, "The Second Coming of Aphrodite: Kate Chopin's Fantasy of Desire," *Kenyon Review* 5 (1983): 42–66.

21. Cynthia Griffin Wolff, "Thanatos and Eros: Kate Chopin's *The Awakening*," *American Quarterly* 25 (1973): 449–471.

KATHLEEN L. KOMAR

Feminist Curves in
Contemporary Literary Space

In her article "The Squaring of the Circle: The Male Takeover of Power in Architectural Shapes," art historian and archaeologist Cillie Rentmeister compellingly explores the "curved/angular" polarity.[1] Rentmeister argues that the originally matriarchal peoples of the Mediterranean and the Near East had a predominantly oval and egg-shaped architectural style. That this style was supplanted by the monumental architecture of Greece evidences the victory of the patriarchy over these earlier matriarchal cultures, or "the male takeover of power in architectural shapes." While Rentmeister wisely cautions against the simplistic transferral of historical knowledge to serve as a model for revolutionary feminist action in the present, her study nonetheless makes clear the importance of space and forms for the explorations of gender. Christiane Erlemann in her essay "What is Feminist Architecture?" takes Rentmeister's analyses one step further: "women's spatial utopias nowadays lean heavily toward curved forms, and if we want to assume that there is more to them than an outline sketch then they must be rooted in a critique of the dominant shapes, a critique which finds symbolic expression in the circular form."[2]

Like Erlemann and Rentmeister, both Sarah Kirsch and Alice Walker acknowledge the association of particular kinds of spatial images and metaphors with males and females—an association common in literary analysis since long before Freud. When the main character in Kirsch's "Blitz aus heiterm Himmel" (A Bolt from the Blue) miraculously changes from a woman into a man, one of her first actions is to replace her apartment's curved spaces, which she had preferred as a woman, with rectangular configurations more appropriate to her new male being.[3] From the opposite perspective, Nettie, of Walker's *The Color Purple,* opts for a round living space that stands in distinction to the rectilinear shapes that define the patriarchal/colonialist structures of school and church in her African village: "I wish you could see my hut, Celie. I love it. Unlike our school, which is square, and unlike our church, which doesn't have walls—at least during the dry season—my hut is round, walled, with a round roofleafroof. It is twenty steps across the middle and fits me to a T."[4] This womblike space not only "fits" Nettie's femaleness but also recalls the native African building style that is being impinged upon and devalued by the colonial powers that have come to "civilize" the dark continent. Both Kirsch's character and Walker's respond intuitively to their new living situations, but their preferences offer support for the findings of art historians, archaeologists, and architects regarding the connection of spaces and spatial metaphors to gender.[5]

All of these thinkers focus on the curved form, reminiscent of the womb and, therefore, of a particularly sororal space, as central to women's conceptualization and actualization of their spatial context. What interests me here is whether the works of contemporary women writers from diverse cultural backgrounds will support such associations, whether specific uses of space and spatial images recur, and, if so, what purpose they serve. I also want to explore how one specific spatial arena, namely, the space of the literary text itself—the unviolated, virginal space of the empty page that waits to give birth to women's suppressed or repressed thoughts—becomes extremely important to women writers. This literary space that is both psychological and physical helps to form a bridge between the outside world and the woman's mind driven deep into its own recesses. Alice Walker's Celie is not alone in her discovery of textual space as a means of female salvation.

Drawing on women's texts from cultures including Germany, France, Africa, Japan, and the United States, I have found two recurrent strategies in the treatment of space. First, women writers identify female spaces in the external world—or indeed they project female spaces onto this outside world. And second, women authors use an opposite strategy for defining and affirming their female selves; they exploit an interior space that is not merely biological (although it is often graphically so) but also psychological. This interior female space is eventually reexteriorized in the form of the literary text, not simply because the women write their stories, but because the space of the text eventually becomes the site of definition and affirmation of the female within and against a male-dominated social structure.

In *Kassandra* Christa Wolf uses traditionally female imagery such as caves and rivers in connection with an alternative female society, gathered around the earth-mother goddess Kybele, which served as an opposition to the male-dominated Trojan court.[6] But Wolf also exploits the traditional assumptions about female imagery for rather startling purposes. She emphasizes the extent of male domination by revealing men's usurpation of womblike, female spaces for repressive purposes. The Trojan rulers, for example, imprison Kassandra in a beehive-shaped, womblike basket in order to keep her from warning Achilles of his impending doom. She is thus physically forced back into the womb and into the preverbal state that deprives her of the speech necessary to alter the political and historical reality that surrounds her. Just as her speech is deprived of authority because of her refusal to submit to Apollo's sexual advances, both her sexuality and her speech are repressed as she is forced to return to the internal space of the womb/tomb.[7] By containing the woman in the space symbolizing that which is most essentially hers, the male political establishment subverts this most female of spaces and turns it against the woman who would participate in history.[8]

Wolf's critique is obviously aimed at the contemporary situation of women writers as well as at the Trojan hierarchy. She implies that no external space, however symbolically "female," is safe from male domination and misuse. Kassandra may refuse Apollo's sexual demands, but she pays heavily for this privilege. What men cannot deprive Kassandra of, however, is her internal speech, a fact I will explore when I look at the second strategy of internalization and textualization of space by women.

The technique of forcing women back into an enclosed space reminiscent of a womb in order to destroy them is an old one. Antigone comes to mind, but so do all the women of fairy tale and myth who are confined in caves or dungeons. The enclosed spaces that echo the biological space of the female become arenas of punishment or at least confinement in which women can themselves be contained and separated from male social space. A metaphorically "female" space thus becomes a weapon with which to combat men's fear of the womb, which Simone de Beauvoir and others have analyzed.[9] Woman is forced back in upon herself to keep her from contaminating patriarchal society. In the case of Wolf's Kassandra, this is precisely what is intended.

Of course, the usurpation of a symbolic womb is only a pale shadow of the violations that are enforced upon the actual space of the female womb itself. Alice Walker's Celie, for example, is repeatedly raped as a child as part of her general subjugation to her stepfather's will. She is additionally brutalized by the rape of her mind as well when her stepfather lays the burden of concealment and guilt upon the defenseless female child, who is told that if she tells anyone about the rape, "It'd kill [her] mammy" (11). Thus two internal female spaces—the womb and the female mind—are both invaded by a patriarchal dominator.

The violated space of the female womb appears repeatedly in texts by contemporary women as the symbol of patriarchal violence. Wolf's Kassandra, for example, is raped by Ajax the Lesser. Classical tradition places the rape in the sanctuary of Athena, thus creating a patriarchal transgression that brutalizes and humbles not only a female mortal, Kassandra, but also a divine female, Athena. Wolf, however, transposes the action to the caverns that constitute the graves of the heroes. The rapist violates both the womblike space of the graves and the literal womb of Kassandra. Kassandra's compatriot, Penthesilea, is not spared even after death, as a frenzied Achilles rapes her lifeless corpse in an act of supreme male vengeance against the Amazon woman who would subdue and vanquish men. The male usurping of the female womb—for personal pleasure or breeding of heirs or simply to prove superior physical strength—is a transgression of female space that recurs often and signals the victory (at least on a temporary basis) of patriarchal powers over the female.

In *Häutungen* (Shedding), Verena Stefan uses specifically anatomical spaces to represent female sexuality and vulnerability, examining female genitalia in precise detail. Woman's body becomes a personal spatial site that she must explore in order to alter her relationship to the surrounding male-dominated cultural and social space.

> I begin to call myself by name. I join the individual pieces together into a whole body. I have breasts and a pelvis. My legs run together in roundnesses folds and lips. I glide and sink with Fenna through meadows of labiate blossoms (only a man could call these erotic women's flowers of the labiate form "lion's mouths" [snapdragon]).
> . . . No, I say breathlessly, we have no "shame lips" [labia]. I look carefully at myself, steep myself in the colors, the shadings, the differences in the skin.

my lips are wrinkled, rolled together. they really look like rolled up flower petals, brownish, when I gently unroll them, shining pink. the many unknown color tones of one's own body! we create ourselves anew through touching looking discussing.[10]

The point of such graphic exteriorizing of the body's intimate, interior space is to transgress those boundaries of tradition and culture that demand that the female body remain hidden and separate from the exterior space dominated by men. Just as Stefan's narrator resents the social repression in men's assumption that she is an object for them to penetrate with their sexually invasive gaze or to fondle at will in the external world they control, Stefan herself resents the repression of the female body within the literary text.[11] Those labiate shapes that surround and preface the womb become not only beautiful natural shapes (flowers), but also lips that speak eloquently of female spaces in general. Stefan's flowerlike shapes recall a similar gesture of exteriorizing the female body by artist Judy Chicago in works such as "Dinner Party."[12] In her startling visual displays, Chicago too seeks to transgress the taboos and boundaries that demand that women's interior being remain hidden. Her aesthetic presentation insists that women rather than men control how women's interior spaces are represented.

In *Les Guérillères,* Monique Wittig explores the space of female anatomy in order to break the taboo assigned to women's being interested in or fascinated with their own bodies. She overemphasizes female genitalia in an attempt to get beyond the need to mythologize the body, to reach a point at which the interest in genitalia will give way to a less gender-fixated narrative.

> In speaking of their genitals the women do not employ hyperboles, metaphors, they do not proceed sequentially or by gradation. They do not recite long litanies, whose refrain is an unending imprecation. They do not strive to multiply the intervals so that in sum they signify a deliberate lapse. They say that all these forms denote an outworn language. They say everything must begin over again. . . . They say that at the point they have reached they must examine the principle that has guided them. They say it is not for them to exhaust their strength in symbols. They say hence-forward what they are is not subject to compromise. They say they must now stop exalting the vulva. They say that they must break the last bond that binds them to a dead culture. They say that any symbol that exalts the fragmented body is transient, must disappear. Thus it was formerly. They, the women, the integrity of the body their first principle, advance marching together into another world.[13]

Until we arrive at less gender-fixated narratives, Wittig must speak the female body emphatically in order to show it in a newly feminized social space. In the group participation in micturition, Wittig produces a much more communal version of the space of sexual exploration than male characters such as those in Günter Grass's *Katz und Maus* enjoy during their group masturbation competitions.[14] This graphic writing of the female body insists on the personal space of the female even in the male-oriented space of the literary tradition. The female body even comes to replace patriarchal religious symbolism as Wittig redefines the quest for the Grail as a quest for the spherical cup containing the blood—or, the vagina.

This focusing on the female body in women's texts produces a new space of comprehension, in which the body becomes nothing less than a new source of understanding equal to the mind. Wolf's Christa T., for example, realizes through her body the need to resist Nazi Germany as she reacts viscerally rather than intellectually to the playing of the German national anthem. Likewise, Suga in Fumiko Enchi's *The Waiting Years* comes to comprehend the nature of men and to sympathize with another woman not by thought but directly through the body: "Ever since her arrival in the Shirakawa household and her discovery of men's nature—a discovery made through her body and in the dark, far from bright colors and music—Suga had cherished in her heart, quite untouched by her direct relationship with Shirakawa, a shining world of enchantment."[15]

After her first, unexpected sexual encounter with Shirakawa, Suga comprehends her own subordinate position of servant who satisfies her master's appetite. Once her internal biological space is violated, only her imagination, her internal psychological space, allows her to conceive of a happier fictional existence. In the same way, she perceives her sympathy for a fellow concubine directly through shared physical—that is, bodily—experience:

> Shirakawa must have done something to Yumi, somewhere, for Suga found her one day standing by the heavy doors of the white-walled storehouse, her narrow shoulders shaking with sobs. "What's the matter? Yumi, tell me what's the matter." . . . Yumi promptly hid her face in the sleeve of her kimono and wept. At each heave of her shoulders Suga felt a vague sensation in her own body that told her quite clearly, with no need to ask, the cause of Yumi's misery. "There, Yumi . . . I know, I know. It was the same with me after all." (70)

Passages such as these correspond to many similar passages in European and American women's literature that assert that the body itself can be a means of comprehending the world. Suga's insight into her social status and her sympathy with Yumi are immediately physical. There is a common sororal understanding that does not depend on cerebration or rationality. Male violation of female internal space cannot destroy this bodily sympathy but, rather, strengthens the unity of physical apprehension for women—a variety of comprehension not open to men in the texts I have examined.

Wittig extends the use of female bodily spaces by also choosing to read external spaces as essentially female, thus subverting the Freudian projection of the phallic onto everything in the world that is longer than it is wide. Wittig literally undertakes a "re-vision" of the external world, even using the symbolic associations of the male-dominated tradition to assert their newly feminized qualities. While Freud, for example, connects weaving and pubic hair to highlight the entangling quality of both for men, Wittig uses spinning as a means of unifying women and giving them wings to escape heterosexual entanglements.

> Whether they are marching or standing still, their hands are always stretched far out from their bodies. Most often they hold them at each side at shoulder height, which makes them resemble some hieratic figure. The fingers of their hands are spread out and in incessant movement. Spinning-glands are at work on each of their limbs. From their many orifices there emerge thick barely visible filaments that meet and fuse together. Under the repeated play of movement in the fingers a membrane grows between them that seems to join them, then prolong them, until eventually it extends beyond the hand and descends along the arm, it grows, it lengthens, it gives the women a sort of wing on either side of their body. (132)

Wittig sees the weaving specific to women as a connecting activity. Discrete female spaces merge in a sororal space that is not so much concerned with entangling men as with uniting women.

Lesbian author Judy Grahn similarly stresses the positively female characteristics of weaving in her poetic text *The Queen of Wands*. Grahn's text revises the myths of Helen of Troy, who was herself textually connected with weaving. (For example, she weaves scenes of battle as she awaits the outcome of the Trojan War.) Grahn takes up the image of weaving (an attribute of Athena as well as of her too truthful rival Arachne and of Helen herself), to produce a spirit called Webster or Spider Webster. "Webster," she explains, "is a word that formerly meant 'female weaver,' the 'ster' ending indicating a female ancestor, or female possession of the word."[16] Punning on the famous Webster dynasty of "word-weavers" who produced many of our dictionaries, Grahn asserts that "language is a form of weaving too" and that its roots are female not male. She thus rejects the idea that language is foreign to women, and she reappropriates the weaving of fate and of words for the female. This strategy paves the way for women to create a new female self in a specifically female textual space.

Grahn continues to focus on weaving as she plays on the word *spinster* as one who spins but also as a name for "women who do not marry, who are sexually self-determined and even lesbian" (100). Grahn explains, "In China women who worked in the women-developed silk industry bribe their way out of marriage, and are notorious as 'bad girls,' militant organizers and lesbians. They are true spinsters, defending the traditional economic independence of ancient women" (100). Spider Webster, therefore, also takes on a note of sexual as well as economic independence and self-determination for women.

In her extensive (and indispensable) "Notes," Grahn extends the importance of weaving in the economic sphere. She describes the beginnings of world economy as being based on clothmaking, and thus "solidly in women's hands" (104). Having redefined the economic foundation, Grahn then argues that the Trojan War was fought, in part at least, in order to capture the economic value and power of the Trojan women tapestry makers. Eventually, men come to control the women and their economic worth, and they forcibly sever the magical and shamanic traditions connected with weaving by instilling fear of spiders and spirits, according to Grahn. In the final step of the patriarchal bid for control, factories replace individual weavers as patriarchal space replaces the female hearthside. "Although the actual closework continued to be done mostly by women, the control of value, use and meaning of the weavings passed into the hands of men—a new kind of men—industrial men" (105). This re-vision of economic history figures prominently in Grahn's version of the horrible and true Triangle Fire story in which 143 young women burn to death in a textile factory because the doors had been locked to keep out organizers.

Both Wittig and Grahn, then, see the female implications of weaving not as entrapment for men, but rather as a spatial connecting force and a focus of unity and power for women. They reject the interjection of male meaning into a symbolically female activity in order to reclaim for women weaving and the aesthetic and narrative spaces it creates. They stress the psychological, physical, and economic strength of a female community and of female space. Their work helps to counter the traditional Western impulse to create all meaning and to judge all value by comparison with male activity. In a similar gesture, Wittig aggressively asserts parallels between women's pubic hair and the Golden Fleece as sacred mythic object. Both Grahn and Wittig return women to the center not only of the space of their individual texts, but to the center of Western aesthetic and mythic space in general.

Other natural imagery is also given a female imprint in Wittig's text: mercury has the properties of the clitoris; water flows in sympathy with women's bodily rhythms. This identification of female body parts or characteristics with natural objects or forces that resemble them in appearance or quality is, of course, an old tradition frequently employed (as the passage from *Häutungen* attests). But Wittig claims the normally male domain of geometry for the female as well, depicting the geometrically enclosed space of the circle or "O" as paralleling the vaginal opening; triangles resemble pubic hair and rectangles the clitoris. Perhaps the most consequent and radical feminist of the authors I discuss here, Wittig refuses to cede to the male any spatial domain, whether natural or abstract. The interior of the circle formed by women together describes a newly female social space in which communality outstrips competition. This female creation of a social space defined by interiority parallels the biologically interior sexual space that is exclusive to the female.

Thus far my examples have focused on the rediscovery of female spaces that are physical and even biological. These women writers also employ a second strategy for defining and affirming their female selves. They exploit an interior space that is not biological but psychological, a space that is eventually reexteriorized in the form of the literary text itself. This turn toward the interior spaces of the mind is a technique long used by women writers. Elizabeth Abel, Marianne Hirsch, and Elizabeth Langland, the editors of *The Voyage In: Fictions of Female Development,* discuss the necessity for protagonists of the nineteenth-century female bildungsroman to turn inward and to "substitute inner concentration for active accommodation, rebellion, or withdrawal," since they cannot participate in the public realm in the same way as men (8).[17] They find, however, that "confinement to inner life, no matter how enriching, threatens a loss of public activity; it enforces an isolation that may culminate in death" (8). Contemporary women writers experience similar limitations. Their characters succumb to madness, death, or both, or they must find a way to reexteriorize their concentrated energies into some public forum. The literary text provides them just such a public space in which to reinscribe their interior experiences.

In contemporary texts by women, the frequency with which the main female characters retreat into the interior space of the mind is striking. The precedent, of course, is again an old one. Female characters have long retrenched in the attic spaces of madness.[18] But contemporary female characters often reemerge from their bouts with near madness to declare a new, relational sense of the self that seems to bear out the developmental models of the psychological school of object relations, which emphasizes preoedipal relationships and interpersonal connectedness rather than separation into a strongly individuated and discrete superego. These feminist revisionist psychoanalysts, such as Nancy Chodorow, Dorothy Dinnerstein, Jane Flax, Carol Gilligan, and Jean Baker Miller, stress the female's relationship to her mother, thus creating a more symbiotic experience and emphasizing continuity, lack of separation, and a fluid, permeable ego boundary.[19] This ego flexibility and relational thinking helps some contemporary women characters to escape madness into a new space of psychological, spiritual, and social relationships.

One striking configuration of female psychological space by women authors takes place in two novels from very different geographical areas and cultures. Both Austrian Ingeborg Bachmann in *Malina* and South African/Botswanan writer Bessie Head in *A Question of Power* depict a female protagonist whose personality is divided into and conditioned by two competing male personae. This psychological splitting threatens to destabilize both women characters as they each teeter on the edge of madness.

Bachmann's unnamed first-person narrator is torn between the rational and practical Malina and the passionate Ivan, who invigorates her imagination but remains largely indifferent to her needs. The two male characters can be read both as discrete characters and as fragments of the narrator's own mind. It is ultimately impossible to decide exclusively for one interpretation or the other. This lack of single interpretation creates an insoluble ambiguity for the reader that mirrors the narrator's own situation. The narrator experiences split and doubled "selves," which cannot finally be integrated or even successfully related to one another. She disappears at the end of the text into a wall that physically protects her but psychologically isolates her and totally suppresses her voice. If this is another forced return of a woman to a kind of womb, it is every bit as destructive as those we have already examined. Only the male persona of Malina remains, as the text closes with the words, "Es war Mord" (It was murder).[20] The female self has been murdered by the overpowering male personae with whom she can neither successfully compete nor psychologically merge. Bachmann's character cannot find that relational thinking that might allow her to survive as a more ego-permeable being. She experiences an intense separation that both bars her from successful relationships and misses Freud's establishment of a strong superego; she is thus stranded in an inescapable and fatal isolation.

Bessie Head's Elizabeth is similarly torn between the spiritual and mythic Sello and Dan, who represents masculinity and physicality. In addition, Elizabeth is doubly marginalized by her mixed racial heritage. Her mother was white, and her father black; Elizabeth is thus "colored" rather than "African."[21] She belongs nowhere. Having been taken forcibly from her white mother (who was sent to a mental institution in punishment for her racial transgression) at birth, the partially black Elizabeth is psychologically wrenched from her a second time by a heartless teacher who informs Elizabeth that her mother was insane and that Elizabeth, therefore, must be on her guard against inherited insanity. Elizabeth is also taken from her foster mother and finally put into a mission school. Having had all her preoedipal contacts so brutally severed, Elizabeth might be expected to succumb to madness or death. However, she eventually learns of her white grandmother's stubborn efforts to retain contact with her despite the social stigma. This female gesture of courage and defiance gives Elizabeth the beginnings of a relationship. After several years of her own psychological hell, Elizabeth finally survives and emerges as a self who has progressed beyond the merely personal. In a gesture opposite to that of Bachmann, Head gives her character a parting vision of unity beyond the insular and isolated self. She succeeds in finding that sense of relationship that allows women to survive psychologically. Returning at the end of the novel to the engendering of life in her symbolic garden plot, Elizabeth realizes that she is part of all humankind and that she stretches beyond either of the male personae that battled for control of her mind.

While Bachmann's character disappears into the socially constructed wall of male language and patriarchal social exclusion, Head's Elizabeth re-appropriates language and the land for a unified human community. Bachmann's character cannot find the interpersonal continuity that marks Elizabeth's final triumph and ties her so strongly to the psychological model of the feminist psychoanalysts. Head's ending is a vision of hope amidst the extreme threat of personal and social madness; Bachmann's text is a lament over loss of both language and social coherence for women.

A chaotic textual surface such as Bachmann's or Head's does not necessarily indicate madness as defining the interior space of the female mind. In Christine Brooke-Rose's structurally radical narrative, *Amalgamemnon,* for example, the "real" space of the text is neither the expansive space of far-flung geography nor the electronic media, which form the very complex and confusing textual surface, but rather the interior space of the mind of the woman thinking—and finally the space of the text itself as an extension of that mind.[22] Every facet of Brooke-Rose's complex mosaic narrative can be understood as an aspect of the woman's consciousness at its center. It is that female consciousness that merges contemporary and ancient literary and historical texts, current conversations, and radio broadcasts to create a multidimensional textual space no longer dominated by an isolated subjectivity. The very form of the narrative reflects a relational model that exploits permeable ego boundaries to the fullest. The space of the literary text and the space of the female mind become identical for Brooke-Rose, thus providing a powerful means of unmediated externalization of this interior female space and giving women direct access to participation in the social world of "man." To occupy the female psychological space of *Amalgamemnon* is not to retreat into internal space, but to assault external, cultural space.

Head's *A Question of Power,* by contrast, depicts women's withdrawal into their own minds. But this movement, like Brooke-Rose's assault, proves to be a therapeutic gesture that allows women to make a space within the larger culture for their more relational thinking. Head's main character hallucinates through much of the text in order to find her way back to a unified identity. Elizabeth's re-vision of her life in the interior space of her mind involves not only her own psychological space, but the space of literature and culture as well. She calls up and literally "re-members" the male and female figures of African, western European, and East Asian cultural tradition in order to create a reunification not just of her own identity, but of the world at large. Figures from Greek mythology and philosophy, Buddha, the biblical David, Egyptian and Hindi mythological figures, and a host of African deities interact and merge in Elizabeth's tortured mind as she struggles to return to sanity. Bessie Head finally arrives at a vision of unification that is inclusive and expansive rather than isolatedly personal. Elizabeth reemerges from the darkness of her own mind to a cultural and social space she has reshaped. She calls up the representatives of the world's cultures in order to redefine their relationships to one another. Elizabeth's mind becomes the site of integration of a new universal culture that is envisioned by a relationally oriented woman rather than by a psychologically separated man.

This re-vision of the textual space that forms the literary and cultural tradition becomes a dominant force in many women's texts. A number of women refashion the myths and texts of Western culture into new shapes that stress different values than do the originals. Christa Wolf's rewriting of the story of Troy, which recasts the "hero" Achilles as a coward and a beast, is the most direct example. Verena Stefan, engaged in the same re-visionary project, realizes that she must reconstruct the male-dominated speech of literature and culture before she can write her own female story. Judy Grahn must retell Helen's myths in order to resurrect the goddess behind the mask of beauty that obscured the classical Helen. These writers and the others I have discussed know that they must transform the traditional spaces of literature and culture in order to create a new, contemporary space that will allow them to establish an unrepressed female identity. Although their works are written largely in isolation from one another, together they form a powerful female chorus asserting the need for a new vision of culture.

In her well-known essay "Double Focus: On the History of Women's Writing," Sigrid Weigel suggests that the space of the literary text constitutes a ground for feminist experimentation:

> Disguise in the form of literature gives protection as well as the chance to overstep the boundaries of the real and to postulate utopias. Fiction is a space in which to learn to walk, to fantasize, and to experiment in order to open up a creative way out of the tension between the "limitations of the strategies

and the unsuitability of the desires" in the real lives of women. . . . If writing/literature is to be a space where the double life can be expressed, opinions exchanged in order to break down the concept of life as the mirror-image of male projections, where freedom can be tried out in order to find a language for our own desires and wishes, then the existing concepts (above all those of the dominant genres) are not adequate, or only at a pinch if their patterns are used in a refracted, paradoxical way.[23]

Many contemporary women writers share Weigel's recognition that literature offers a space in which women can redefine themselves and their surroundings. And many of them depict this process directly by portraying female centers of consciousness who are writers, who are explorers of textual and cultural space. Karin Struck's Karin in *Klassenliebe* (Class Love); the first-person female narrator of Ingeborg Bachmann's *Malina;* Beatriz, Laura, and the narrator Morgner in Irmtraud Morgner's *Leben und Abenteuer der Trobadora Beatriz nach Zeugnissen ihrer Spielfrau Laura* (The Life and Adventures of the Troubadour Beatriz, According to the Testimony of her Accompanist Laura); Wolf's narrator and her Kassandra in *Kassandra,* and her narrator and title character in *The Quest for Christa T.;* Alice Walker's Celie in *The Color Purple;* Verena Stefan's first-person female narrator in *Häutungen;* and the women who record themselves in Wittig's "feminaries" in *Les Guérillères* all turn to the space of the literary text itself as a place in which they can unfold and solidify their interior psychological spaces. The literary text gives women—as Weigel suggests and as Abel, Hirsch, and Langland argue we must have—a social and cultural forum in which they can reinscribe their interior experiences in a public space.

This process is a complicated one, because, as Verena Stefan's narrator points out, a woman is always colliding with a language and tradition that are distinctly not her own in which the male vocabulary, point of view, and method of conceptualization have long dominated. Women must, therefore, recast this space as their own; they must "feminize" it in order to create a textual space defined by their own interiority and relational orientation.

This feminist rethinking of textual space is closely bound up with the difficult task of creating a self in language. Perhaps we can appreciate the complexity and importance of being able to declare a self in language by referring to Monique Wittig's essay, "The Mark of Gender":

For when one becomes a locutor, when one says I and, in so doing, reappropriates language as a whole, proceeding from oneself alone, with the tremendous power to use all language, it is then and there, according to linguists and philosophers, that there occurs the supreme act of subjectivity, the advent of subjectivity into consciousness. It is when starting to speak that one becomes I. This act—the becoming of the subject through the exercise of language and through locution—in order to be real, implies that the locutor be an absolute subject. . . . I mean that, in spite of the harsh law of gender and its enforcement upon women, no woman can say I without being for herself a total subject—that is, ungendered, universal, whole. . . . Language as a whole gives everybody the same power of becoming an absolute subject through its exercise.[24]

Wittig's comments make evident why language and particularly the written text are so important to contemporary women. By being able to declare themselves in language, women can create a female subjectivity that can claim a place in the larger social and cultural world. Language literally creates a space in which women can gain universal validity as subjects, in which they can escape both silence and reification into the objects of someone else's spatial creation. When it becomes inscribed and perpetuated in a literary text, language helps women to recreate cultural space to include their own particular multivalent sensibilities. The space of the literary text becomes a powerful re-visionary site within which women can create new relational models of culture and society.

Despite the difficulties of the project, women authors have discovered that the space of the text gives them a stable platform on which to examine, re-form, and recapture the identities of women. The narrator of Christa Wolf's *The Quest for Christa T.* realizes as she begins her story that Christa T. can only gain an identity and duration through the narrative she creates.[25] But the narrator also realizes that her own self-definition is at stake as well. The text thus becomes a joint exploration of identities for two female characters who have reacted differently to the boundaries imposed upon their actions and thoughts by a society they do not control. The text forms a metanarrative, a site for understanding not only the self and a [female] other but the essential interrelatedness of the two. The pages of the literary work become the space in which a female identity can emerge and be sustained both for Christa T. and the narrator, and for Wolf and her readers.

In a similar process, Celie in Alice Walker's *The Color Purple* finds her voice and identity only in the act of writing. She writes into existence a self distinct from the repressed slave of a male world. Her physical and psychological brutalization by the men in her life drive Celie into a space that is personally defined—the space of her written pages. After a good deal of exploration of her own feelings through writing, Celie begins to experience and record sororal relationships that replace the hierarchical patterns of patriarchal culture. The act of writing (whether to God, her sister Nettie, or her own inner being) enables Celie to survive and develop internally in an external world of hostility and repression. Writing becomes for women a privileged port of entry into a psychological development that often cannot take place in the society at large.

In her essay "One Is Not Born a Woman," Monique Wittig similarly stresses the importance of constituting a self in literature:

> To become a class we do not have to suppress our individual selves, and since no individual can be reduced to her/his oppression we are also confronted with the historical necessity of constituting ourselves as the individual subjects of our history as well. I believe this is the reason why all these attempts at "new" definitions of woman are blossoming now. What is at stake (and of course not only for women) is an individual definition as well as a class definition. For once one has acknowledged oppression, one needs to know and experience the fact that one can constitute oneself as a subject (as opposed to an object of oppression), that one can become someone in spite of oppression, that one has one's own identity.[26]

Bessie Head's Elizabeth in *A Question of Power* as well as Christa Wolf's Christa T., Nelly, and Kassandra, and Wittig's own fictional characters join Alice Walker's Celie in realizing the importance of this task for contemporary women writers.

For Verena Stefan's narrator, it is also the act of writing, of re-forming language into a tool of female sensibility, that enables her to redefine her self and its relation to the larger world—literally to make a distinctly female space for herself. The fleeting third-person narrator who opens Christa Wolf's *Kassandra* comes to a similar realization. This modern narrator visits the site of Agamemnon's fortress and begins to remember the Trojan Kassandra and her story. Within a few paragraphs, the consciousness of this modern female narrator merges with that of the Kassandra of ancient literature to produce a first-person voice that contains both women. The space of the literary text allows the two voices and two female selves to fuse in order to recreate a living woman whose story helps to redefine the contemporary woman writer as well as her ancient mythic counterpart.

The space of the literary text is thus critically important not only to the rethinking of women's roles in today's world, but also to the very declaration of a female self. Contemporary women writers have expanded the essential critique of patriarchal space that Christiane Erlemann calls for in her essay on feminist architecture to include a feminist re-vision of literary space as well. The space of the literary text becomes a site of critical rethinking and often of female rebirth. The textual space allows women writers to create new psychological shapes that displace the hierarchical patriarchal structures in favor of relationship, communality, and interiority. This new literary space author/izes women to throw a few new curves into contemporary culture.

NOTES

1. Cillie Rentmeister, "Die Quadratur des Kreises—Die Machtergreifung der Männer über die Bauformen," *Bauwelt* 31/32 (1979): 1292ff.

2. Christiane Erlemann, *Feminist Aesthetics,* ed. Gisela Ecker (Boston: Beacon, 1986) 130–131, translated from "Was ist feministische Architektur?" *Feminismus, Inspektion der Herrenkultur,* ed. Luise Pusch (Frankfurt: Suhrkamp, 1983).

3. Sarah Kirsch, *Blitz aus heiterm Himmel* (Rostock: Hinstorff, 1975).

4. Alice Walker, *The Color Purple* (1982; New York: Washington Square Press, 1983) 146.

5. The 1970s and 1980s offered a concentration of investigations of space in literature from several cultures. Studies of Italian, German, American, French, and other literatures took up the topic, and six different congresses in the 1980s treated space in Anglo-American literature, in Spanish and Latin American literature, in Canadian literature, in modern poetry, in "la poésie spatiale," and finally in Comparative Literature. Although much of this work did not treat gender specifically, recent calls for papers of the Modern Language Association and other national congresses show that the topic of space is of growing interest to scholars examining gender issues, as Daphne Spain's recent *Gendered Spaces* (Chapel Hill: North Carolina UP, 1992) also evidences.

6. Christa Wolf, *Kassandra* (Darmstadt und Neuwied: Luchterhand, 1983). The lectures preceding it form a second volume, *Voraussetzungen einer Erzählung: Kassandra* (Darmstadt und Neuwied: Luchterhand, 1983).

7. According to tradition, Apollo desired Kassandra. She required of him that he give her the gift of prophecy in return for sexual favors. He gave her the gift, but she then refused to sleep with him. Since Apollo could not revoke his gift, he added the stipulation that no one would believe Kassandra's accurate prophecies.

8. The usurping of a specifically female symbol by male authorities occurs often in history. Klytemnestra's double-headed axe, or *labrys,* for example, was originally wielded as a scepter by the ancient Amazonian goddess Rhea. A ceremonial weapon, the labrys may also have been used by women warriors. A male priesthood that took over the goddess's shrine at

Delphi adopted the labrys as its own symbol. The symbol was eventually reclaimed by women, however, as lesbians readopted the labrys in memory of the female community of Lesbos and its founding mother. See Barbara G. Walker's *The Woman's Encyclopedia of Myths and Secrets* (San Francisco: Harper & Row, 1983) 523.

9. Simone de Beauvoir, "Dreams, Fears, Idols," *The Second Sex* (1953; New York: Vintage, 1974) 157–223.

10. Verena Stefan, *Häutungen* (Munich: Frauenoffensive, 1975) 98; my translation.

11. For perspectives on the body within narrative space, see Laura Mulvey, "Visual Pleasure and Narrative Cinema," *Screen* 16 (Fall 1975): 6–18; Alice Jardine, "Pre-Texts for the Transatlantic Feminist," *Yale French Studies* 62 (1981): 220–236; Luce Irigaray, "When Our Lips Speak Together," *This Sex Which Is Not One,* trans. Catherine Porter (Ithaca: Cornell UP, 1985) 205–218; and Hélène Cixous, "Castration or Decapitation?" trans. Annette Kuhn, *Signs* 7 (Autumn 1981): 41–55.

12. A similar association is noted in passing by Sandra Frieden in her essay, "Shadowing/Surfacing/Shedding: Contemporary German Writers in Search of a Female *Bildungsroman,*" *The Voyage In: Fictions of Female Development,* ed. Elizabeth Abel, Marianne Hirsch, and Elizabeth Langland (Hanover: UP of New England, 1983) 314.

13. Monique Wittig, *Les Guérillères,* trans. David Le Vay (Boston: Beacon, 1985) 66, 72.

14. Günter Grass, *Katz und Maus* (Darmstadt und Neuwied: Luchterhand, 1961).

15. Fumiko Enchi, *The Waiting Years,* trans. John Bester (Tokyo: Kodansha International, 1971) 67.

16. Judy Grahn, *The Queen of Wands* (Trumansburg, NY: Crossings, 1982) xiii.

17. The following also explore the inward, psychological turn of women characters: Nancy K. Miller, *The Heroine's Text* (New York: Columbia UP, 1980); Joanna Russ, "What Can a Heroine Do: Or Why Women Can't Write," *Images of Women in Fiction: Feminist Perspectives,* ed. Susan Koppelman Cornillon (Bowling Green, OH: Bowling Green U Popular P, 1972) 3–20; and Annis Pratt, *Archetypal Patterns in Women's Fiction* (Bloomington: Indiana UP, 1982). Carol P. Christ characterizes the inward turn as a spiritual rather than psychological quest in *Diving Deep and Surfacing: Women Writers on Spiritual Quest* (Boston: Beacon, 1980).

18. See Sandra Gilbert and Susan Gubar, *The Madwoman in the Attic: The Woman Writer and the Nineteenth-Century Literary Imagination* (New Haven: Yale UP, 1979).

19. See Nancy Chodorow, *The Reproduction of Mothering: Psychoanalysis and the Sociology of Gender* (Berkeley: U of California P, 1978); Dorothy Dinnerstein, *The Mermaid and the Minotaur: Sexual Arrangements and Human Malaise* (New York: Harper & Row, 1976); Jane Flax, "The Conflict between Nurturance and Autonomy in Mother-Daughter Relationships and within Feminism," *Feminist Studies* 4.2 (June 1978): 171–191; Carol Gilligan, *In a Different Voice: Psychological Theory and Women's Development* (Cambridge: Harvard UP, 1982); and Jean Baker Miller, *Toward a New Psychology of Women* (Boston: Beacon, 1976). See also Jessica Benjamin, "The Bonds of Love: Rational Violence and Erotic Domination," *Feminist Studies* 6.1 (Spring 1980): 144–174; and Marianne Hirsch, "Mothers and Daughters: A Review Essay," *Signs* 7.1 (Autumn 1981): 200–222.

20. Ingeborg Bachmann, *Malina* (Frankfurt: Suhrkamp, 1971).

21. Bessie Head, *A Question of Power* (London: Heinemann, 1974).

22. Christine Brooke-Rose, *Amalgamemnon* (Manchester: Carcanet, 1984).

23. Sigrid Weigel, "Double Focus: On the History of Women's Writing," trans. Harriet Anderson, *Feminist Aesthetics,* ed. Gisela Ecker (Boston: Beacon, 1986) 67, 75.

24. Monique Wittig, "The Mark of Gender," *Feminist Issues* 5.2 (Fall 1985): 6.

25. Christa Wolf, *The Quest for Christa T.,* trans. Christopher Middleton (New York: Farrar, Straus and Giroux, 1970).

26. Monique Wittig, "One Is Not Born a Woman," *Feminist Issues* 1.2 (Winter 1981): 51.

BARBARA HARLOW

Sites of Struggle: Immigration, Deportation, Prison, and Exile

In her 1977 essay "The Chicana Labor Force," Rosaura Sánchez presents an analysis of the recent history of Mexican American working women and examines the consequences of such an analysis for rethinking the interference of issues of race and class in the construction of a women's movement in the United States. The place of Chicana laborers in the field and within the family, followed by their subsequent displacement in the process of urbanization, provokes a further critique of traditional family and kinship structures and the differentials of ethnicity that can be enlisted both in the service of and in resistance to capitalism and patriarchy. Sánchez concludes her analysis of the Chicana labor force, however, by addressing herself to Chicanas in the academy: "It is imperative that those few Chicano women attaining professional status or higher education recognize the low economic status of the majority of Chicano women and identify with their struggle rather than with feminist middle-class aspirations, for most of us Chicano women have working-class roots."[1]

The emphasis on class differences within the Chicana constituency and the attendant need to organize around the issues of working-class women is established in Sánchez's essay on the grounds of "identity," the "working-class roots" of "most Chicano women." Chicana feminism in its development over the last decade, and through the internal debates it has waged over identity and categories of gender, sexual orientation, race, and class, thus becomes exemplary in important ways for the history of the U.S. women's movement more generally. Not only has it become necessary, that is, to "identify with" with other struggles—on an individual or personal level, or even on the basis of "roots"—but furthermore to participate actively in identifying those struggles according to political and historical exigencies. The very question of identity is at stake, a question that Chicana writing poses in ultimately urgent ways—for non-Chicanas as well as for Chicanas, for cannery and field workers no less than for academics. Too limited a definition of identity politics only leads, as Jenny Bourne has pointed out, to a "discourse of equal oppressions."[2] How then is it possible to "identify with" the struggle so that the struggle is itself identified in such a way as to enable collective participation, political participation of the kind that Cornel West has enjoined, in the Afro-American context, as "strategies (as opposed to personal moral duties) of struggle against racism."[3]

Immigration, deportation, prison, and exile—each differently, but nonetheless complicitously, indicates what might be called "extradiscursive formations," institutions and mechanisms initiated by state bureaucracies to control the borders of dissent within their territorial domain. As such, they serve too to manipulate a "discourse of boundaries" from within the sites of hegemonic power. The supervision of national borders is part of this "discourse of boundaries" described by Rosaura Sánchez in her 1987 essay, "Ethnicity, Ideology and Academia": the legislation of entry, rights of passage, and expulsion.[4] Nationalism itself legitimizes its position of ideological ascendancy as a cover for more coercive stratagems of power, from the U.S. Immigration and Naturalization Service (INS) to the university's literary critics who superintend the distinctions of genre and national literatures and discipline their practice. These external borders are again internalized inside the national confines through the state prison itself.

If prisons, deportations, immigration control, and enforced exile indicate a nexus of bureaucratic power and its deployment in the service of the state, functioning as "structural constraints [that] impose limits upon historically constituted agents," they also provide at the same time "conjunctural opportunities [that] can be enacted by these agents" (West 24). The borders they define and on which they are premised determine sites of struggle and potential social transformation. Prison, deportation, immigration, and exile have in recent decades become central to the contemporary historical experience of much of the world's population. Rampant statistics and the documentation by individuals and organizations, details that have become almost legend, attest to the decisive interference in daily life practiced by systematic state oppression against various peoples. In Argentina, for example, at least eleven thousand people were "disappeared" between 1976 and 1983 under the dictatorship of the generals and the army. Approximately 30 percent of the Palestinian population living in Israel or under Israeli occupation in the West Bank and Gaza have passed through the Israeli prison system.[5] In South Africa, some ten thousand individuals, many of them children, have been detained since the state of emergency was declared in 1986. And there are an estimated thirteen million refugees in the world today. According to the Independent Commission on International Humanitarian Issues (ICIHI), seven hundred people per day have been forced to leave their country over the last thirty years.[6] In El Salvador as in Cambodia and elsewhere, internal exile and displacement characterize the existence of a large proportion of the country's inhabitants.

Although what is currently known as the Third World functions as the primary locus for these figures and data, this same geopolitical category—Third World—can also serve rhetorically to distance the self-appointed First World from the political phenomena isolated for attention by such statistics and to obscure further the degree to which they transgress and challenge the protective barriers of national borders. Similar figures are produced as well from within certain neighborhoods, barrios, and ghettos in the United States. The social pattern of systematic oppression and displacement that they reveal exemplifies the daily lives of First World ethnic minorities no less than those of Third World populations. In 1960, for example, 1 out of every 26 black men between the ages of twenty-five and thirty-four was in prison on an average day, as compared with 1 out of 163 white men in the same age group.[7] Two and a half decades later, according to a report from the California state attorney general's office, among a group of 240,000 California men, "65.6% of the blacks were arrested at least once, compared to 33.9% of the whites. Latinos were included with the whites because law enforcement agencies often list them that way."[8]

Two stories by Chicana writers, each based on the narrative and political manipulation of a discourse of boundaries, strategically collapse the apotropaic distance granted by the very term *Third World* and expose the political complicity in these data of the dominant ideology. "The Ditch" (1929) by Rosaura Sánchez is the story of an INS raid on migrant workers picking in the cotton fields. Alerted to the approach of the officials, the pickers run. The short narrative, which tells the tale of their flight toward the ditch and safety, contextualizes the personal fate of the illegal aliens from south of the border within the larger historical narrative of U.S. predations in Vietnam: "He ran fast, head down, stepping on whatever was in his path, be it cocklebur or thorny plants. He saw himself running through the field as others before him had run through rice paddies in Vietnam, as he himself had run when he crossed over the wire fence on the border."[9] The "illegal aliens'" historical consciousness acknowledges the political duplicity of a hegemonic language of nationalism: "It was an often repeated scene. They had only recently set up the radars on the border: it was hardware left over from the Vietnam War" (182). That same consciousness further reveals the agenda of destruction concealed in the duplicity: "Immigration officials were planning to clear the thicket with a little Napalm, left over as well from Vietnam" (183).

Whereas "The Ditch" premises the historical continuity between First and Third Worlds concealed in and by U.S. policy and the complicity of its domestic and foreign agendas, thus collapsing the dichotomies from within the system itself, "The Cariboo Café" (1985) makes the border between the United States and its Central American "neighbors" a site of contestation.[10] In Helena Maria Viramontes's story, borders become bonds among peoples, rather than the articulation of national difference and the basis for exclusion enforced by the collaboration of the United States and Salvadoran regimes. Borders, that is, function as sites of confrontation between popular and official interpretations of the historical narrative. "The Cariboo Café" is set in an unnamed U.S. city that numbers Salvadoran refugees among its populations. Much as these refugees transgress national boundaries, victims of political persecution who by their very international mobility challenge the ideology of national orders and its agenda of depoliticization in the interest of hegemony, so the story refuses to respect the boundaries and conventions of literary critical time and space and their disciplining of plot and genre. No markers indicate the narrative's breaks and shifts from the United States to El Salvador, and history remains to be reconstructed. Implicit in Viramontes's storied narrative, as Sonia Saldívar-Hull has pointed out, is a documentary critique not only of the INS and the Salvadoran semiofficial paramilitary death squads, but of their active collaboration as well.[11] The story of the Salvadoran woman refugee, expelled from her country when her son is abducted, and the Chicano children, locked out of their home when they lose the key, thus enjoins an historical awareness and a political reading on the part of its audience no less than from its characters. It proposes too another historical narrative. Restructuring the traditional family order, "The Cariboo Café" assigns to women the task of a reformulation across borders of gender and race and insists on their place in the construction of identity and political struggle.

Stories such as "The Ditch" or "The Cariboo Café," like Sánchez's critical essays "The Chicana Labor Force" and "Ethnicity, Ideology, and Academia" or the international reports of nongovernmental human rights agencies, and irrespective of genre distinctions, collectively challenge on the discursive level the arbitrary deployment of boundaries, both as practiced by the U.S. government and as professed from within the academy. Area studies programs and departments of national literatures discover their extracurricular analogues in the state bureaucracy that closes its internal borders as readily as it allows for a calculated permeability of its external boundaries. On 29 October 1986, for example, the U.S. Bureau of Prisons opened at the cost of some several millions of dollars a maximum security prison for women in Lexington, Kentucky. Designed to house sixteen inmates, the facility until recently contained only two detainees, Alejandrina Torres, a Puerto Rican nationalist, and Susan Rosenberg, a "self-proclaimed revolutionary" from New York City, both confined under extremely brutal conditions deemed by Amnesty International as constituting "cruel and unusual punishment."[12] Less than a year later, in July 1987, death squads from El Salvador extended their sphere of activity into the United States, to the streets of Los Angeles, when three Central American women were abducted, tortured, and then returned to the street badly beaten, as a "message" to them and their supporters.[13] The ultimate intended effect of such a "message" and the dominant discourse of boundaries and border defenses that it bespeaks is to disenfranchise the political for the sake of the national patriotic.

The writings of Third World women participants in the political arena challenge that message and the discourse of boundaries that underwrites the construction of domestic prisons and the practices of foreign death squads. The politics of place are problematized in these writings, and their analysis in turn allows for an immanent reading of the "conjunctural opportunities" contained in these spaces. I examine here a not altogether random selection of texts from across the geopolitical divide of First and Third Worlds that elicit the collective cultural habits of survival and resistance as these have developed among social groups growing up under conditions of political oppression and dispossession. Implicit in this examination will be the further question of how the U.S. academy, itself a political institution, can respond to the conditions that have generated this oppression—without falling into what Armand Mattelart has aptly criticized as "ethnocentric cosmopolitanism."[14]

Sahar Khalifeh is a Palestinian woman novelist from the occupied West Bank. Her second novel, *Wild Thorns,* published in Arabic in Jerusalem in 1976, engages the problem of intersecting and competing borders, both territorial and ideological, that interrupt the contemporary situation of Palestinians living under Israeli occupation in Gaza and the West Bank since the June war of 1967 when these territories were captured by Israel from Egypt and Jordan.[15] A Green Line, recognized internationally but effaced, for example, on maps distributed by Israel's tourism industry, separates the state of Israel from the territories it has occupied militarily for more than twenty years. These Occupied Territories, the setting for *Wild Thorns,* delineate a liminal geopolitical space, created by historical circumstances and contested by multiple parties with divergent political agendas. The most significant opposition remains that between the state of Israel and the Palestinian people, but equally dramatic, and critical to Khalifeh's novel, are the divisions among the Palestinians themselves. Such divisions are created by borders between those living in exile (*manfā*) and those living under occupation (*taht al-ihtilāl*), or by borders, under occupation, between those who live in Israel proper and those living in occupied Gaza and the West Bank. But the divisions are produced by economic differentials as well, as indicated in the novel in a conversation among passengers in a service taxi: what is the difference, after all, they argue, between working "inside" or "outside," in the Arab gulf states or in Israel, since wealthy Palestinians and Arabs are no less guilty than Israeli employers of class exploitation. Within this contested space, which functions as the setting of the novel, a Palestinian *feda'i,* a commando from the resistance organization in Jordan, has been sent to sabotage the system of economic cooptation between Israel and the Palestinian work force by blowing up the buses that transport Palestinian day laborers from the Occupied Territories to the factories and construction sites on the other side of the Green Line.

If *Wild Thorns* is premised on a history of territorial occupations and settler colonialism, the force of the novel's plot is to disrupt the Western historical narrative organized according to a linear stages-of-development model for progress and the cultural synchronicity that such a model entails. By locating prisons and factories as primary sites of confrontation, *Wild Thorns* challenges not only the Zionist program of Israel but the romantic idealism of Palestinian cultural symbolism and its focus on land and peasant. The feudal estate lies untended in the novel, its patriarch surviving only with the aid of a kidney dialysis machine and unaware that his eldest son travels daily across the "border" as a worker in Israeli factories. In the prison, meanwhile, young Basil, arrested for hurling epithets at Israeli soldiers on patrol, attains symbolic manhood, and Zuhdi learns the significance of solidarity and collective endeavor. The Israeli factories, by contrast, are scenes of violence and strife provoked by ethnic and racial contentions fostered by the state's discriminatory labor policy, which divides Israeli and Palestinian workers among themselves. Adil, however, the landowner's proletarianized son, who seeks indemnification for his co-worker and compatriot who has lost his hand in a work accident, emerges as a proto–trade union organizer.

The country/city dichotomy, based like the rhetorical division between First and Third Worlds on an unreflected idealism and exploitative nostalgia as models of development and underdevelopment, is collapsed in *Wild Thorns,* thus requiring another explanation of historical exigencies, one that would involve what Cornel West has called an "explanatory commitment" invested in an "emancipatory vision of the future" (25). In the end, Usama, the commando, and Zuhdi from the workers' buses are killed in the attempt to explode the process of the proletarianization of the Palestinian peasantry. Buses, then, which traverse the space between rural and urban, like prisons and factories situate new forms of struggle and immanent historical change through organized resistance. In Luz Garzon's story, "Going for a Ride," the INS buses "repatriate" illegal Mexican aliens.[16] But in *One Day of Life,* by the Salvadoran writer Manlio Argueta, the buses that carry peasants to demonstrate in the capital city are attacked by government forces and their passengers assassinated. *Cuzcatlán,* a sequel to *One Day of Life,* opens in turn with Beatriz, nicknamed Ticha, a partisan in the Salvadoran resistance, reflecting to herself as she rides the microbus to San Salvador, "If the [North American] advisers knew our history, would they still treat us the same? I don't know. Besides, our history is sad and boring. Maybe they're not interested in hearing about it. We're interested, though, because it gives us strength. It teaches us to survive. We've learned how to survive. That's why I use an alias."[17]

The current debate over the "proletarianization of the peasantry," which informs Sahar Khalifeh's novel *Wild Thorns* and which critically determined Rosaura Sánchez's analysis of "the Chicana labor force," is a debate that focuses on class issues and eschews finally a strict nationalist position, whether on the part of dominant institutions or as an ideology of resistance. It raises too the question of the "task of the intellectual" and the class position of an intellectual partisan within the opposition. The problem, however, becomes again more complicated when the class relationship of the woman is at stake, and more urgent still when her role within the resistance movements that have emerged out of traditionally patriarchal social orders is examined. How, that is, beyond "identity," does the university-educated Chicana "identify" with "the struggle of the Chicana labor force"? How does the Western academic, more generally, participate in Third World forms of resistance? In *Wild Thorns,* the role of Palestinian women in the opposition remains unspoken, tacit: a female fellow passenger, her arm in a plaster cast, in the service taxi that takes Usama into the Occupied Territories to carry out his mission is shortly afterwards observed in Nablus with her arm finally exposed to view and no evidence as to its erstwhile sheath. The other women, more prominent in the novel, remain to varying degrees confined by tradition: Um Usama, the *fedāᵢ*'s mother, consigns her fate to Allah, and Niwar, a university student, refuses to defy openly her infirm father's wishes. Her engagement to a comrade from the resistance in prison is in the end revealed by her younger brother.

The decades from the 1950s to the 1970s have been described as the era of national liberation, an era that culminated in the national independence of most formerly colonized territories. This epoch has given way now to variant forms of neocolonialism or neoimperialism, of cultural, economic, and political dependency, which have replaced the classic versions of territorial imperialism from the nineteenth and early twentieth centuries. Two ongoing national liberation struggles continue, however, still unresolved, as if "left over" from the decades of "high" national liberation: Palestine and South Africa. Are these resistance movements then avatars? atavistic anachronisms? remnants of a past abandoned by historical developments? Or has their own development in response to changing historical conditions so proceeded as to enable perhaps a renewed "emancipatory vision of the future," one that ultimately intersects with the immanent agendas of liberation within the Chicana/o context, for example, as well as with the programs of other Third World population groups located under First World territorial dominion? These movements provide new critical possibilities for a rethinking of traditional nationalism and its attendant discourse of boundaries, and strategic means too for intervening in the broader debate over the conflicted relationship between the First and the Third Worlds. Together with nationalism, this dichotomous, even separatist, relationship demands now a historical reformulation.

According to George Katsiaficas, for example, "Because the extreme economic, political and social problems of the Third World demand radical solutions, it is in the underdeveloped countries that revolutionary movements today are most viable. As in 1968, social movements in the industrialized societies will continue to be motivated by international dynamics, but the differing material conditions of existence which define the core and the periphery of the world system make the organizational models of Third World movements highly problematic for social movements in the capitalist metropoles."[18] Among these conditions, Katsiaficas cites "different immediate aims: decentralization of increasingly powerful centers vs. national consolidation of power in the face of international imperialism" and "different primary contradictions: technological and economic overdevelopment and political/cultural overdevelopment vs. economic underdevelopment and intense class struggles/cultural awakening" (207). While acknowledging the urgent significance of organized resistance in the Third World, as well as the historical specificity of these different movements, Katsiaficas's analysis reasserts once again the binarism of First World/Third World relationships and with it the primacy of place conventionally assigned to the First World. The borders remain still unassailed, and the political potential of the question, What does the First World have to learn from the Third World? unanswered. The "border problems" that traverse Chicana and other Third World women's writings begin to suggest the important strategic possibilities inherent in such a question for a reconsideration of nationalism and a critique of various forms of fundamentalism.

Black Gold, a study of Mozambican migrant workers in the mines of South Africa, appeared in 1983 under the name of Ruth First, a white South African woman active in the African National Congress (ANC) and the South African Communist Party in the 1960s. A journalist and a historian of Africa as well, Ruth First was arrested during the Rivonia raids on the ANC in 1963 in South Africa and sentenced under the ninety-day detention law. Her prison memoir, *117 Days*, takes its title from this law, which allowed for automatic renewal of the detention period at the discretion of the authorities. Eventually, following various banning orders and restrictions on her work, and later a period in England where she coauthored a biography of Olive Schreiner with Ann Scott, First went into exile in Mozambique. Her activities as a researcher at Eduardo Mondlane University in Maputo came to an end when she was assassinated by a parcel bomb in 1982. At Mondlane University, she had been part of a large research collective studying migrant labor patterns in the countries of southern Africa and their effects on historical transformations in the indigenous social structures. The volume entitled *Black Gold* was part of that collaborative research effort and combines historical background and sociological analysis of the "proletarianization of the peasantry," interviews with miners and their families, and work songs composed and sung by male migrants in the mines as well as by those—men, women, and children—who remained behind.[19]

Black Gold was published in the year following Ruth First's death, posthumous only if one considers the function of "author" according to the most limited definition of the word, as referring to the personal identity of the authorial individual. The contribution of *Black Gold*, however, to a reconstruction of political strategy and the ideology of literary critical practice is manifold and includes an implicit critique of authorship and the "task of the intellectual" in the resistance struggle. The reformulation of genre, together with its textual analysis of class and race in the migrant labor movement, which confute "nationalism" as an enabling paradigm, are reiterated on a sociopolitical level over the issue of authorial identity. The very circumstances of "exile" that condition First's participation in the research require a particular construction of nationalism and departure from it. Unlike her compatriot Nadine Gordimer, for example, for whom exile from South Africa is construed as escape to Europe, as in her novel *Burger's Daughter*, or as existential flight in the case of Maureen Smales's headlong plunge at the end of *July's People*, Ruth First would seem to have reworked exile imposed by the South African state as continued participation in the popular history of African resistance. Ruth First's biographical narrative intersects with the labor history of the migrant worker, and *Black Gold* can be read critically as an active, indeed committed, conflation of the two modes, otherwise separated by disciplinary strictures and a cult of individual authorship. If *Black Gold* is read as the autobiography of the partisan intellectual subject in which a personal itinerary is assimilated into a larger historical narrative of resistance and struggle, then First's own exile becomes crucial as part of the means to the narration of the history of the migrant workers. Her political task as an intellectual is subsumed by the cooperative research project in which the laborers themselves acquire authorial voices and historical agency. The issues of authorial identity and the work of the intellectual are reconstituted across national borders. Ruth First's identification with the resistance movement thus allows as well for an identification of the resistance movement within an expanded emancipatory agenda.

The same interplay and continuity of authorial identity and sociopolitical critique are rearticulated, as informed from within the First World territorial context in and against which she writes, by the Chicana writer Gloria Anzaldúa in her self-critical autobiography *Borderlands/La Frontera*. Whereas *Black Gold* displaces the author's persona and relocates it within the problematic of migrant labor in southern Africa, *Borderlands/La Frontera* foregrounds the issue of the personal identity of the subject and complicates it by an analysis of the mythic and historic elements that have contributed to its constitution: the legacies of Aztec civilization and Spanish culture, a mestizo heritage and the recent past of legal and illegal Mexican American immigration across the U.S. borders, and women's traditions of compliance with and opposition to the machismo-sanctioned practices of their men. That already complex identity is fragmented further in the bilingual, even trilingual, multigeneric textual composition that disarticulates Anzaldúa's expression—at once intimate and scholarly. The academically footnoted autobiographical narrative of the first half of the book, with its combined sense of fabled past and political present, gives way in the second part to a collection of poems that offer a more lyrical disquisition on the contradictions of class and race as these are implicated in questions of gender and sexual identity.

The poems are in Spanish and English, some (but not all, thus enjoining not only a historical consciousness but a linguistic responsibility from the reader) in both their Spanish and English versions, while others combine both languages in challenging even a coherent linguistic identity. The poems are further sequenced critically to move along a personal trajectory, from childhood's sense of fullness and loss to the painful rewards of women's homosexual love. That personal axis is embedded in the historical itinerary of development and the passage from field to city that charts the narrative of a "proletarianization of the peasantry." Central to this fragmented developmental process are two poems that speak to the emergent historical consciousness of their narrators and the ways in which that historicity both interrupts a prelapsarian sense of self and posits the conditions for its historical reconstruction under political pressures. Each of these poems further elicits the issue, already posed in "The Chicana Labor Force" and elaborated by Ruth First, of the "identification" of the educated Chicana with "the struggle of the majority of Chicano women." In "Nopalitos":

> I left and have been gone a long time
> I keep leaving and when I am home
> they remember no one but me had ever left.
> I listen to the *grillos* more intently
> Than I do their regaños.
> I have more languages than they,
> am aware of every root of my *pueblo;*
> they, my people, are not.
> They are the living, sleeping roots.[20]

Again, in a critical change of person, the narrator observes of herself, in "Sus Plumas el veinto":

> If she hadn't read all those books
> She'd be singing up and down the rows
> like all the rest. (117)

Is it that books and their writing intervene/interrupt/inhibit the identification of the woman intellectual with the resistance, the class struggle, the struggle against racism, the independence movement? "The insider-outsider dilemma," according to Patricia Zavella, who did anthropological fieldwork among Chicana cannery workers in California's Santa Clara Valley, "is still salient for minority researchers doing fieldwork in minority communities."[21]

The fields upon fields of rows up and down which Gloria Anzaldúa, privileged now by her learning, no longer moves, have become proletarianized as factory assembly lines for the cannery workers in whose midst Patricia Zavella carried out her academic study, and for the women too of northern Mexico who are employed in the *maquiladoras* on the southern side of the U.S.-Mexican border, whose story is told by María Patricia Fernández-Kelly in *For We Are Sold, I and My People.* In July Lucero's prison poem, "Jail-Life Walk," these rows are in turn made part of the "politics of punishment." The poem, signed like all of her writing by the poet-detainee's prison identification number, uses ellipses and the letter "U" to transform the sense of self in a struggle against the coercive machinery of the prison apparatus:

Walk til you . . . See the sign
Look at the sign . . . Walk in line
. . . .
The only thing free
is your mind
Free to count
As U walk in line.
#21918[22]

The reconstruction of identity practiced in Lucero's poetry from prison is located in topography and the neighborhood in Sandra Cisneros's volume, at once novel and collection of prose poems, *The House on Mango Street.* The disassembled narrative is premised on the alienation between the young girl's emergent sense of a socially conditioned self and the new neighborhood where the Mango Street house has failed to actualize the child's aspirations of status and comfort raised by the promise of "moving," a promise critical to the inherently political ideology of the American dream. That ideology is subjected in Cisneros's book to a radical critique when the flawed discrepancies are realized in the anecdotes and stories that follow, stories that recount the short histories of the neighborhood's inhabitants embedded in the longer history of Hispanic immigration, relocation, and political displacement in the United States. In *The House on Mango Street,* alienation becomes a border problem: the isolated women who sit daily, routinely, at their windowsills are as much of a piece with the neighborhood as Geraldo No Last Name, the illegal immigrant who refuses to identify himself in the face of threats from the INS.[23]

The internal borders that disrupt the Mango Street neighborhood and redefine its characters are reproduced by the cordon principle of immigrant and ethnic neighborhoods in the major cities of the United States, where urban planners provide the blueprints for the dominant discourse of boundaries. According to the labor historian Mike Davis, such designs, from skyscrapers and Hyatt Regency hotels to freeways, are indicative of the "decisive role of urban counter-insurgency in defining the essential terms of the contemporary built environment."[24] These hegemonic urban plans, in containing the ghettos and the barrios and their "Third World populations," serve also to sabotage their internal coherence and historical continuity. Helena María Viramontes's story "Neighborhood" narrates the deterioration of community in the life history of Anna Rodriguez, who "always stayed within her perimeters, both personal and otherwise, and expected the same of her neighbors. . . . People of her age died only to leave their grandchildren with little knowledge of the struggle. . . . Like those who barricaded themselves against an incomprehensible generation, Anna had resigned herself to live with the caution and silence of an apparition . . . without hurting anyone, including herself" (102).

The revisionary rebuilding of such neighborhoods is part of the larger task of a counterhegemonic ideological production. The "structural constraints" force as well "conjunctural opportunities," as when the neighborhoods of the past are reconstructed in the prisoners movement, in the Chicano movement, and in Raúl Salinas's 1969 prison poem from Leavenworth penitentiary, "Un Trip through the Mind Jail."

> LA LOMA
> Neighborhood of my youth
>   demolished, erased forever from
>   the universe.
>   You live on, captive, in the lonely
>   cellblocks of my mind.[25]

The relationship of the prison system to its inmates, and the connection between the inmates and the sociopolitical world outside, is exemplary of the need to politicize the "discourse of boundaries." Erik Olin Wright studied the U.S. prison system from within through ministry work with prisoners in the early 1970s, particularly with reference to the ethnic populations and "political prisoners" it incarcerated. According to Wright, "in certain situations, the relationship of crime to political decisions is very direct . . . [but even] broadly speaking, the pattern of crime in America is a product of the basic political choice to maintain the existing structure of wealth and power in this society" (4). The calculated distinction between criminal offenses and political activities is one that is manipulated by the dominant ideology precisely in order to maintain its control over the borders of dissent. As Lorri Martínez writes in her collection of prison poetry, *Where Eagles Fall:*

> Remember—technically,
> I'm doing time
> because I used to be
> a drug addict.[26]

That punctuated technicality is decisive to the hegemonic discourse of depoliticization and its legislation of the "extradiscursive formations" of coercion at its disposal. It is a technicality that the prison counterculture exposes as illusory and ideologically overdetermined. As Judy Lucero writes in "I Speak in an Illusion," "the bonds are real" (396).

Even the critique of the prison system, however, is subjected to the consent of that same prison system and its apparent insistence on a language of authority and objective responsibility requiring a complicit compromise from the would-be researcher and attempting a usurpation of his or her own project. Thus, R. Theodore Davidson, who investigated social formations and networks among Chicano prisoners in San Quentin, introduces his study with an explanation of his own situation within that system: "Prison administrators realized the delicate nature of the information I would probably encounter if I were to accomplish my task, so it was agreed that I would not have to reveal any confidential information to the staff. The only exception would have been if I had learned that someone was going to be physically harmed or that the prisoners were going to destroy the prison in some manner."[27] This "only exception," however, is twofold, and the requirements of the prison administration and the unitary language serve only to conceal a concern for the stability of the prison system itself ("destroy the prison in some manner") under an ostensibly humanitarian sensitivity for the safety and well-being of the anonymous prisoners ("someone was going to be physically harmed").

In the introduction to the collection of essays entitled *Women and Political Conflict,* Rosemary Ridd describes what she calls a "counterweight to this privileged insider [and outsider] view." This counterweight is the "particular responsibility the writer has to the community she studies and to her informants who may risk much danger in sharing information with her. Sensitivity to this danger then calls for some commitment to the community on the part of the writer and, in many cases, makes it unfeasible and inappropriate for her to become involved with people on more than one side in an issue."[28] The insider/outsider contradiction is neither an academic question nor a scholarly dilemma over scientific objectivity or neutrality. "Identification with" is not a "personal moral duty" but a political choice. What these writers—Chicana, Palestinian, and South African—writing from "inside the struggle" discover through their writings is that borders and the discourse of boundaries that patrols them are designed as part of hegemony's self-interest in maintaining its border controls intact. It is these border controls, which govern national boundaries and university disciplines alike, that must be dismantled. An "identification with" the struggle requires other strategies in the identification of the struggle, strategies suggested by these writers. As Rosaura Sánchez puts it in her essay "Ethnicity, Ideology, and Academia," "all that is inside is not center" (82).

NOTES

This chapter was originally published in *Criticism in the Borderlands: Studies in Chicano Literature, Culture, and Ideology,* ed. Hector Calderon and Ramon Saldivar (Durham: Duke UP, 1991), and is reprinted here with permission.

1. Rosaura Sánchez, "The Chicana Labor Force," *Essays on La Mujer,* ed. Sánchez and Rosa Martínez Cruz (Los Angeles: Chicano Studies Center, UCLA, 1977) 14.

2. Jenny Bourne, "Homelands of the Mind: Jewish Feminism and Identity Politics," *Race and Class* 29 (1987): 11.

3. Cornel West, "Marxist Theory and the Specificity of Afro-American Oppression," *Marxism and the Interpretation of Culture,* ed. Lawrence Grossberg and Cary Nelson (Urbana: U of Illinois P, 1988) 19.

4. Rosaura Sánchez, "Ethnicity, Ideology, and Academia," *Americas Review* 15 (1987): 80–88.

5. This number has increased significantly since the beginning of the *intifada* in December 1987.

6. Independent Commission on International Humanitarian Issues, *Refugees* (London: Zed, 1986) 9.

7. Erik Olin Wright, *The Politics of Punishment: A Critical Analysis of Prisons in America* (New York: Harper & Row, 1973) 31–32.

8. "Third of Men in State Arrested At Least Once between 18 and 29, Study Shows," *Los Angeles Times* 1 March 1987: see 1, 35.

9. Rosaura Sánchez, "The Ditch," *Requisa Treinta y Dos: Bilingual Short Story Collection* (La Jolla: Chicano Research, 1979) 182.

10. Helena María Viramontes, "The Cariboo Café," *The Moths and Other Stories* (Houston: Arte Publico, 1985).

11. Sonia Saldívar-Hull, "Feminism on the Border," *Criticism in the Borderlands: Studies in Chicano Literature, Culture, and Ideology,* ed. Héctor Calderón and José David Saldívar (Durham: Duke UP, 1991) 203–220.

12. William A. Reuben and Carlos Norman, "The Women of Lexington Prison," *Nation,* 7 June 1987, 881–884.

13. *NACLA* 21.3 (1987): 4.

14. Armand Mattelhart, "Communicating in Nicaragua between War and Democracy," *Communicating in Popular Nicaragua,* ed. Mattelart (New York: International General, 1986) 7.

15. Sahar Khalifeh, *Wild Thorns,* trans. Trevor Le Gassick and Elizabeth Fernea (London: Al Sagi, 1985).

16. Luz Garzon, "Going for a Ride," *Requisa Treinta y Dos* 165–167.

17. Manlio Argueta, *Cuzcatlán Where the Southern Sea Beats,* trans. Bill Brow (New York: Pantheon, 1987) 5; and see *One Day of Life,* trans. Bill Brow (New York: Random, 1983).

18. George Katsiaficas, *The Imagination of the New Left: A Global Analysis of 1968* (Boston: South End, 1987) 207.

19. Ruth First, *Black Gold: The Mozambican Miner, Proletarian and Peasant* (New York: St. Martin's, 1983).

20. Gloria Anzaldúa, "Nopalitos," *Borderlands/La Frontera: The New Mestiza* (San Francisco: Spinsters/Aunt Lute, 1987) 113.

21. Patricia Zavella, *Women's Work and Chicano Families: Cannery Workers of the Santa Clara Valley* (Ithaca: Cornell UP, 1987) 20–21.

22. Judy Lucero, "Jail-Life Walk," *The Third Woman: Minority Women Writers of the United States,* ed. Dexter Fisher (Boston: Houghton Mifflin, 1980) 395.

23. Sandra Cisneros, *The House on Mango Street* (Houston: Arte Publico, 1984).

24. Mike Davis, "Urban Renaissance and the Spirit of Postmodernism," *New Left Review* 151 (1985): 113.

25. Raúl Salinas, "Un Trip through the Mind Jail," *Un Trip through the Mind Jail y Otras Excursions* (San Francisco: Editorial Poncho-Che, 1980) 55.

26. Lorri Martínez, *Where Eagles Fall* (Brunswick, ME: Blackberry, 1982) n.p.

27. R. Theodore Davidson, *Chicano Prisoners: The Key to San Quentin* (New York: Holt, Rinehart & Winston, 1974) 1.

28. Rosemary Ridd and Helen Callaway, eds., *Women and Political Conflict: Portraits of Struggle in Times of Crisis* (New York: New York UP, 1987) 10.

INDIRA KARAMCHETI

The Geographics of Marginality: Place and Textuality in Simone Schwarz-Bart and Anita Desai

. . . if there is anything that radically distinguishes the imagination of anti-imperialism it is the primacy of the geographical in it. Imperialism after all is an act of geographical violence through which virtually every space in the world is explored, charted, and finally brought under control. For the native, the history of his or her colonial servitude is inaugurated by the loss to an outsider of the local place, whose concrete geographical identity must thereafter be searched for and somehow restored.—Edward Said

The terms *Third World* and *postcolonial* both register imperialism, "geographical violence," as the center of thinking about literature from the former European colonies.[1] The *Third* in *Third World* posits geographic distance from, as well as economic and political subordination to, centers of imperial power; *postcolonial* takes the territorial usurpations and physical violations of colonialism as the originating point of its literary canon. If imperialism is an act of geographic displacement, anti-imperialism is, as Edward Said points out, an imaginative recovery of a "local place," a particular soil.[2]

Geography is so deeply embedded in our thinking that it remains largely unexamined as an active force in the ways we understand literature, particularly the ways we produce significance in postcolonial texts by women. The grid of geography intersects here with that of gender. The spatial dislocations through which we understand "woman" coincide and collude with the geographic losses imposed on the subjects of colonialism. The following pages explore imaginative geography from connected viewpoints: first, as an epistemological "act of violence" in culture and criticism constructing the categories of "postcolonialism" and "woman" in the Third World; and second, as an imaginative recovery of local place in literary representation, to enable the liberation and recovery of the colonized self. My essay engages four interrelated terms as they affect each other: geography and gender, domination and resistance.

For writers characterized as "Third World" and "woman," anatomy and geography are equally destiny.[3]

The placement and labeling of Third World countries at the edges of conceptual maps graphically illustrate their textual marginalization, revealing our fixed ideology about geographic centrality. Terms like the *Middle East,* the *Far East,* or *South* America assume a geographic center. Hawaiians look west to find the Far East with no more than a shiver of absurdity. Europe is home, the metropole at the center of a world map. The rest of the world is reduced to frontier outposts.

Similarly, the terms *longitude, latitude,* and *Greenwich mean time* (also known as *universal time,* in an even larger arrogance) derive from a system based on local civil time at a small borough of Greater London. Greenwich mean time, the standard for establishing time throughout the world, is measured at the prime meridian; this Greenwich meridian in turn is zero degrees longitude, from which all other longitudes are measured. Thus international cartographic spatial and temporal measures historically spring from and refer to a small English site notable for no longer housing the Royal Observatory. The rhetorical figure has escaped all ties to a physical universe, assuming symbolic power to control our knowledge of the world. This way of understanding the world is an ideological operation.

Geographic ideology, a kind of epistemological cartography, dictates the interpretation of postcolonial literature. Said articulates "imaginative geography" as a "dominating discourse" that "[distributes] geopolitical awareness into aesthetic . . . texts."[4] This dominant discourse constructs relationships between geography and various kinds of power. Political power maps the remoteness of colonial texts from imperial metropoles; cultural power distances "native" texts from European "orthodoxies and canons of taste, texts, values" (12); and "moral power" traces the boundaries of our understanding of the distant other and his or her inability to understand us.

Imaginative geography enables readers and writers alike, whether in the dominant First or the marginalized Third Worlds, to generate textual meaning.[5] When readers help create the text through "gaps of indeterminacy," they draw upon codes of reading common to interpretive communities of readers and writers.[6] Imaginative geography provides some of these gaps or windows of opportunity in a text where the reader can connect the work with prior socially constructed assumptions about the world and thus generate meaning. In presenting the Third World as by definition the unknown, these codes create the indeterminacy necessary to generate meaning. At the same time, geographic codes reinscribe severe limits on what may be known about a postcolonial text: what we know about it is its remoteness, its difference, its ultimate unknowability. On this conceptual map, the self of the Third World woman, both as fictional character and as author, is likewise constructed by geographic positioning.

Third World women are colonized equally by geography and by gender. As women, they are spatially constrained within their own cultures in locally specific ways. In turn, they are usually objects of literary interest rather than voices producing literature: spoken for, rather than speaking subjects.

As writers, postcolonial women are triply marginalized. Their geographic placement distances them from the European metropolitan centers of publishing and marketing. Their gender further limits access to the metropolitan centers of production and consumption within their own cultures. Finally, their relegation to the margins of their cultures because of their gender alienates them internally from the act of writing.[7]

Given these degrees of marginalization, imaginative geography provides a frame that shapes writing by women within the Third World and simultaneously delimits our understanding of those texts.[8] No less than their male counterparts, women writers register geographic violence as the origin of their writing and attempt to recover local geography as a way to contest colonial and gender domination.

When articulated with gender, imaginative geography offers three strategies for signification that become sites for eventual contestation.[9] One "legend" that the received map of reading codes provides is *stasis,* which construes both the exotic and woman as signs connoting stillness, timelessness, lack of change. A second legend, *binarism,* divides the world into pairs of dominant and dominated opposites, male/female, European/native, and so on. The legend of *atextuality* presumes that certain texts lack power to convince of the "truth" of their representation.

Just as colonial space encodes distance from metropolitan centers, colonial and postcolonial "woman" conventionally signifies remoteness and lack of movement. Like Donne's "fixed foot," the immutable female other enables male dynamism, discovery, and growth. Her stasis emblematizes the Third World's temporal constriction to an exotic lack of change that foregrounds European modernism and progress. Moreover, the "native" woman is often physically confined to limited spaces: not only the national landscape as opposed to the international metropole, but the countryside as opposed to urban center, domestic place as opposed to public space, and even the individual body because it is not her own property. The movement of the individual female body is also regulated, whether by European norms of proper physical expressiveness and restrictive dress, such as high heels or tight garments, or by Third World practices such as foot binding. All such restrictions imply cultural prohibitions against the free physical movement of women and their bodies. More important, the West identifies Third World woman with the withdrawal of the female from the world, defined as human and male, to geographic areas both physically bounded and female, stereotypically the harem and purdah.

The legend of binarism dictates that females be constructed *with reference to* maleness and geocentricity. Within this frame the Third World woman is *unlike* the male European. In a world defined as binary, she is that necessary element whose exclusion makes the constitution of the male, of the European, possible. She herself, however, remains a negative quantity, constituted by what she is not.

The negation that flows from such binary operations, finally, informs what I call *textuality*. I use this term in the sense suggested by Gayatri Chakravorty Spivak, as the making known or real of a part of the world assumed to have been previously unknown. In her words, textuality "should be related to the notion of the worlding of a world on a supposedly uninscribed territory. When I say this, I am thinking basically about the imperialist project which had to assume that the earth that it territorialised was in fact previously uninscribed. . . . Now this worlding actually is also a texting, textualising, a making into art, a making into an object to be understood."[10]

Atextuality, as I use it in discussing writing by women from the Third

World, points to either (1) the lack of a written (textual) tradition that makes real the world these writers describe, or (2) the all-too-real presence of a world described through imperialist eyes, which the writers then contest.

Certainly, anything represented has textuality; it enters an arena of struggle for representational authority. Texts from the geopolitical First World presume to tell *truths* about the Third World. In corresponding ways Third World texts engage with and contest those strategies of self-authorization to achieve the power to represent their own cultures' histories and societies.

In discussing the problems of being a postcolonial writer, V. S. Naipaul points to the geopolitical bases of literary authority: "When one was young one behaved as though there was God—that God was publisher, editor, and critic, and if you were good, regardless of your background and your themes, you would be received into the pantheon of writers. But in fact virtue is not rewarded. If you're a Yugoslav, for example, there's no God for you, for God is going to have to go through an awful lot of English and French writing before He comes to Serbo-Croat."[11] Postcolonial women writing from the outposts of empire also write in a literary universe from which God has turned his eyes, and their geopolitical marginality translates into a search for literary authority.

The geographic figure of marginalization further positions Third World women as literary marginalia. Etymologically, the term *margin* has ancient imperialistic origins, as well as literary meanings, referring to border territories, as in Northern Marches, or margrove. Texts by Third World women writers are dominated, colonized territories relegated to the edges of the European canon. Imperial hierarchy and power delineate the "marks" separating the center from the edge, printed text from vacant margins. By definition negative space, margins through their emptiness define the text, their blankness constituting the presence of discourse.

Graphically located at the edges, marginalia add surplus discourse to a prior text. A dependent form, they comment, correct, or expand the dominant text, centered on the page. Similarly, the marginalized writings of Third World women writers assume the status of commentary or apocrypha to the authorized texts of the European or the male canon or both. This contrast defines these writings as nontext, or supratext; they occupy a space reserved for silence.

Thus, the violence of our imaginative geographies occasions a loss of textual authority that flows from a denial of cultural authority. Geopolitics determine the understanding of the terms *Third World* and *woman:* curiously, where you are is what you speak, and what you mean is where you are. As Said states, all "texts are fundamentally facts of power, not of democratic exchange."[12] Third World texts function in a "discursive situation . . . typified by the relation between colonizer and colonized, the oppressor and the oppressed" (181–182).

Third World women writers work with and against the textual significations afforded by imaginative geographies. It is not easy to "gain voice," as some simplistic versions of the discourse of resistance would have it. How is that voice heard? In what terms is it interpreted? Since women writers from the Third World do not pretend to claim virgin territory for literary representation but instead move to retake ground already heavily appropriated by the same (neo)colonial powers that have appropriated their physical land, the terms within which they can speak their political and literary resistance are those of the representational strategies and interpretive grids within which their fictions are read.

Resistance to imaginative geographies, whether political or literary, as an instance of representation necessarily operates within the boundaries of the same imaginative categories. Since representation in itself recasts its subject as object, contestatory representations are complex and paradoxical, further complicating the objectifications that constitute and maintain imperialisms and neocolonialisms. The objectifying power of geopolitical, economic, and literary forms of domination is daunting, because one way by which any system maintains its domination is to represent its own power as total. However, as Foucault and others have shown, power continually shifts, negotiates, and renegotiates the terms of its continuance. Consequently resistance, however complex and difficult, is not impossible.

The interpretive grids of postcolonialism and gender are *generative:* without such discursive frameworks we writers and readers have few strategies to generate meaning within texts by Third World women, given the ignorance of postcolonial conditions often found amongst their audience. Necessarily we read and understand texts from outside our own cultures through the mechanisms our own cultures provide. Yet those interpretive strategies convey forceful political subtexts that marginalize or erase the subjectivity of the Third World woman at the same time that they enable readers to perceive meaning within the literary text.

Thus, texts by Third World women, regardless of the writer's intentions, in the interactive process of reading always battle geography to redraw the world map and reclaim local place. The battle against imaginative geographies in literary terms is the battle for freedom from the violence of imperialism and patriarchy that defines and confines Third World texts and women. Recovering local place is at least one strategy for recovering the agency and subject status of the postcolonial woman.

But countermoves against imaginative geographies threaten the ability to generate meaning at all. Without these links to the world known by the reader, the text loses its reality, further marginalizing it and casting doubt on the possibility of escape from the tyranny of geography. As Spivak phrases it, "Can the Subaltern Speak?" Is it possible to have access to the consciousness or experience of Third World women unmediated by either gender or geocentrality?[13] Are attempts to create such unmediated access always preempted by the necessary presence of imaginative geographies for the reader and the writer? We need not reach the grim conclusion that resistance is impossible; rather, we need to be aware of the limited and limiting terms within which resistance can be spoken.

Many Third World women writers attempt to turn imaginative geographies to their own purposes by reshaping the three reading codes of stasis, binarism, and atextuality. Stasis must be transformed into movement or somehow dynamized; it must acquire a different value. A world constructed in binary terms must be either reconstructed as multiple or more simply wrenched by revaluing, reversing, or displacing its binarisms. Atextuality may be countered by moves to textualize place and so to give fresh local authority to the text. Third World women writers thus attempt to construct and teach alternate interpretive strategies. They are simultaneously engaged in textualizing geographic place and in (re)placing their texts in a newly drawn geopolitical and literary cartography.

Simone Schwarz-Bart of Guadeloupe and Anita Desai of India, while very different in cultural background and literary style, are important examples of writers who attempt to retake geographic space and textual authority. Schwarz-Bart is particularly illuminating in the way she clearly registers geographic marginalization as the premise of her narrative. Her *Between Two Worlds* (1981) begins with an ironic concession:

> The island on which our story takes place is not well known. It floats, forsaken, in the Gulf of Mexico, and only a few especially meticulous atlases show it. If you were to study a globe you could wear your eyes out peering, but you'd be hard put to it to find the island without a magnifying glass. . . .

To tell the truth, it is a completely unimportant scrap of earth, and the experts have once and for all dismissed its history as insignificant . . . as for the people, they believe nothing happens on the island, never has and never will until the day it goes to join its elder sisters at the bottom of the sea. . . . They say that real life is somewhere else.[14]

Between Two Worlds and a later Schwarz-Bart novel, *The Bridge of Beyond* (1982), both center on Fond-Zombi, a small settlement on this island whose distance from the center is stressed: "If Guadeloupe itself is hardly more than a dot on the map, it may seem even more hopeless and futile to try to summon up an atom like Fond-Zombi" (*Between Two Worlds*, 4). It is a place "not the forest, but beyond the forest, not the back of beyond but the back of the back of beyond" (5).

Schwarz-Bart insists on Fond-Zombi's distance from any metropolitan center, even those towns in the island that might tacitly form a community of shared understanding between her text and the reader. But she also attempts to redraw that geographic measure, to make Fond-Zombi the center of the world by textualizing it: by writing it into being, onto the globe. Schwarz-Bart repeatedly contests "the experts," by telling us that the island is worthy of epic: "it has had its bad times, its past great upsurges, fine copious bloodlettings quite worthy of educated people's attention" (3). Even Fond-Zombi, that "atom," "has a long history, full of wonders, bloodshed and frustrations, and of desires no less vast than those that filled the skies of Nineveh, Babylon or Jerusalem" (4). While the analogy draws on the ancient capitals of Western mythic maps, this claim challenges their imaginative domination and centrality to what is understood to be "epic."

Fond-Zombi and analogous Third World places bear a burden of atextuality, as V. S. Naipaul explains: "If landscapes do not start to be real until they have been interpreted by an artist, so, until they have been written about, societies appear to be without shape." To textualize place then becomes an evaluative act that attempts to reverse our definition of the center: "Fiction or any work of the imagination, whatever its quality, hallows its subject."[15]

Schwarz-Bart retrieves local place by giving detailed descriptions that endow Fond-Zombi with textual amplitude. As if drawing verbal maps, directions for reaching the village, she traces the path from the town of La Ramée to smaller and smaller tracks through the coastal plain into the interior, deep into the forest covering the mountain, and so on. Thus, she pencils in areas of the world map that have been previously untraced.

Schwarz-Bart's attempt to recenter the world map and to give place textual life moves beyond simple description or contestation of experts to what might be called invocation by incantation. The enunciation of place names, the repetition of name and detailed description, textualizes Fond-Zombi, translating it from ephemeral orality into the authoritative Logos of text. Schwarz-Bart intones the names of regional trees in a litany that calls them into being: "mahogany and galpas, genipaps and locust trees, the now extinct bois rada, and balatas entwined in lianas, screening you in, shutting you away in a separate world" (6). She seeks to hallow them by simple enunciation until repetition makes the list of names reverberate.

It is arguable whether this method of intoned place names can succeed altogether in avoiding the objectification associated with representation. In effect, the list of undifferentiated names may reduce the trees to visual and auditory images that trope the exotic. Said notes that "representation, or more particularly the *act* of representing (and hence reducing) others, almost always involves violence of some sort to the *subject* of the representation, as well as a contrast between the violence of the act of representing something and the calm exterior of the representation itself, the *image*—verbal, visual, or otherwise—of the subject."[16] The strategy of incantation, far from freeing Fond-Zombi from Western imaginative geographies, runs the risk of reinforcing them. Likewise, when Schwarz-Bart attempts to create a subjectivity where it had never existed before, it could be argued that the objectifying processes of representation work against her project. She is evidently aware of an audience that appropriates the world she represents as the "other." However, I am less interested in arguing the success or failure of resistance in Schwarz-Bart's work than I am in pointing out the complex and subtle ways in which she carries out a specifically literary resistance. Her foregrounding of geography enables, it seems to me, both the generation of meaning in her text and resistance to the power and dominance of these interpretive grids. Her resistance may be more performative, implicitly in process, than achieved, but it is resistance nonetheless.

If Schwarz-Bart redraws the world map by recentering it, she does so also by decentering it. *Between Two Worlds* was originally titled *Ti Jean l'horizon,* literally, Little John Horizon, pointing us toward the world map. Surrealistically, this book overturns conventional cartography. In Fond-

Zombi, a Beast swallows the sun, so that time throughout the world loses sense. The worlds of technology and of nature are equally overturned. The hero, Ti Jean, enters the mouth of the Beast to set things to rights, only to discover a cosmography in which space and time are not just reversed but operate in one great interpenetration. He finds himself in Africa among his ancestors, during a time when the Europeans are only rumors (not yet authoritative texts), before slavery and the importation of Africans into the Caribbean. Seeking Egea, the woman he loves, he finds her in the lineaments of another woman, who has dreamt of the island Ti Jean has left: "She remembered that she had been living in a strange country, a strip of land surrounded by water that never saw the sun" (163). He lives an entire life, visits the underworld of the shades and France, returns (still inside the Beast which is on Fond-Zombi) to Fond-Zombi, kills the Beast, releases the sun and several worlds, and resumes his youthful form. By means of this surrealistic geographic movement, the novel subverts a cartography oriented toward Europe. Having redrawn the map according to a precolonial Caribbean and diasporic reality, Ti Jean is able to return to a remade conventional world.

But if Ti Jean can travel over space and time on such a scale, Schwarz-Bart's female characters have no such freedom. Both his mother and Egea, the only major—though secondary—female characters, are caught in stasis; they do not move spatially or spiritually. Swallowed up by the Beast, Egea is sought by the hero. Ti Jean's mother moves only from the heights above Fond-Zombi to Fond-Zombi below. Nor does she learn anything during her life; there is no transformation of the self, change in understanding, or gain in the power to transform the world comparable to the changes in Ti Jean wrought by his journeys.

Similarly, the aged heroine of the second novel, *The Bridge of Beyond*, Télumée, never moves beyond the small villages around Fond-Zombi in her entire life. In fact, during the course of the novel she does not move at all from her garden, for the entire text takes place in her memory, where she dreams of her past and waits for death. Télumée remembers and tells about the lives and (mis)fortunes of her mother and grandmother, the legendary Lougandor women who suffer but find the fortitude to continue. Yet, having stepped into her own remembered life, like Ti Jean entering into the Beast's mouth, Télumée makes time elastic, connecting her individual life to generations of Lougandor women, the history of slavery, and the African heritage represented by the witch Mama Cie.

In her representations of Fond-Zombi and Télumée, Schwarz-Bart works to convert geography and female stillness into values denied by Western imaginative geographies. This village and character may be a mere "scrap" in the conventional world, but they are, Schwarz-Bart suggests, nonetheless a whole world. Télumée's last words underscore her supposed constriction and her paradoxical freedom: "I shall die here, where I am, standing in my little garden. What happiness!"[17]

Schwarz-Bart's subversions of imaginative geography and female stasis bear a cost: she reinscribes the hierarchical values of our imaginative geographies while reversing them. First, her desire to reverse stasis and atextuality leads us toward a myth of origins. The reader's entry into Fond-Zombi, Ti-Jean's reentry into Africa, and Télumée's containment in the "back of beyond" are equated: all three places, marginal and static, become glamorized into a dream of prelapsarian Eden. Télumée's constriction—like that of the Lougandor women preceding her—is a measure of her worth and constancy, contrasting with the movement of the men who invariably fail her and her predecessors. She is in her place; her placement in fact is her virtue. The courage and joy in adversity of Toussine, Télumée's grandmother, strengthen everyone to believe in his or her own significance. Her stature in the community is expressed in specifically geographic terms: she is "not a woman, for what is a woman? Nothing at all, they said, whereas Toussine was a bit of the world, a whole country, a plume of a Negress, the ship, sail, and wind, for she had not made a habit of sorrow" (*Bridge of Beyond* 14). Her ability to accept the limitations of her life, as remote and marginal as it may seem to be, recenters the world around her. Similarly, Télumée identifies what she is with where she is: "The next morning I woke with the feeling I was fulfilling my destiny as a Negress, that I was no longer a stranger on the earth. . . . I looked at Fond-Zombi in relation to my cabin, and my cabin in relation to Fond-Zombi, and felt I was in my right place in life" (83). Her "place" is simultaneously devalued and held up as the highest value: in fact, Fond-Zombi becomes a lost—that is, unrecognized—paradise, an Eden belonging to African Antilleans and especially to women. This lost and "strange" Eden is prior to European marginalization of it: "And so, when [the Blacks of Fond-Zombi] thought of themselves and their fate, arisen out of nowhere in order to be nothing, these forgetful ones would . . . drearily shake their poor battered heads, and reassured by a familiar face or shrub or a broken-down hut still standing among the rocks, would send a great shout of laughter skyward. All was well: they knew where they were again" (*Between Two Worlds* 5). To lose this Eden is equivalent to the loss of self and subjectivity.

Schwarz-Bart's return to a myth of origins is also a return to a Lacanian realm of the mother to Toussine or Télumée. Africa and Fond-Zombi, in the writer's corrective recentering, serve as metonyms of subjectivity, of wholeness, of proper placement, where the self is not yet fragmented by the Law of the Father, here the imaginative geography of the European. Yet, an entry into the realm of the symbolic marks the beginning of narrativity. Schwarz-Bart's desire to place her fictional world in the realm of the mother and the imaginary is undermined by the placement of her own narratives within the genre of diaspora: they are narratives of displacement, texts growing out of the Law of the Father. Her dilemma is just this: can she present the realm of the mother in a narrativity that can only exist under the Law of the Father? Again, the point here is not her success or failure, but the way in which her resistance works and reworks the interpretive grid of geography.

The problem of creating a specifically Afro-Caribbean, female, and at the same time geographically centered subjectivity surfaces most clearly in Schwarz-Bart's definition of a West Indian identity. *The Bridge of Beyond* locates that identity in various ways—linguistic, botanic, and cultural. Schwarz-Bart locates identity in objects geographically associated with the Antilles: breadfruit and madras cloth. Since these local products are not indigenous to the region (they come from Polynesia and India, respectively), her attempt to textualize place ironically points to other places, tying Antillean identity not to the Antilles, but to other regions of the imperium. Her attempt to center West Indian identity cannot succeed in isolating it from the geographic movements of colonialism; however, it does intensify the fragmentation and the contingent nature of the positioning of the subject in the West Indies.

Several questions arise from Schwarz-Bart's attempts to counteract Antillean marginalization. Is the movement toward the realm of the mother perceived by the reader as further marginalizing the Caribbean? Does Schwarz-Bart's strategy in centering her world map on the constricted, static spaces of women in Fond-Zombi only succeed in promoting isolation and removal from the centers of power? Next, although Schwarz-Bart herself is rigorous in acknowledging the historical context of her fictional world, does her strategy of tying identity to objects familiar from the cult of the tropical exotic (breadfruit, madras cloth) nonetheless reinforce the reader's imaginative geographies, rather than correct them? Finally and most important, do Schwarz-Bart's texts remain caught in binarism? She reverses the values assigned to the European center and West Indian marginality by insisting on the textualization of the marginal. In doing so she "transgresses," to use Stallybrass's and White's term, against the accepted geographic binary structure. While she commits infractions against that binary structure, she does not, however, move "into an absolutely negative space *beyond the structure of significance itself*," where the imaginative geography of the Caribbean would not depend for significance upon the centrality, admitted or combatted, of Europe.[18]

Indeed, it could be said of Schwarz-Bart that she has constructed a "world upside down" or a hierarchy inversion. As Stallybrass and White define it, "Inversion addresses the social classification of values, distinctions and judgements which underpin practical reason and systematically inverts the relations of subject and object, agent and instrument, husband and wife, old and young, animal and human, master and slave. Although it reorders the terms of a binary pair, it cannot alter the terms themselves" (56). Schwarz-Bart's Edenic world of Fond-Zombi inverts the imaginative geographies of literary signification, although it may not create a new system that would leave them behind. If her works remain caught in a binarism that reinforces while it confronts European centrality, Schwarz-Bart nonetheless remains notable for the ways in which she foregrounds and problematizes the power of imaginative geographies.

Anita Desai too can be seen as grappling with marginality and imaginative geographies, especially the problem of binarism. Three novels in particular compose an extended meditation on stasis, atextuality, and binarism. *Fire on the Mountain* explores stasis and retreat from the problem as a possible resolution. *Bye-Bye Blackbird* investigates atextuality and assimilation as its possible answer. Finally, *Clear Light of Day* endeavors to move beyond binarism, to reach an uneasy, ambiguous space beyond marginality/centrality—perhaps the "negative space beyond the structure of significance."

Fire on the Mountain establishes an entirely female world.[19] As such, it is also an entirely static world. There are only three females involved, each a variation on the female position, all three without men. Nanda Kaul, a widow, has had what seems to be a privileged life; she is a beauty, the daughter and widow of wealthy, influential men; and the mother of busy and successful children. She has seemingly experienced everything desirable for a woman, but as a widow she has rejected the world that has so blessed her. Her lifelong friend Ila Das is her opposite, without beauty, wealth, family, or skills. Unlike Nanda Kaul, she has aged gracelessly. Never married, she lacks male protection. She has not voluntarily retreated from the world; rather, she has been forced to accept a job as a social worker so poorly paid that she lives in a hut and starves slowly. Similarly the prepubescent Raka, Nanda Kaul's great-granddaughter, is a sickly child so thin her flesh seems almost pared away, insectlike. She is the child of a mother suffering in a bad marriage.

All three live in the small Indian hill station of Kasauli, an imitation of more fashionable Anglo-Indian towns like Simla, which themselves imitate small English country towns. Thus, Kasauli seeks to erase, not merely marginalize, one geographic reality and replace it with another seen as more "real." The text underscores the fictionality of the enterprise by noting its fraudulence in an ironically nostalgic retrospect: "Back in those English country towns, so unexpectedly and prematurely, they sighed and said no, these were nothing like Kasauli, let alone Simla. But there was nothing to be done, no going back" (9–10).

The hill station is firmly placed in its historical context; in fact, the second chapter of the novel chronologically lists all the English occupants of Nanda Kaul's home during colonial times, when Indians were not allowed to live there. But the overbearing colonial presence stresses the major characteristics of present-day Kasauli: isolation, marginality, barrenness. It is a town not only where nothing happens, but where almost nothing actually lives. "What pleased and satisfied [Nanda Kaul] so, here at Carignano, was its barrenness. This was the chief virtue of all Kasauli of course— its starkness. It had rocks, it had pines. It had light and air. In every direction there was a sweeping view—to the north, of the mountains, to the south, of the plains. Occasionally an eagle swam through this clear unobstructed mass of light and air. That was all" (4). The nothingness in Carignano and Kasauli matches the lack of change in the three females' lives. Nanda Kaul wishes to spend her last days here; Ila Das has reached the bottom of a long journey down the social ladder and in fact dies in Kasauli; Raka has not yet begun to move in the world and by the end of the novel commits a deed that may place her forever outside it. The text's geography actualizes the marginality of women's place without men and the marginality of India in the world map.

Fire on the Mountain intimates that to recenter the world map is not possible; the three females are powerless to move from their marginal positions, and all three are betrayed by men. Nanda Kaul, the only one who seemingly has or had some power, actually has none. Her past life, while supposedly that of a beautiful, happily married wife and busy mother, is revealed to be a barren fraud. Her husband maintained a longstanding love affair with another woman; she felt alienated from and unhappy with her children. Carignano, far from being a gladly chosen and embraced freedom, is the involuntary refuge of penury: "She did not live here alone by choice—she lived here alone because that was what she was forced to do, reduced to doing" (145). Ila Das, for whom marriage has never been conceivable because of her ugliness and poverty, counsels villagers against child marriage in a voice so raucous that even friends flinch on hearing it. A virgin, she is raped and strangled in revenge by an enraged father prevented from selling off his daughter to a rich landowner. The girl Raka, like her betrayed mother, is ultimately at the mercy of her father, parked at Carignano only because there is no place for her in her parents' lives. She has more power than either of the old women, but a negative one: she can answer marginalization and stasis through destruction. She sets fire to the mountain, destroying the male and European imaginative geographies that have imprisoned and oppressed Nanda Kaul, Ila Das, her mother, and other Indian women.

Although destruction is the only resolution *Fire on the Mountain* offers to the problem of stasis, *Bye-Bye Blackbird* posits a somewhat more hopeful answer to the problem of atextuality. Set in London in the immigrant Indian community, the novel immediately establishes that this city has accrued a reality more textually dense than the unlimned geography of India. Textualization has actualized it for a recent immigrant:

> he took in, recognized and named the "[mullioned] windows," the "horse brasses" shining against the stained woodwork, the "casks" and mugs and portly British faces. He had known them all, he had met them before, in the pages of Dickens and Lamb, Addison and Boswell, Dryden and Jerome K. Jerome; not in colour and in three dimensions as he now encountered them, but in black and white and made of paper . . . this world had been constructed for him, a paper replica perhaps, but in a sense larger than life, so

that what he now saw and touched and breathed was recognisably the original, but an original cut down to size, under control, concrete, so that it no longer flew out of his mind and hovered above him like some incorporeal, winged creature.[20]

Sarah, an Englishwoman married to Adit, an Indian travel agent, has in her turn constructed a picture of India. But it is the India of exotic orientalism, composed of bits and pieces from books about "Himalayan flowers or bandits in Rajasthan" (43), "the droughts, monsoons, famines and floods of which they read in the papers" (44), "Kipling, Hickey's Diaries, Todd's *Antiquities of Rajasthan*" (210), as well as stray oddments of received opinion: "the whiterobed widows who, she had heard, lined the banks of the Ganges in Benares, . . . the composition of henna that women used, she had heard, to draw patterns on the palms of their hands and the soles of their feet" (44). Adit, her husband, knows the difference between this picture of the perfumed, flowery romance of Indian miniatures and the reality of his home in Calcutta, far from such imaginings: "He became aware of the great gulf between her country home in Hampshire and his own over-filled city home in Calcutta. . . . When he saw her at work in her kitchen—neat, organised and quick—he tried to picture her transferred to the sprawling noisiness, untidiness and unpunctuality of his mother's kitchen" (213).

England, that greenly glowing gem of a land already hallowed in texts, is given substance and further hallowed in Desai's work. Dev, a recent immigrant, while at first hostile to the lure of the land because of the race prejudice he encounters, cannot resist once he experiences the England of his reading. A walk in the English countryside converts him to pleasure and near worship. The birds, the cows, the trees, flowers, bees:

> It was something he was visiting for the first time in his life, yet he had known it all along—in his reading, in his daydreams—and now he found his dreams had been an exact, a detailed, a brilliant and mirrorlike reflection of reality. English literature! English poetry! he wanted to shout and, instead, raised his arms to the sky, clasped them, in pagan worship, in schoolboy excitement. (170)

Dev goes "through every step of the paradisiacal walk in his mind, again and again, richly in detail, as though to imprint it all on his mind as one memorizes a poem one knows one will want to recite to oneself later, again and again" (172). The prior textualization of place reifies the location; its reification produces heightened textuality.

Ironically, as Dev "imprints" these details on his mind, the novel does so on our minds, more firmly securing England's place in the center of our imaginative geography and further marginalizing such countries as India. Desai, however, counters the centering of Britain with a meditation on the marginality of India. Dev's growing enchantment with England is balanced by Adit's disenchantment. It is as if "some black magician had placed an evil pair of spectacles on his eyes which led him to see, not what was before him," but the spectacle of a desolate India superimposed on that of a lush, fertile, and rich England (177). India is textualized, not as the Edenic landscape of Orientalism or the Mogul miniatures, but as a marginal, impoverished country, a

> vast moonscape of dust, rock and barren earth, broken only by a huddle of mud huts here, a dead tree there, a tree that raised its arms helplessly, dead before it had ever borne bud or flower, leaf or fruit . . . hordes of soundless Indian cattle, all rib-cage and meditative eyes and spatterings of dung . . . he saw the vultures of India, those great, heavyboned birds with their reptilian necks rising out of rhinoceros shoulders and blood-caked feathers, perched on thorn-bushes around the corpse of a buffalo that had collapsed of starvation, or a pariah dog run over in the street, or a pile of ashes in a river-bank crematorium. (177)

This ostensibly realistic landscape of death, dirt, and destitution is familiar as part of the European imaginative geography: it is the obverse of the Mogul miniatures. As a geographic trope of stasis, it too further entrenches the centrality of England, the marginality of India.

Through Adit, Desai opens up the possibility of a world map centered in India. While Dev falls in love with England, it grows increasingly unreal to Adit against the backdrop of India's war with Pakistan. In Adit's growing allegiance to India, Desai gives the text of India a growing authority and presence. He decides to return to India; Sarah goes with him, carrying their unborn child. She does not regret leaving England, the place, the novel tells us, although she does regret the loss of her own English identity (221). Her friend Mala, heretofore all frivolity and gold-bordered saris, suddenly becomes pragmatic and substantial when giving advice to Sarah about what to pack for India: "Mala looked busily through Sarah's packed trunks and turned quite unexpectedly practical, making Sarah wonder if, in her proper setting, she was not quite an efficient and able person after all" (212). Thus, India is drawn as a place of reality in potentia, where identity can be born. But it remains in the future; the novel perhaps cannot textualize India as more than an imagined destination, rather than a place of actual arrival.

As Adit becomes obsessed with India, gradually his anguish over the contrast between India's poverty and England's prosperity gives way to repeated mentions of India's "wild, wide grandeur, its supreme grandeur, its loneliness and black, glittering enchantment" (180). But his unfocused and vague endorsement lacks the specific details that create a mental map, a vivid and persuasive sense of place comparable to the details that textualize England. The novel ends not with the journey to India, but with Dev's trip by bus to his new home in London, during which he feels he is "riding into the heart of a painting by Turner," suggesting the aesthetic power of a textual England to pervade the imaginative geographies of the colonized, if not the reading audience of the West as a whole (230).

Unlike *Fire on the Mountain* and *Bye-Bye Blackbird, Clear Light of Day* attempts to transcend the accepted world map by contrasting two sisters.[21] Bim, unmarried, has remained in the increasingly dilapidated family home in Old Delhi with Baba, a brother whose mental incapacity makes him unfit for anything but playing old phonograph records over and over again. Thus, Bim represents a female constriction and stasis, which her sister Tara has escaped through marriage to a diplomat with whom she travels throughout India and the world. A remaining brother, Raja, is estranged from Bim.

There is no attempt to textualize either Delhi or Bim's home, only concentric circles of increasing constriction, stasis, and marginalization. India is marginal to the larger world accessible to Tara but closed to Bim. Old Delhi is marginal to New Delhi. The fortunes of Bim and Baba, a manless woman and an "unmanly" man, are marginal even in Old Delhi. But Bim nonetheless by virtue of her emotional strength becomes the center of the narrative, the heart of the family, stable and three-dimensional in a way none of the other characters is. She is the one who receives the epiphany of the title, the great truth of abiding familial love rooted in the family house:

> she saw how she loved him, loved Raja and Tara and all of them who had lived in this house with her. There could be no love more deep and full and wide than this one, she knew. No other love had started so far back in time and had had so much time in which to grow and spread. . . .

Although it was shadowy and dark, Bim could see as well as by the clear light of day that she felt only love and yearning for them all. (165)

In their dilapidated home the novel works out an ambivalent space, both marginal and central. Constriction and stasis are acknowledged; conventional textualization of place does not occur: Desai's "truth effects" are not based on realistically detailed place description. Rather, while allowing that the center of the map may indeed be male and European, the novel formulates a rival center based on the home of the self, whose fullness and depth emotionally root a sense of place. That self may be static, circumscribed, and marginal on the map of the world, but in its individual life imposes itself on the narrative map. Thus, two maps exist simultaneously: the one asserting European/male centrality and another indifferently acknowledging that political truth but focused on the marginal as its own subjective center.

Clear Light of Day ends with a reconfirmation of that oxymoron. Mulk Misra, a shiftless neighbor living on the pittance earned by his unmarried sisters, gives a concert where he sings with his singing master. His song ennobles him and occasions another epiphany for Bim:

> With her inner eye she saw how her own house and its particular history linked and contained her as well as her whole family with all their separate histories and experiences—not binding them within some dead and airless cell but giving them the soil in which to send down their roots, and food to make them grow and spread, reach out to new experiences and new lives, but always drawing from the same soil, the same secret darkness. That soil contained all time, past and future, in it. It was dark with time, rich with time. It was where her deepest self lived, and the deepest selves of her sister and brothers and all those who shared that time with her. (182)

These epiphanies suggest transcendence of both understanding and language; fittingly the novel ends with song, rather than discursive language. Discourse proves inadequate for the representation of these personal and lyrical truths; only song can represent it. The song Mulk's teacher sings is praise for the God who has created this world of pain and love:

> "In your world I am subjected and constrained, but over my world You have dominion."
> "Vah! Vah!" someone called out in rapture . . . and the singer lifted a shaking hand in acknowledgment. (183)

Song bypasses language; the response of rapture can be couched only in nonlanguage. "Vah" is a signifier that has no external object for referent: it signifies only the internal response of pleasure. The singer's acknowledgement further slides language into insignificance: his lifted hand alone signs the community of shared place and identity. Desai's creation of this aporia, two contradictory but equally valid geographies, the value of individuals devalued by the world, suggests that it is possible to surpass the judgments of the world as it is possible to surpass the understanding and the power of language to signify. By the end of this novel, she asks us to consider that "negative space beyond the structure of significance itself."

Schwarz-Bart and Desai do not resolve the problem of writing against the imaginative geographies that oppose European centrality to Third World marginality, and a male center to a female periphery. However, they do suggest the extent to which writers marginalized by gender, race, class, or geography may engage those structures whose signifying codes determine their narratives. The attempt to respond to those marginalizing structures of imaginative geographies also establishes how much literary understanding is a contextualized understanding, that is, a matter of recognizing the already known in language, narrative, and extraliterary context.

Among other things, Third World women's writing is characterized by this dialogue between the reader, attempting to determine the text by imaginative geographies that marginalize the text, and the writer, attempting to counter those strategies and teach new ones. Thus, it is always dialogic, polyphonic, and novelizing, to use Bakhtin's terms. It always contains a double narrative, composed of the surface narrative, the individual and varying story, and the deeper narrative, the unvarying dialogue between reader and text over the literariness of the text.

This dialogue takes place within the context of geopolitics and gender. If geographic provenance, no less than gender, often results in marginalization, the Third World woman writer, in asserting the legitimacy and value of her specific place and gender, simultaneously asserts the literary authority of her text.

NOTES

1. Though unsatisfactory terms, *postcolonial* and *Third World* occur throughout this paper. *Postcolonial* reinscribes the centrality of the imperialism it wishes to overturn. I agree

with Aijaz Ahmad and Timothy Brennan that the term *Third World* has limited theoretical usefulness in a discussion of literary texts; it does, however, spotlight the battle for dominance, and the contestation of literary, political, economic, and sociological categories. I use *Europe* as shorthand to encompass Europe and the cultures historically derived from it.

2. Edward Said, "Yeats and Decolonization," *Nationalism, Colonialism, and Literature* (Minneapolis: U of Minnesota P, 1990) 77.

3. To refer to "Third World women writers" may seem a form of imperialism, creating a fictional construct to substitute for, and so erase, real women in various countries. I do not presume to speak for these women, nor do I imply belief in some monolithic entity in the "real" world at all. My concern is to consider the ways texts about women in the Third World and by them are understood by means of interpretive strategies within the First World. The construction of geography is one of those strategies; I wish to explore what it means, how it works, and whether it can be successfully turned to contestatory purposes.

4. Edward Said, *Orientalism* (New York: Pantheon, 1978) 12.

5. That writers and readers of First and Third World literature receive similar literary training is borne out historically and sociologically. It was a part of French and British colonial policy to educate natives in the European literary masterpieces; the European canon is still central in postcolonial educational systems. Moreover, those texts associated with postcolonialism are produced, generally speaking, by Western-trained authors, marketed by Western publishers, and consumed by Western or Westernized audiences. Thus, imaginative geography and the unequal power relations it represents operate on both the producers and the consumers of this genre.

6. See Wolfgang Iser, "Indeterminacy and the Reader's Response in Prose Fiction," *Aspects of Narrative: Selected Papers from the English Institute,* ed. J. Hillis Miller (New York: Columbia UP, 1971) 1–45; and Stanley E. Fish, "Interpreting the Variorum," *Contemporary Literary Criticism: Literary and Cultural Studies,* ed. Robert Con Davis and Ronald Schleifer, 2nd ed. (New York: Longman, 1989) 101–117.

7. Sandra Gilbert and Susan Gubar's *Madwoman in the Attic: The Woman Writer and the Nineteenth-Century Literary Imagination* (New Haven: Yale UP 1979), although specifically a study of Victorian British women writers, is valuable for a postcolonial critic who examines what enables women to write in any culture where writing and masculinity are equated. That is, if being a woman is equated with being an object acted upon rather than an agent with the power to represent and change culture, how can a woman write?

8. When I refer to "our" understanding or to how "we" read Third World literature, my terminology casts up a complex theoretical issue: how to acknowledge individual variation within the readings of any one group and also acknowledge that there is a rough consensus within a given community of readers. This problem of the supposed unity of the group as opposed to the difference of the individual reader has dogged reader-response criticism, to which I subscribe, since its inception.

9. The following pages about stasis, binarism, and atextuality do not delineate a universal strategy that applies equally to all readers. Rather, they sketch general codes of signification and maps of reading that direct and misdirect us in our progress through a text. At the crudest level, the signposts are stereotypes; at the most complex, they belong to the elaborated networks of literary genre and convention, as well as cultural ideology, that frame meaning.

10. Gayatri Chakravorty Spivak, *The Post-Colonial Critic: Interviews, Strategies, Dialogues,* ed. Sarah Harasym (New York: Routledge, 1990) 1.

11. Israel Shenker, "V. S. Naipaul, Man without a Society," *Critical Perspectives on V. S. Naipaul,* ed. Robert D. Hamner (Washington, DC: Three Continents, 1977) 52–53 (rpt. *New York Times Book Review* 17 October 1971, 4, 22–24).

12. Edward Said, "The Text, the World, the Critic," *Textual Strategies: Perspectives in Post-Structuralist Criticism,* ed. Josue V. Harari (New York: Cornell UP) 178.

13. Gayatri Chakravorty Spivak, "Can the Subaltern Speak?" *Wedge* 7 (1985): 120–130.

14. Simone Schwarz-Bart, *Between Two Worlds,* trans. Barbara Bray (New York: Harper & Row, 1981) 13.

15. V. S. Naipaul, "Jasmine," *The Overcrowded Barracoon and Other Articles* (London: Andre Deutsch, 1972) 25 (rpt. *Times Literary Supplement* 4 June 1964).

16. Edward Said, "In the Shadow of the West," *Wedge* 7 (1985): 5.

17. Simone Schwarz-Bart, *The Bridge of Beyond,* trans. Barbara Bray (London: Heinemann Educational Books, 1982) 173.

18. Peter Stallybrass and Allon White, *The Politics and Poetics of Transgression* (Ithaca: Cornell UP, 1986) 18.

19. Anita Desai, *Fire on the Mountain* (Harmondsworth, Eng.: Penguin, 1981).

20. Anita Desai, *Bye-Bye Blackbird* (Delhi: Orient, 1985) 10–11.

21. Anita Desai, *Clear Light of Day* (Harmondsworth, Eng.: Penguin, 1980).

DEBRA A. CASTILLO

Borderliners: Federico Campbell and Ana Castillo

Late in Federico Campbell's novella, "Todo lo de las focas" (Everything about Seals), the voices of the two main characters alternate in a fragment, one of their many vignettelike exchanges. The nameless narrator has apparently received from Beverly a copy of Leo Lionni's children's book, *Little Blue and Little Yellow*. Campbell's characters summarize Lionni's plot: two spots, one blue and one yellow, hug each other until they are green, go out to play, and return home to be rejected by both sets of parents until they decompose themselves from a single green entity back into a blue spot and a yellow spot once again.[1] In their dialogue, significantly, the two voices also merge; neither is marked or inflected in any way to readily identify the speaker as a Mexican man or a woman from the United States, and the conversation begins with a rejoinder to an unrecorded question about Lionni's story. The giver has inscribed it with a dedication—"so that you learn how to disobey"—and the recipient assures the giver that the book was read and will be treasured forever. The same speaker ends the brief conversation with the elliptical remark, "A children's story . . ."[2]

Lionni's book, so prominently cited in Campbell's novella, clearly suggests something other than just another children's story. It is, as both characters agree, one of the formative texts of their border reality, an unforgettable book that taught them the virtues of disobeying restrictive parents in the name of friendship, and that graphically showed them how other limits and borders, including the borders of the body, could be dissolved. Campbell, himself a Tijuana native, in this novella and other stories from the collection *Tijuanenses* imagines numerous retellings of that simple story of the borderlands between one shape and another, of the interactions of "blues" and "yellows" in that border space, of the insights achieved by the intermittently emergent "green" friendships, and of the shocks created in the inevitable and repeated crashing of one reality against another.

The collision of realities is also a central theme in Ana Castillo's first novel, *The Mixquiahuala Letters*. Castillo's narrator, a Mexican American woman named Teresa, recalls for her "semi-white" friend Alicia a long-ago summer school weekend spent in the pre-Columbian village named Mixquiahuala. Says Teresa, with apparent approbation: "for years afterward you enjoyed telling people that i was from Mixquiahuala," and, as the title of the book suggests, that once seen and now mythic town represents less an actual place than the state of mind that pervades these letters.[3] It marks the unease of someone who, in Lionni's and Campbell's terms, would be a green patch in a world that is sometimes blue and sometimes yellow. In many ways, Mixquiahuala is an earlier version of the country that Castillo identifies in her second novel as Sapogonia: "a distinct place in the Americas where all mestizos reside, regardless of nationality, individual racial composition, or legal residential status—or perhaps, because of all these."[4] Castillo goes on: "Sapogonia (like the Sapogón/a) is not identified by modern boundaries" (6). It is a place both spiritual and physical that recognizes and celebrates the overlapping of two realities, two myths, two cultures, two ways of living and dreaming, two different political and economic modes of perceiving the world. Thus, the two-thousand-mile political boundary drawn between the United States and Mexico for both the Mexican male writer and the Mexican American female writer identifies a notional truth, a reality that is also, like all things that merge blue and yellow, a fiction.

What is not at question in these books is whether that notional truth about Mixquiahuala or about Tijuana matches a geographer's or a politician's truth. These writers focus rather on the task of delimiting the soul in the borderlands of these invented truths. And in both books that spiritual element is sought in the other country, the other sex, the other race. This encounter, however, differs from the friendly embrace of two children who disobey their parents' unfair strictures in order to play together; both books draw narrative reality painfully against the norms of daily truth and even common sense. What has seemed to be knowledge reveals itself as a cultural practice open to question and interpretation. The encounter between two cultures and two people opens a site of exchange, but also of bitter cultural contest. With bicultural usages, as Lionni's parable reminds us, figural assumptions and metaphors for abstract relations spring from a practice that dislocates the language of the text. Confronted with such border-conscious texts, critics (myself included) tend not to be wary enough.

One of the most ambiguously negotiated sites in both novels is that of female identity. The borderlands seem to bring to consciousness the most extreme variants of each culture's stereotypes about itself and about the other culture. These stereotypes focus on and through the feminine and suggest ambivalence toward female sexuality. Homi Bhabha writes that "cultural difference is to be found where 'loss' of meaning enters, as a cutting edge, into the representation of the fullness of the demands of culture," and in these novels the "cutting edge" invariably takes the form of the encounter between two versions of male and female stereotypes about each other.[5] Meaning is not so much lost as subject to negotiation, as are the other products of cultural conditioning, and in such renegotiations of identity cultural constructs are both eroded and reinforced.

For Castillo's Teresa, the cultural conflict is particularly intense, as the Mexican American woman straddles the razor edge between two cultures, neither of which satisfies her spirit. The barely remembered, poetically reinvented pre-Columbian Mixquiahuala represents for her a spiritual homeland. "There was a definite call to find a place to satisfy my yearning spirit," she writes to her friend Alicia, "i chose Mexico" (46). Nevertheless, Mexico functions as a spiritual home only from the U.S. side of the border; once she actually begins to live in that country she finds it antagonistic to her sense of self. She recalls to Alicia, "i'd enough of the country where relationships were never clear and straightforward, but a tangle of contradictions and hypocrisies," and she captures her frustration in a poem: "This was her last night / in the homeland / of spiritual devastation" (54–55).

In fact, what Teresa finds spiritually devastating is not the contradictions and hypocrisies in relationships between men and women in Mexico, but rather their excessive clarity and directness. Teresa's relationship with Ponce, a Mexican engineer, is a case in point:

> He began, "I think you are a 'liberal woman.' Am I correct?" His expression meant to persuade me that it didn't matter what I replied. In the end he would win. He would systematically strip away all my pretexts, reservations and defenses, and end up in bed with me.

> In that country, the term "liberated woman" meant something other than what we had strived for in the United States. In this case it simply meant a woman who would sleep nondiscriminately with any man who came along. . . .
> Liberal: trash, whore, bitch. (73)

In this brief exchange, Castillo establishes two sets of cultural norms with their attendant illusions. For the Mexican man, liberated and liberal fold into each other, and both words stripped of their decorative rhetoric come down to the same thing when applied to a woman—that she is a willing prostitute who does not even require payment for her services. For the Mexican American woman who dedicates herself personally and politically to the struggle for women's equality, such narrowmindedness is appalling. But what makes the exchange devastating is that she also recognizes Ponce's equation of liberated = whore as to some degree an accurate, if pitiless, reading of a personal reality she strives to reject, while her own politically advanced positioning becomes infected with a hypocritical and highly selective attitude toward both dominant white culture in the United States and her own Mexican heritage. For both the Mexican man and the Mexican American woman, the whore is the grounding signifier where cultural difference and loss of meaning come to rest. But that signifier, so shocking, so stripped of pretext, stubbornly resists interpretation.

Campbell, too, grounds signification in the feminine other, in the liberated U.S. woman apparently open to any man's sexual advances. His Mexican narrator says of Beverly, in announcing his intention to seek her throughout the entire world, "You were always the same woman with different names—the little girl from the neighborhood, the companion in junior high school, the recently married young woman, the casino prostitute—or the same person, yourself, when at a certain distance you allowed me to follow you through the passageways of the airport" (81). Campbell's parallel series is subtly shocking. He molds his image of the beloved woman as a sequence of snapshots representing the different phases in her life—child, student, married woman, prostitute—where the final profession suggests not only a logical next step in the sequence of a woman's growth in the borderlands, but also a culminating identity. The images of femininity come down to this image, before dispersing in Beverly's resistance to the narrator's reading, her obscurity in his photographs.

It is not coincidental that the narrator of Campbell's novella identifies himself through his camera, which steals snatches of life, and through photographic products. In this manner not only does he evoke, in a minor key, the profession for which Beverly Hills is best known, but his emphasis on the camera's view also reminds us of the doubleness of the development process—from negative to positive print, where shadow and light echo and reverse each other. For the photographer, the United States is the specular space in which he contemplates his other self. "We live in different, divided worlds," the narrator says to Beverly, and he is both right and wrong.

This is a border region in which, as Emily Hicks acutely observes, "two or more referential codes operate simultaneously." Hicks continues, "in the U.S.-Mexico border region, there is no need to 'become-other'; one is 'other' or 'marginal' by definition, by virtue of living between two cultures and being 'other' in both."[6] Says Campbell in another context, "And your eyes would go back and forth, from one side to another, from Los Angeles to the DF and viceversa, like a ping-pong game. You never could figure out which pole attracted you most; it was never very clear if the latest innovations in speech or dress . . . came from Tepito or from the East Side."[7] For the alienated narrator of "Todo lo de las focas," the constant to-and-fro from L.A. to the D.F., the increasing slipperiness of people and places, leaves him oddly isolated. Togetherness is illusory for the narrator as he drives Beverly up the Mexican coast toward the Tijuana–San Diego border, their car paced and accompanied by a herd of seals offshore, also floating north. The end of the novella returns to the opening frame: the car reaches the international border, and a border guard discovers that Beverly has died sometime during the night. In the central part, the narrator, a Tijuana native, goes back in time to trace his on-again, off-again relationship with the elusive and mysterious woman from the other side of the border. Their story also and inevitably evokes the history of the border region and of Tijuana's growth from the isolated ranches of the early part of the century through the casino boom during the Prohibition years to its dubious fame as a major way station for illegal immigration and its growing prosperity as a center of *maquiladora* plants. What the novella mostly explores, however, is the borderlands' soul.

For the narrator, the political reality of the border does not cease to impinge upon his self-imposed egoism. At one pole, central Mexican culture and the Spanish language exert a strong pull, but Los Angeles's popular culture and the appeal of a secure income exert an equal and opposite attraction: "Where have you been, in Los Angeles?" asks a character in one of Campbell's stories, and the narrator muses, "The question presupposes a myth. Every absence is related to an adult destiny in Los Angeles' East Side" (152). And yet, for the Mexican national, the Ping-Pong game has clear rules and a clearly marked net—the fence between Tijuana and San Diego. Campbell reminds us that illegal border-crossers in the Californian sister cities are not "*mojados*" (wetbacks) but "*alambrados*" (fence climbers) or perhaps "*alambristas*" (high-wire walkers), who do not wade the river but instead confront the entanglements of the fence. In the unresolved exchange between L.A. and the D.F., this fence rises up to divide the narrator's world, and to divide himself—a steel fence in the soul dividing self from body, spirit from mind. Language, reality, truth, nationality: all are subject to the driving force of the divided being, transfixed by the steel fence of a borderline's liminality, allowing one culture to bleed into the other in the between time, between place of the borderland self. Campbell's narrator longs for safe limits—but not the external limits imposed by an all-too-real fence. He longs for an end to the dizzying Ping-Pong game—but that game defines his border self. He wants to be firm and compact and self sufficient—but the aching need for Beverly recalls to him that without her inscrutable presence to complete him and to complete his map of California, upper and lower, he is only, in Lionni's terms, a blue spot, and not a green whole. In terms of the profession he has adopted, he is only half the photographic process.

For Castillo's characters in *The Mixquiahuala Letters,* too, personal and cultural identity rest on the borderlines of a loss corresponding to an ambiguous surplus of stereotypical identities. Like the Mexican male protagonist of Campbell's novella, Castillo's Mexican American female defines herself against the other culture and other sex, only to find her own fragmented sense of self forced into an unacceptably narrow mold, or her undecidability uncomfortably confirmed. There are crucial differences, however. While Campbell's narrator focuses on a concrete border and a psychological profile of the border self, Castillo broadly emphasizes a spiritual borderlands and the interplay of race, culture, and economic position, the "unholy trinity" that defines for Anseleme Remy the concept of ethnoclass.[8]

Teresa looks to Mexico to cure the discomfort she feels with the markers of her ethnoclass in the United States, where she is made to feel an outsider to her own country with the copper skin and fuller body type that marks her racial heritage, the slight accent that betrays her cultural background, the often angry reactions that betray her efforts to resist the traditions of her family's economic class. Teresa is attracted to Mixquiahuala largely because it satisfies in her a yearning for some concrete correlative of her own lightly marked Indian features: "it explained the exotic tinge of yellow and red in my complexion, the hint of an accent in my baroque speech, and most of all, the indiscernible origin of my being" (20). Like Campbell's narrator, Castillo's Teresa suffers the scars of a divided self that drives her to foreground those specific features she describes, but to do so in minimalizing terms: "the *tinge* of yellow and red," "the *hint* of an accent," "the *indiscernible* origin." Alienated from her ethnoclass by education and experience yet unable to find anonymity in the dominant society, like Campbell's protagonist she looks to the idealization of another culture for clues to her lost or fragmented identity—but with a difference. Whereas Campbell's provincial Mexican rebounds between two modern, very cosmopolitan centers, Teresa, as a product of the large U.S. city, projects herself backwards, toward an indiscernible but determinably provincial origin. That homeland, as she knows, functions best in dreams and is too fragile to stand up to waking reality:

> i too suffer from dreams.
> It was a provincial town, with cobblestone streets, shattered windows, and aged wooden doors and gates. In the scale of history: between the sixteenth century and the present. . . .
> The people were of mixed blood, people of the sun and earth. . . .
> i too was of that small corner of the world. i was of that mixed blood, of fire and stone, timber and vine, a history passed down from mouth to mouth since the beginning of time. (95–96)

Teresa knows that this terrain, although intimately hers in dreams, belongs to her only in those dreams. When she is awake, her own words distance her from Mixquiahuala. Likewise, when she travels in Mexico, only one part of her divided self comes home; the rest of her visits an exotic and unfamiliar land. She, like the people in her fantasy, is of mixed blood, but she has not grown up in the out-of-the-way provincial village of her dreams where copper-colored skin is the norm. Her skin color is racialized and defined by her U.S. reality in a way alien to that half-imagined utopic town. Her color is, as she says, "exotic," her origin, even to herself, "indiscernible."

Accordingly, Teresa's motivation for her trips to Mexico is divided. On the one hand, she goes to Mexico to find people like herself, to understand her roots, to reaffirm the value of the ethnoclass from which she has sprung. On the other hand, like any gringa tourist, she seeks those aspects of Mexico that are for the dominant U.S. culture exotic, foreign, and for that very reason, seductive. Describing one visit to a "quaint Mexican town," Teresa evokes a seduction scene in which a man named Alvaro appears in her bedroom from a balcony: "From behind his back he produced a mango the size of which i hadn't seen before. Isn't this what you said you craved back in Califas? i smiled. As he peeled back the skin, releasing the exotic juice, he entertained me with another of his fantastic stories" (50). The exotic and the virile merge in an episode that is half-real, half-fantasy, and attractive in its strangeness. As in fairy tales, enchantment and passion intertwine. Yearning for so much, both Teresa and her friend Alicia find Mexican men strangely recalcitrant; such men have their own dreams of seducing "liberated" gringa tourists, after all. For them, the definition of the exotic is inverted, but their Mexican reality enters Castillo's novel only in distanced and rejected dystopic moments of unpleasantness.

Neither Alicia nor Teresa finds in Mexico any solution to the conflicts deriving from their ethnoclass situation in the United States, although distance and exoticism provide them with a space to imagine an idealized other world. From the U.S. side of the border, Mexico seduces as the tabula rasa upon which they may rewrite their pasts, and that familiar but alien other provides a more malleable form for this self-imagining than the resistant molds of their own country. To the degree that Mexico confirms her fictional image, including her dream of a seductive exoticism, Teresa loves it and its people; to the degree that it insists on deviating from her dream, on confirming a stubborn incomprehensibility—or worse, a matter-of-fact counterstereotype—she rejects it utterly. Again and again, in each visit to Mexico, Teresa's dream of finding a simple, exotic homeland fragments against the staged exoticism of a pragmatic seduction attempt. Each encounter is wounding, and each wound reconfirms her divided self. Castillo's epistolary novel does not attempt to resolve the tension of this double vision. Instead, the strained theatricality remains highlighted in the text, pointing directly at the heart of Teresa's confused longing, her double and distanced misreadings of two cultures' typical tropes.

Campbell too is concerned with tropes, and with imagined cities such as L.A. and the D.F. that inflect and corrupt border reality. Equally illusory are the novella's Hollywood, seen through the eyes of a Tijuana native who has watched Rita Hayworth dance and Charlie Chaplin get drunk, and the tourist's exotic and tacky "T.J." Tijuana graphically, geographically, illustrates the confluence of many types of borders, some of which negate others, and all of which are presided over by a modern totem. One border is, of course, the political boundary between the United States and Mexico, physically impressed upon the consciousness of border dwellers in the form of the fence that slices through the San Diego–Tijuana metropolitan area. Some roads, suggests the narrator, lead up to the fence and then abruptly cease to exist. A few break off at a border post presided over by an immigration officer and then resume mysteriously, discontinuously, on the other side. Anyone who drives a car in the border region is always aware of those possibilities opened by the paved surface or foreclosed. Campbell refers frequently to a second border created in the encounter between land and sea. Humans follow the surfaces of the land or the traceries of its roads; fish swim the sea roads, and only those strange, ambiguous creatures, the seals, slip back and forth easily across the borders between them. Land and sea answer to each other in this borderland, just as the United States and Mexico must: the two borders, seashore and manmade fence, run perpendicular to each other. This symmetrical conversation, these competing and cacophonous monologues—of land and sea, United States and Mexico, fence and shoreline, English-speaking woman and Spanish-speaking man—pervade both Californias. In each case, the perfect answering of negative to print, the to-and-fro movement of the Ping-Pong ball, also reminds the reader of untranslatable, unspoken abysses that mark the uncrossable limits of two disparate realities.

It is Campbell's task to disrupt the borders and shift the axes. He does so first of all by taking to the air. The narrator as a child haunts the airport and is an avid constructor of model airplanes. Typically, the narrator's gang of school friends chooses a name that reflects their yearning to soar as well. They call themselves "*pegasos*" (Pegasus) and wear red jackets with winged horses copied after the famous Mobil Oil symbol, jackets they only remove in order to fly, downward this time, from the springboard into the water of a local swimming pool (52–53). In these boys obsessed with flight and afraid of flying, we see the opening of a new conversation over other borders—Greek myth and U.S. advertising, winged horse and amphibious seal, air and water.

Even more pervasive in the novella than the airplane/Pegasus images, however, are the recurrent images of the seals. Like airplanes, they inspire a fearful fascination. The seals, says the narrator, are "Halfway beings; metamorphosed borderliners; halfway on the road to terrestrial life; the laughing inhabitants of the waves; sleepy, mute floating dolls; androgynous beings" ("seres a medias: metamorfoseados, fronterizos, en medio del camino hacia la vida terrestre, habitantes risueños de las olas, muñecas flotadoras, somnolientas, mudas, seres andróginos") (66). Like their human counterparts who live on other borders, the seals are denizens of an indeterminately inhospitable intermediate zone, in this case the ambiguous space between land and sea. There is a price, the narrator hints, for their border-crossing abilities—he tends to evoke the seals in a context of mutilation, or death. In a complex sequence of associations, the seals become associated with those other deformed "halfway beings," the human border dwellers, who also seem pathetic and mutilated when they cross the line from one space into another. Himself terrified of surfacing, the narrator's personal identity is caught in helpless awareness of a bifurcated cultural and historical memory, both poles of which are necessarily foreign. His typical gesture points less to writing and more toward the ghost of a culturally coded graphism displaced or encrypted amid the proliferation of signals, a graphism both full and empty, energized and repressed, the mediation between them inevitably unintelligible.

Beverly, the woman who descends from the airplane and who rises from the sea, appears in the text in close association with references to the herd of seals floating offshore. When she and the narrator go to the shore to see the seals, they observe a lifeguard rescuing a woman from the sea. From the protagonists' vantage point above the beach, seals and human beings lose their distinguishing physical characteristics and bleed into each other. Later, as the narrator drives a dying Beverly north toward San Diego after her bungled abortion, the seals also float northward, toward Alaska (12). The seals stand in contrast to the humans as examples of the optimally adapted border dweller, and yet they too, on land, seem clumsy, laughable, mutilated. They are by nature what the narrator yearns for and fears in his obsession with Beverly. He desires paradoxically to sink into the other, and yet at the same time to reject fragmentation or division and to soar heavenward in splendid isolation.

Thus, while this book proposes to tell us "everything about seals," it ultimately can speak only around those strange border creatures who escape definition, who achieve the floating existence, the self without foundation to which the narrator aspires, and that he fears. They are, then, an ambiguous but powerful symbol of social values that remain fluid and ill defined. They come to land as awkward, mutilated spectators of terrestrial life, and they move with an incomprehensible grace in that other, incommensurable world of the sea. Like airplanes, they belong to two worlds and to neither and are sublimely indifferent to borders; they cross fences and shorelines with impunity.

Beverly too is a border crosser, a pilot who in one of her incarnations flies planes in the air-taxi service between Hollywood and the Agua Caliente casino (17). Piloting a plane makes her, in the narrator's point of view, another order of being: "The fact that she knew how to fly a plane meant that I saw in her hands a potency and superiority that separated her from me insurmountably, as if she came from another world" (16). Beverly differs from ordinary women in other ways. She is separated from the narrator because she is a woman with a past. He senses "that she was someone marked forever by other hands, that there was something fatally irrecuperable in her" (34). This irrecuperable element, the unknown experience from the other side of the border, continually interrupts the narrator's efforts to construct her and, through her, himself. He creates her with his tongue, his hands, his body, his lens, but there is always some element of her that escapes him, that remains on the other side. Even her name (but can we even know if it is her "real" name?) evokes nothing so much as a place marker in the border man's incessant Ping-Pong vision of two unknowable wholes—D.F., L.A. She marks the Hollywood side of the transaction; her name reminds us of the flight of U.S. popular culture over the border, uninhibited by fences. She is Beverly Hills incarnate, raising in his heart all the conflicting emotions of rejection and attraction to her romantic dream vision and to an alien, culturally coded myth. Her past is nothing he can imagine, and there are no recognizable faces assigned to it.

At one moment, he conjectures that this other element, the unimaginable presence of her past, might be located in the English-speaking man who sometimes accompanies her on her flights to Tijuana. That man too has a place in this story, but in all the confusions of time and place and circumstance, the narrator is unable to write him in: "He, that cold and distant man who accompanied you in the Blue Fox bar, he ought to be the third character. Your husband, your fantasy lover. The master pilot. The captain. The aviator devoured by the sky" (93). The fantasized master pilot should have been the third character in this tale, the apex of the romantic triangle, but he is not. Instead, phantomlike, he suggests all the possibilities of Beverly's life on the other side of the border, without concretely defining any of them. That other man, the Hollywood counterpart to her glamourous and distanced self, keeps Beverly unclassifiable; he is what makes the narrator, land-bound and border-transfixed, almost too obviously defined. Like the seals, she escapes his obsession with her yet becomes at the same time the absolutely alien other and the embodiment of his border dream.

Beverly gives shape and language to his surroundings—he, in an earlier passage, gives her his language: "Each morning that dawns restores Beverly to the objects and to my first words. . . . I taught her to read in Spanish: 'Susi. This is Susi. Susi cleanses herself. Such is Susi'" (20). The string of words, "Susi, Ésa es Susi, Susi se asea. Así es Susi," borders on nonsense, anchored in the repetition and variation of a woman's name that is not Beverly's. The repetition "Susi" figures the narrator's desire to name and to fix the woman, a naming undone by the sing-song of the word echoes that tends to fragment and dissolve the words into their component syllables, mere alternations of vowels and sibilants. The song of her voice stays with him, however; scanning their rhythm gives order to his thoughts and imaginings. Much later, perhaps, resting with his head on Beverly's belly, he recalls these words and takes obscure comfort in them (117). They provide a background murmur to his meditations, much like the comforting sound of the sea washing against the shore.

The narrator, caught on the fence, suffers from indecision. Not so Beverly, who finds his inaction exasperating. Says the narrator about her, "The important thing about her was her way of be-ing, of really being, and not asking herself too many questions" ("Lo que importaba era su manera de estar, estar realmente y no plantearse demasiadas preguntas") (22). Campbell inaugurates here an untranslatable play between the two Spanish verbs of being, where "manera de estar" stands in for the more orthodox "manera de ser." Beverly herself, with her limited Spanish, is not likely to capture such nuances, but the narrator delicately hints at two different ways of being. Beverly's fluid "estar" stands in implicit contrast to the narrator's more intractable "ser." Moreover, her unrooted manner of being coincides with a tendency to embrace certainties rather than ask herself "too many questions." Beverly aspires to "know" the city; for the narrator, such knowledge is fraught with danger: "But the streets were question marks" (22), he reminds us, his abstraction, uncertainty, and surfeit of questions more than compensating for her lack of them and her confidence.

For Beverly, the narrator's hesitation and propensity for concretized abstraction remain inexplicable. Whereas she seemingly can stand (the etymological root of "estar") on her own, the narrator—despite his frequent and unconvincing declarations of independence—requires her reality to prop up his own indistinct sense of self. "I am the only way I can be," he tells her, "I am what you believe me to be." To which she responds: "Go away to where new countries are being created every day. Do something, good or bad, but do something. Shake yourself out of your funk. . . . Go to the corner and buy an ice cream cone" (33) Typically, of the options for action that she gives him, he chooses the last, and they share the ice cream cone: the abstract becomes concrete, and consumption turns it ephemeral once again.

In these versions of their tale, Beverly is wholly strange to him. Remembering her, inventing her, makes Beverly—the unforgettable but unknowable seal-woman—into the focus and impulse for narrative. Even as he tries to forget her, her silence or absence surrounds him and gives him shape. Intermittently, we intuit that the same constraint does not hold for her; for example, when she asks the narrator, "Why yearn after what we don't know?" she continues, answering his unheard question: "It hurts me to tell you this, but there is nothing you can do for me. . . . Why do we never coincide? You, after all, have not been the most important thing in my life" (36). Abjectly, he discovers that her indifference too is precious to him. Their relationship echoes the epigraph to the novel, from *Las sergas de Esplandián,* a chivalric novel by Garci-Ordóñez de Montalvo published for the first time in the portentous year of 1492: "on the right hand of the Indies there was an island called California . . . totally inhabited by women, without a single man" (10). The women of that island, writes Garci-Ordóñez de Montalvo, although not in the passage Campbell cites, ride to war on griffins—great flying monsters, half-lion and half-eagle—border-crossing animals contemporary with the Pegasus, but more fierce and terrifying. Ominously, the California women feed their mounts with the bodies of their male infants, supplemented with occasional male voyagers who happen onto that island.

Mexican California is virtually an island—almost surrounded by water on three sides, separated from the mainstream of the country by its border character, and separated from its northern continuation by the political boundary with the United States policed by the modern griffins of INS helicopters to which the narrator's pathetic border Pegasus offers no concomitant threat. Though the novella is narrated by a man, the city he describes is a woman's territory, contained and defined by fences and water boundaries. And, like the imagined California of Garci-Ordóñez de Montalvo's romance, this island-California is located precisely "to one side of terrestrial paradise" (10). In modern terms, seen from the Mexican side, it lies just down the coast from Beverly Hills and celluloid heaven. Seen from the U.S. side, the Mexican island-California is the home of easy women and cheap nightlife, only a short air-taxi ride away.

What then, of the men in this island-California? They, like the narrator of this story, are originary immigrants, foreigners whose anxious spinning of tales and photographs only confirms their belatedness. They have no names, no country, and a language borrowed from and propped on a female whose presence defines and destroys them. Enrique Lihn's parody comes close: "We are nothing: imitations, copies, phantoms: repeaters of what we understand badly, that is, hardly at all: . . . the animated fossils of a prehistory we have lived neither here nor there, consequently anywhere, for we are aboriginal foreigners, transplanted from birth in our respective countries of origin."9

In the island-California, the narrator invents an island-self, carefully inventing borders that he must but cannot cross, defining picture frames to organize a fragmented existence, going out into the city to look for, to invent, to ignore that solitary other who defines him and frames his existence and his desire. "I would try to search for you throughout the whole world," he says once. A bit later he adds, "In other words, I would invent you. I would organize things to make of you an irreconcilable enemy and in that way to maintain you outside myself, more myself" (83). Only by making her, and making her other, can he make her his own, discovering himself finally in the mirror, and her in the photographs, both in framed and multiply appropriated realities.

His framed and fragmented writing suffers from amnesia when the borders of life and language fail to overlap. Juan Flores and George Yúdice say that in the borderlands, "even for the most monolingual of Latinos, the 'other' language looms constantly as a potential resource, and the option to vary according to different speech contexts is used far more often than not."[10] In Campbell's work, the other language, like the other culture and the other sex, looms more ominously. The narrator's resources are impoverished by the need to keep both options open. The necessary encounter he seeks will eventually deprive him of speech and turn him into a "bilingual cripple."[11] He tells Beverly, "I only wanted to preserve the threads of what we provisionally call . . . What do we call it?" (113). He has no name for the writing of Beverly that is taking place around him and by his hand; nevertheless, he forces himself on, stutteringly, hesitantly, by indirect allusion. Beverly has warned him earlier that "things dilute" (97), and in the absence of a camera to fix the images of "things" or of Beverly to fix the order of speech, language too becomes an uncertain tool. By the end of the novella, with Beverly's death, the threads of narrative break off entirely. It is a loss of language felt as the slippage of sounds from the tongue and performed in the text in the abrupt breaking off of the narrative:

> my words are not my words. I use terms that signify nothing to me, or that change meaning with the years, or that are diluted in a diction that doesn't even serve me. They lose themselves gutterally and I have no option left but to fall mute, as you fell mute, although your silence always belonged to another order of ideas. . . . I confess; I confess to being here, before the world . . . as soon as possible I will disappear, whatever you say, whenever is convenient for you, I'm here to serve you, it's just that I thought, it's just that. (124–125)

The narrator focuses on his own alienation from language before ending with a sequence of nearly meaningless Spanish courtesy formulas. In his self-silencing, he evokes the physical apparatus of sound production and the useless body that remains behind, uselessly, when words stutter into silence. The truncation of the novella, with its fall into meaningless commonplaces, paradoxically reminds us that discussions of border reality, border identity, and border politics must be framed and situated.

Beverly, then, maps and defines the boundaries of the island-California, while at the same time she represents its antithesis. Seeing Beverly descend from an airplane brings to mind her emergence from the sea—both cases evoking a kind of birth the narrator urgently needs to capture and preserve in his photographs (91). The narrator as a Mexican both frames the geography of her body and accounts for her (and his) paradoxical deterritorialization. Even his meticulous analysis of their almost prelinguistic verbal pact, his geographer's awareness of their bodies' living territorial compact, represents only one of the permutations of this relationship. Other narrative moments privilege the enforcement of bodily, cultural, and political boundaries, when he cannot find the manner to enter into her body or to capture her living presence. In order to understand her life and his own city, he must account for her death and her nationality. In a larger sense, he can do neither. Thus, he falls back on the evocation of a chiasmic encounter that takes place between land and sea, earth and air, man and woman, life and death, voice and silence. In variations on the story of his search for the elusive Beverly, he tells of one who is only marginal to his life and another who dominates every aspect of it; a Beverly who says "tengo frío" and "Susi se asea" before falling into silence, and another who defines the possibilities of speech; a Beverly he barely knows and another who dies aborting his fetus; a Beverly who drowns in a beach accident, and one who seal-like, Pegasus-like, slips smoothly between two realms; a Beverly who defines a borderlands existence and another who refuses to let lines and divisions of any sort enter into her logic.

Campbell's starkly poetic novel ends abruptly. The truncated potential of the aborted child, "A baby that slid from her vagina, aiming at me" (63), hints at the impossibility of recovering the lost text of any enabling ritual whatsoever. Their aborted child points itself toward the narrator in an accusing gesture, evoking the narrator's own aggressive handling of the camera, and points as well towards an aporia, the deeply ambiguous ending of a ruined bond that is as much transhuman as transnational. Both child and camera signal the presence of a rhetorical tradition in which the imagination and reality are discrete spaces, susceptible to metaphorical bridging. As critics we may theoretically construe that metaphorical bridging by the upflinging of the Hegelian *Aufhebung*, the minimal slippages of the Derridian *différance*, or the bar between signifier and signified. The disjunctions in Campbell (and, as we shall see, in Castillo as well) respond to a recognition that the abysses of metaphor are artificial cultural products, with temporal and spatial limitations. The metaphorical border site makes concrete the underpinnings between two vaguely shifting forms—insubstantial memoir, insubstantial world. It is painted out of the double haunting of an experience and a language that is also dual. These delicate distinctions and subtle displacements cipher a particular repertoire of linguistic practices that respond and correspond to the need of bicultural-bilingual writers to encode in a more than superficial manner their shifting set of mutually exclusive, equally valid, alternate roles. Furthermore, the underlying scene is compacted and complicated by the need to represent not only the temporal and spatial disjunctions, but also those imposed by a living awareness of multiple cultures, multiple languages, multiple time frames that impose their own rules and offer their own separate opportunities for distancing and irony.

Ana Castillo also uses the aborted child as a narrative frame, as the image of something that is unresolved or irreconcilable, but at the same time unforgettable. Teresa and Alicia have both had abortions, and both still reside to some extent in the territory of that remembered pain. The narrator evokes Alicia's experience as a pitiless awakening to reality and to a kind of bodily ending that will nevertheless remain with her for the rest of her life:

> Even while i dreamed, you had stopped waiting for knights in shining armour. . . . You were seventeen and, at first, had wanted the child, romanticized motherhood. . . . When Rodney stopped coming around, you were afraid to be exiled alone.
>
> A friend of a friend lent you her welfare card. . . . The nurse . . . drew up forms that were not presented to you until you were on the table, sedated, feet in stirrups and exposed to the world the way you had never been exposed before in your life.
>
> You were sterilized. (120)

Teresa too has suffered an abortion, a decision made in hate and rage, when, as she puts it, her "womb is attacked" and her body betrays her with a man she no longer loves. Afterwards, she says, "i'm much better now and will be up and around soon to gather the pieces of the woman who was my self. . . . i had sent our child away, i told him, to wait out its turn to take part in this miserable world, where once being born it would no longer be innocent, for being was to survive and to survive, one must hurt weaker beings" (108–109). By the end of the novel, however, one sign of Teresa's newfound self-confidence is her decision to bring her baby to term when she once again finds herself with child by another faithless lover.

Alicia's forced sterilization allows her no way back into the redemptive potential of childbearing. These failed relationships and the abortions that violently mark their definitive dissolution define these two women's lives.

The way they see themselves and imagine future relationships are affected by the scars of past failures. Teresa describes both abortions at considerable length because these difficult and painful experiences of "having life sucked out from between [their] legs" are strongly defining elements of the context in which these women see themselves (109–110). For the life that is sucked out is not just the life of the potential child, but the potential life of the not-yet-mother, who must work harder at reerecting a definition of herself once she has been sucked dry.

The women in Castillo's novel seem doomed to being sucked dry, and not only by abortions. Early in the novel, the narrator asks why "so many of our ideals were stamped out like cigarette butts when we believed in them so furiously" and answers her own question, "Perhaps we were not furious enough" (16). Certainly the protagonists in this novel suffer for their efforts to define themselves and their lives. When they furiously declare their independence and their right to a relationship of equality with the men they choose as husbands and lovers, their fury wears down in the relentlessness of everyday life. Like infants, the men in these women's lives suck dry their wives and lovers. Teresa writes, "A woman takes care of the man she has made her life with, . . . as if he were her only child, as if he had come from her womb. . . . There isn't a woman who doesn't understand this deathtrap" (112). Yet she repeatedly falls into it. Teresa reminds Alicia, who is grieving over the suicide of her lover: "Abdel was a weak man, Alicia, and he had already sucked you dry of more than what a child can demand of its mother," for unlike a child, a man remains dependent on the woman—mother figure (129).

Women's losses risk codification as failures. She who fails to attract and keep a man is considered unwomanly, or too experienced to deserve a relationship with a desirable man (93–94). The cultural production of standards of beauty and desirability is very much at issue here. Teresa is bitterly aware of the triple bind of the beauty system: attractive experienced women attract the wrong kind of men; attractive inexperienced women attract danger; and unattractive women are not only valueless but guilty for the lack of effort they put into attracting men. One of Teresa's dream-poem narratives slices through the hypocrisy of her society, describing a drag beauty pageant haunted by danger and violence:

and no scene such as this is complete without Eric the Rapist . . .
and i didn't understand., Alicia
how you danced with such carefree abandon

when an hour before you escaped violation at the point
of a gun (77)

Alicia's almost blithe inattention to her own danger represents a basic character trait that Teresa refers to frequently throughout the letters. It is a
tendency that alternately attracts and exasperates her friend, but mostly
Teresa suffers from her helplessness to protect Alicia as if it meant an assault
on her own physical reality. In this metaphorical/real situation in which
Alicia is sandwiched between two versions of masculinity—one whispering
sweet nothings in her ear and the other whispering death threats—only Teresa understands that both men in effect appropriate Alicia's dancing body
through repetition of the same story used for ages to entrance women.
Teresa's whispers go unheeded, and her words cannot compete with the
force and power of the men's words and weapons. Teresa, who does not
dance, constitutes herself the unnoticed guardian, but she recognizes that
she is ineffective and equally susceptible to men's voices and knives: "there is
little in the end i can do, i have a vagina too" (78).

Teresa and Alicia look elsewhere for their earthly paradise, going to
Mexico to reinvent themselves and recover their past, to seek an alternative
present, to dream a Mixquiahualan future. Only in that utopian realm can
Teresa achieve real self-sufficiency. In her nightmare about a revolution,
when the peaceful town finds itself subjected to violent attack, she imagines
herself as a powerful woman, armed, a resistance leader. When the government troops arrive in her dream town to confront her, she is ready to die
defending her people: "My weapon. It was my own and i had used it
before, fit into my hand like that of a faithful lover" (97). In her dream of
mestizo resistance to oppression, Teresa vindicates herself and finally over-
comes the self-imposed limitations that flow from her hyperawareness of
her woman's body. Significantly, Teresa can only contemplate such a step
when she is doubly exiled: in her nightmare, and in Mixquiahuala. Even
there her revolutionary potency has limits; Teresa stops short of actually
firing the weapon. She ends the retelling of the dream with the moment of
lifting the weapon and preparing to fire.

When Teresa steps back from her dreams and into the contemporary
reality of the Mexico she has visited with her friend, she finds no real
alternative to the dilemma posed by the parable of the woman dancing
between twinned threats of seduction and death. Mexico rejects the young
women even more firmly than had the patriarchal United States. It is not

just that they are seen as legitimate prey, but that they go through the country unacknowledged and unaccounted for. Despite their longing to belong to an alternative reality, Mexico refuses to recognize them and, as Teresa notes, snips them out of the societal pattern. They are anomalies. Insofar as they exist at all in Mexican consciousness, they exist as exotic creatures outside normal laws: "We would have hoped for respect as human beings, but the only respect granted a woman is that which a gentleman bestows on a lady. Clearly we were no ladies. What was our greatest transgression? We travelled alone" (59).

Not only did they travel alone; they did so in what is practically the uniform of U.S. tourists. In one encounter, when the women hitch a ride with a trio of heavily armed men, the men ask Teresa and Alicia if they are from the United States. Teresa replies: "i tried to laugh, as if the suggestion was ludicrous. How could they possibly think that? Couldn't they see by our color that we weren't gringas? It's the blue jeans, one said, as if stating a statistical fact" (63). In this key scene two clichés about the United States are played off against each other. The U.S. women of color assume that they can "pass" as non-U.S. by virtue of their race; underlying their presumption is a painful and deeply inbred feeling that the "typical American" (ugly or not) is necessarily white. Under that assumption, they do not fit in the United States, and thus it is both shocking and distressing for them to be immediately identified with a rejecting and rejected nationality in the country to which they wish to escape. The Mexican soldiers recognize the women despite their native Spanish by clichéd cultural markers the women don't care to disguise: their travel together without a man for protection (U.S. women are independent) and their clothes (all and only U.S. women wear blue jeans).

It is a scene replayed again and again, and Teresa has a hard time catching on, perhaps because she so badly wants reality to match her dreams and therefore refuses to accept the realities that present themselves. In another encounter with two men in a Veracruz restaurant, one asks if they are gringas: " 'What makes you think we're gringas?' i asked, trying not to give away defensiveness. 'Easy. Your blue jeans,' he replied smiling" (69). The ubiquitous jeans that in the United States seem an invisible, class-dissolving fact of life for young people become in their chosen dreamland a marker of exotic and vulnerable femininity to the Mexican men. Pointedly, Teresa and Alicia meet very few Mexican women except in dreams, where those women are motherly mestizas who work the fields and care for their children in provincial homes. They are not blue jean–clad adventurers. In fact, they look and act uncomfortably like Teresa's own mother and aunts in unromantic Chicago.

What makes this novel an interesting counterpoint to Campbell's novella is that Teresa does not rest on the gendered clichés of a romantic deterritorialization. Although in Mixquiahuala she holds up an unused dream weapon, her dreams eventually become a weapon to attack her own prejudices: her hatred of middle-class Chicano "brothers" with their intermittent and hypocritical commitment to "barrio" causes, her resentment toward white women as the ultimate in desirable possessions, her intransigent romanticism about Mexico. Her friendship with Alicia and the dialectic between them contribute most to this reevaluation.

These women define themselves antithetically in terms of attractiveness to men. Alicia, plain and flat-chested, "bore no resemblance to the ideal of any man / you encountered anywhere" (44). She hates herself and "would not be loved," although she allows men to copulate with her frequently in a semblance of relationships. Of the two, it is brown-skinned Teresa that men want: "i never had problems attracting men. You pointed out the obvious, the big breasts, full hips and thighs, the kewpie doll mouth" (113). Their skins, like their blue jeans, shape superficial perceptions of what they are, but neither woman is that physical object. Nevertheless, the perceptions change them, at least partially, into a person matching the physical image. Taught to valorize themselves through their attractiveness to men, both women hate the tyranny of the physical. Alicia feels rejected because of her unattractive body; Teresa feels insulted by men's purely physical interest.

In effect, their very differences—of build, race, temperament, and background—bring them together as mirrors for each other and their own self-reflection. They deterritorialize themselves, first in Mexico, where they devise a dream that fits them, and then in each other, where they discover opportunities for both support and battle. They reserve their sharpest weapons for each other, and their most thoughtful and loving exchanges: "Each time we parted it has been abruptly. We picked, picked, picked at each other's cerebrum and when we didn't elicit the desired behavior, the confirmation of allegiance, we reproached the other with threatening vengeance. . . . We begged for the other's visit and again the battle resumed. We needled, stabbed, manipulated, cut and through it all we loved, driven to see the other improved in her own reflection" (23). Teresa calls their intense relationship "a love affair," although of a particular, nonsexualized kind: "we were experts at exchanging empathy for heart-rending confusion known only to lovers, but you and I had never been lovers" (39, 121). This love affair between the two women is different from any relationship they share with their various male lovers. The men are exclusively interested in the physical being, in the mechanics of conquest, the triumph of possession, the fierce joy of imposing themselves indelibly upon the woman. The men use women's bodies as markers of status, they use their own bodies as weapons, and they use weapons to mark women's bodies. In the ultimate instance, exemplified by Abdel, they narcissistically turn the weapon on themselves so that the woman can never escape the memory of finding the violent suicide and will remain indelibly scarred by his death.

With each other, the women's battles have more productive ends. They learn to cut through the racialized distinctions and look into each other's brains and souls. No longer merely objects, no longer smooth surface beings for male reflection, they actively reflect and reflect upon each other, and while they see the mirror in the other, they also seek the depths. Yet the novel frames this constructive relationship with the ruptures of abortion, sterilization, and suicide.

Both Castillo and Campbell thus finally invoke cultural loss through a violent act that cuts off further contemplation: the excision of potential life with an abortion and the cutting off of narration after recounting a lover's violent death. Literal cuts coincide with literary breaks. In the borderlands between loss of meaning and the fullness of culture's demands erupt images of these violent woundings of identity. The implications of this violence at the border unsettle my own interpretive strategies. Where is the edge of the cut? To paraphrase a question asked in another context by Marcos Sánchez-Tranquilino and John Tagg, What is the arc of the knife?

Sánchez-Tranquilino and Tagg interrogate another cultural and social figure of the borderlands, the *pachucos/as*, who in their aggressive zoot-suited self-construction seem to shrink the limits of the heterotopia to the highly restricted space of their own bodies and the clothing they wear.[12] These critics provide an essential clue for a reading of the cut in Campbell and Castillo. The pachuco/a culture, they find, "repudiated *subordination* in a hierarchy of national cultures" moving through and appropriating the cultural markers of both Mexican and U.S. Anglo culture. If the pachuco's refusal to choose either a Mexican or a North American identity represented for Octavio Paz a "scandal of civilized meaning," neither the scandal nor the civilization is quite what Paz imagined, and the question of meaning is likewise problematic. The pachuco first needs to be put in the context of a fuller cultural and sexual spectrum, to include both pachuco and pachuca. One of the scandals of Paz's analysis and of much subsequent mythologizing about the pachuco occurs because his counterpart is cut off and made invisible. In turn, we must ask which civilization the pachuco and pachuca affront, for as Sánchez-Tranquilino and Tagg point out they repudiate and appropriate both poles. Zoot-suiters resisted the dominant cultural representations of Mexico and the United States with a strategy that "was neither 'inside' nor 'outside': it ruptured their structures of Otherness, at least for a moment, at least for the best times of the week." This momentary interruption of cultural structures and strategies was both a fugitive phenomenon and a visual confrontation of bodies marked by tattoos and decorated with razor blades: "The clothes made meanings with their bodies. They made them hateful and desirable. They made them visible. But, worse than that, they made them readable in a way that had to be denied" (559–560). In 1943, white servicemen responded by stripping and battering zoot-suiters in East L.A. The pachuco/a, then, like the other borderliners studied here, crosses the field of interpretation not as resistance to reading, but as a discursive product that offers too many readings and yet has been consistently underread from both sides of the violent, divisive cultural cut.

"What is unraveling now," Sánchez-Tranquilino and Tagg conclude, "is the discursive formation of a discipline—the conjunctural effects of its practices, institutions, technologies, and strategies of explanation" (557). This unraveling is particularly noticeable in such borderline texts as those by Campbell and Castillo that take the multiply-valenced identity of the border dweller as their subject. Such novels cannot be easily accommodated to the cultural histories of either nation. To paraphrase Sánchez-Tranquilino and Tagg again: these novels not only mark, but provoke, a certain kind of internal cultural crisis in narrowly conceived imaginations of nation, just as they mark, but refuse to inhabit, the gender roles, subject positions, and nationalistic spaces limned for them in the violent conflicts of cultural miscegenation. These wounds, these transgressive cuts, characterize a practice in which the conjunctural describes only one side of the seam.

NOTES

1. Leo Lionni, *Little Blue and Little Yellow* (New York: Obolensky, 1959).

2. Federico Campbell, *Tijuanenses* (Mexico: Mortiz, 1989), 102–103; my translation. This collection also contains "Anticipating Incorporation" ["Anticipo de Incorporación"], "Tijuanenses," "Los Brothers," and "Insurgentes Big Sur."

3. Ana Castillo, *The Mixquiahuala Letters* (Binghamton, NY: Bilingual, 1986) 20.

4. Ana Castillo, *Sapogonia* (Tempe, AZ: Bilingual, 1990) 5.

5. Homi Bhabha, "DissemiNation: Time, Narrative, and the Margins of the Modern Nation," *Nation and Narration,* ed. Homi K. Bhabha (London: Routledge, 1990) 313.

6. D. Emily Hicks, MS, review of Herbert Blau's *The Eye of the Prey.*

7. As D.C. stands for Washington, so D.F. (Distrito Federal) is shorthand for Mexico City. Tepito is a lower-class Mexico City neighborhood, whose inhabitants are instantly recognizable for their distinctive accent and phrasing; the "East Side" refers to L.A.

8. Anseleme Remy, "The Unholy Trinity," *Caribbean Review* 6.2 (1974): 14–18.

9. Enrique Lihn, "El arte de la palabra" (Barcelona: Pomaire, 1979) 82.

10. Juan Flores and George Yúdice, "Living Borders/Buscando America: Languages of Latino Self-formation," *Social Text* 8.2 (1990): 75.

11. Abdelkebir Khatibi, *Love in Two Languages,* trans. Richard Howard (Minneapolis: U of Minnesota P, 1990) 24.

12. Marcos Sánchez-Tranquilino and John Tagg, "The Pachuco's Flayed Hide: Mobility, Identity, and *Buenas Garras,*" *Cultural Studies,* ed. Lawrence Grossberg, Cary Nelson, and Paula Treichler (New York: Routledge, 1992) 556–570. This important theorization of a specific, controversial border identity responds to Octavio Paz's classic demonization of the pachuco in "The Pachuco and Other Extremes," from the Mexican Nobel Prize winner's 1959 collection of essays on Mexican identity, *The Labyrinth of Solitude,* trans. Lysander Kemp (New York: Grove, 1961). The article responds to the more recent aesthetic appreciations of the pachuco phenomenon in such works as Luis Valdez's 1978 play (now a movie) "Zoot Suit." Originally referring to an attitude, a style of dress, and a type of bilingual slang originating in El Paso, since the 1943 "zoot-suit riots," pachucos/as and their descendants have been closely identified with gang activity in Los Angeles.

JANE MARCUS

Registering Objections: Grounding Feminist Alibis

Come, let us counsel some cold stranger
How we sought safety, but loved danger.
So, with stiff walls about us, we
Chose this more fragile boundary:
Hills, where light poplars, the firm oak,
Loosen into a little smoke.
—Louise Bogan

The Hottentots [exiles from Southern Africa in England] then,
saw themselves as having fetched up, by great misfortune upon a
miserable island. They had fallen among the master race. They
wished to register their objections. They had, it was true, learned
too many of the master's ways. They drank his liquor, caught his
diseases, traded with him and accommodated him. All right,
they'd compromised. But they would not give in. . . . They would
never go over to the enemy.—Christopher Hope

Feminists, like other avant-gardes of intellectuals, artists, and social critics
in history, are always scrambling for the high ground. They wish to separate themselves from the enemy, and often the best position from which to
pontificate against error seems to be above. These modernist and postmod-
ernist articulations of self-exclusion are certainly as predictably spatial.
Feeling stranded in an alien land, exposed and vulnerable, they wish at
every stage to "register their objections."[1] They/we want to make it perfectly clear that accommodation to patriarchy (or its equivalent in power)

was necessary for survival. We object to imprisonment in the miserable spaces alloted to us, recalling instead a geography of grand spaces, high mountains, and deep canyons in a utopian space and time before empire and colonization created an us and them as margin and center of our cultural maps.

Registering objections, then, names much of our practice as feminist critics. Registering objections is what we do when we enter and continue the discourse of accusation and complaint sung by those who are, like Christopher Hope's exiles, profoundly uncomfortable at having fallen among the master race. One may note how often this discomfort is expressed in purely verbal protest.

In genres from fiction or political protest songs to literary criticism or autobiographical ethnographies, such discourse often turns on images of fields or grounds of geographical exploration and colonization in which the languages of race and gender twist together. But there is more to an oppositional discourse than simply (or complicatedly) registering one's objections. It is always already problematic in its elitist occupation of an untainted elsewhere from which it may ethically abstain from social responsibility. It could be argued that the practice of registering one's objections merely creates an alibi in case freedom does prevail and the master race is overthrown . . . someday.

A Very Fine Negress

The noticeable contradiction in the social practices of many white Western women—that is, as Louise Bogan's poem "Last Hill in a Vista" so poignantly reminds us, the ways in which we simultaneously seek safety and love danger—is worth exploring.[2] Both in that masterpiece of registering objections, *A Room of One's Own* (1929), and in *Three Guineas* (1938) Virginia Woolf outlined what we may call a *politics of trespass,* urging those excluded from the institutions of power by gender, race, or class to step on the grass of the cloistered quadrangles of ancient and privileged universities and by extension on the territories, material or intellectual, of all such closed elites. Her Outsider is, of course, by virtue of her own oppression, never implicated in the oppressions of her own society against others. It is never her fault, and she cannot and will not be blamed for the sins of those she calls the patriarchs. ("Patriarchy" was a shocking word in 1929, and Woolf took it from Jane Ellen Harrison's discourse of feminist anthropology.) There was no discourse available to her, one could argue, in which gender, race, and class oppressions could be explored together. (I appreciate, but still disagree with, some responses to this paper which excuse Woolf's remarks as ironic.) But we have other options and need not limit our critique to the rhetoric of registering objections, articulating an ethics of elsewhereness or a politics of trespass, seeking safety while loving danger, anticipating the need of an alibi before the court of history.

Righteously asserting that *as a woman* she has no reason to feel guilty about the oppression of others by white men, Virginia Woolf proclaims her innocence. In what is now a basic text in the history of the struggle for freedom of her sex, she proposes to collectivize the innocent oppressed into a body of outsiders, a society of those who cannot be blamed, a fellowship as it were of the marginal. But we who come after her in history cannot maintain the fiction of her (or our) innocence. As we learn to confront her with her own words, using the (partial) methods of feminist cultural critique she drafted (despite the lack of discourses in which to express her insights), we are forced to deal, however inadequately, with our own record on class and race. The difficulties of such self-scrutiny have produced some disturbing writing by white feminists in the West.[3]

"It is one of the great advantages of being a woman that one can pass," Woolf asserts, "even a very fine negress without wanting to make an Englishwoman of her." Woolf is here dissociating herself from nationalism and imperialism by attributing the desire to possess the other to a specifically European male "instinct, which murmurs if it sees a fine woman go by, or even a dog, Ce chien est à moi." "And, of course," she continues, "it may not be a dog, I thought, remembering Parliament Square, the Sieges Allee and other avenues; it may be a piece of land or a man with curly black hair."[4]

It is, of course, one of the great advantages of being a feminist critic that one cannot pass even a very fine example of "registering objections" without commenting on its self-serving racism and appallingly problematic assumptions. A white middle-class woman reader may easily assume that Woolf's tone is deeply ironic: The narrator has shown in fact few advantages to being a woman in England in the 1920s or before. For black readers of different nationalities and ethnicities, as Alice Walker once eloquently adumbrated in *In Search of Our Mothers' Gardens,* passing over this passage in a primary feminist text is a problem.

Objecting first to those powerfully loaded words, *negress* and *English-*

woman, we might begin by examining the cultural freight they carry. Heavily gendered, both words exist as variants of the masculine normative nouns *negro* and *Englishman.* Both carry the burden of gender, but it is not distributed equally. *Negress* is far more negatively marked than *Englishwoman,* in its feminizing diminutive "ess." Like *laundress* or *waitress,* it devalues and diminishes, distances and disempowers. It seems to feminize the black woman but not to "womanize" her as an equal. The figure of race in the first is bound as tightly to gender as the figure of nation is bound to gender in the second.

Added to their already secondary status as exceptions to the male rule, the unequal way each is marked as feminine makes it look unlikely that these words might signify sisterhood. Since in Woolf's passage "negress" carries no national identity and "Englishwoman" carries no racial identity—all the English are white, and negroes have no countries—there is no possibility of linguistic bonding. How was this passage to be read by the "negress" herself? Did Virginia Woolf presume she couldn't read English, being illiterate, or wouldn't be likely to read a white feminist's polemical essay? Can we presume that the "negress" was an African national subject? Not very likely in 1928 in England. As a colonial subject, which seems likely, she would have been deprived of a national identity, and politically disenfranchised. The "negress" might not share Woolf's impassioned pacifist rejection of "nation" in *Three Guineas:* "As a woman I have no country; as a woman I want no country; as a woman my country is the whole world."[5] Because of white European colonists, she might have experienced the loss of national identity, exile, displacement, or homelessness. But her gender status might have been more valued in her native culture than Woolf's was in the England that had only that year, reluctantly and after a century of struggle, granted the vote to members of her sex.

If we track the origins of the narrator's legacy of five hundred pounds a year in Woolf's text, we find that the white Englishwoman's economic freedom has been earned at the expense of colonial expansion, in the form of a legacy from an aunt. Her aunt died after a fall from her horse while taking the night air in Bombay. The point may be subtle, but it is made. Woolf's acknowledgement that middle-class Englishwomen of her generation owe their freedom to the legacy of colonial exploitation is, I believe, a conscious radical move, telling us that the five hundred pounds that free an Englishwoman like her to write derives from territorial expansion and the exploitation of her sisters in India and Africa.[6] The precious room of her own, so symbolic of feminist struggles in the twentieth century, has been bought with blood money. The white woman reader is reminded of her fall, the original imperialist historical sin committed by her ancestress in farthest India or darkest Africa that funds her freedom to write.

But if Woolf and her narrator are aware of these connections, and surely on some level they are, then how ironic is the narrator's claim that she has no wish to "make an Englishwoman" of the "very fine negress"? Does this signify a difference from the attitudes of her fore-aunts? If she tells us so clearly that gender did not exempt her aunt from responsibility—that there is indeed no feminist alibi for imperialism—does she signify her and our own guilt as well? Is she saying we have rooms of our own because they don't—because the "First World" largely functions on the labor of our sisters in the former colonies? The answer is yes, whether or not you attribute such an intention to the writer or the narrator of *A Room of One's Own*.

Perhaps we may undo some historical damage if we join this text in the classroom with a black woman's text that explores race and gender issues in terms of space, such as Harriet Jacobs's *Incidents in the Life of a Slave Girl*, which relates confinement to gender and race, suggesting the historical legacy of the horror of the holds of slave ships in the narrator's seven-year confinement in a garret.[7] We might then ask why Woolf claims such a small space for the woman artist's exercise of freedom, why she plays on the domestic locked in/locked out trope of the prison transformed to a private workspace.

A Room of One's Own, like much feminist protest literature, uses the tropes of slavery to make the case for women's oppression. Woolf's Englishwoman, the fifteenth-century daughter cited by Trevelyan who refused to marry the man of her father's choice and was "locked up, beaten and flung about the room" (44), is projected in her text as a slave, not a "freeborn Englishwoman," through the repetition of this scene throughout the text. In staging the scene of women's history as "An Englishwoman Is Being Beaten," and calling upon the historian George Macaulay Trevelyan as her authority in so doing, Woolf links the "very fine negress" and the "Englishwoman" as victims of male violence, as female bodies hurt and imprisoned against their will: "in fact she was the *slave* of any boy whose parents forced a ring upon her finger" (45). The rhetorical energy gathered in the repetition of the scene of an *Englishwoman* being beaten is used to fuel the feminist complaint.[8]

The oppressive aspects of both race and gender are conceived in terms of space. As a woman Woolf was intimidated by the overpowering geography of gender domination in the public streets of European cities, with their public spaces like Parliament Square and the Sieges Allee, arrogantly asserting the power of generals and kings with their statues of heroes and great men, streets and squares built for military displays of soldiers and weapons. The equally splendid private male spaces of the courts and quadrangles of the men's colleges at Oxford and Cambridge (where the narrator was forbidden to step on the grass) offer another version of the same privileged topography.

Yet one of Woolf's most charming personae is that of the *flaneuse,* the English version of the *flaneur,* the European walker in the city, the dandy and artist-observer. I have compared her to Water Benjamin in her exploration of London, the Capital of the Patriarchy. She calls herself a street haunter and makes clear that she is breaking a gender taboo by her eccentric pattern of walking and looking, since those activities are usually reserved for men. As a woman she is supposed to be looked at, not to look herself. A lady's eyes are cast down in public. A woman's bold look is culturally attributed to a prostitute. Virginia Woolf personally wilted under the gaze of strangers in the streets and in shops. Her own observation overlooks the possibility that the "negress" might return her gaze, seeing a pale, thin, pop-eyed, straggle-haired woman whose clothes are held together with safety pins. When Woolf/the narrator assumes the privileges of the gaze as she looks at the negress, how does she differ from the men who make her so uncomfortable by staring at her as she walks the city streets?

The narrator's gaze is race-d as well as gendered, and powerfully erotic. The use of the word *savage* in this text is equally problematic. Readers also stumble on the passage about "kissing a negress in the dark" in *Orlando.* What's the difference, we want to know, between passing and kissing? Was Woolf aware of the racial meaning of the word *pass?* Drawing on the literary and social insights about racial "passing" offered by contemporary black feminist critics Hortense Spillers, Mae Henderson, and Deborah McDowell, one senses in Woolf's narrator "who passes" a negress the assumed confidence of the white male whose gaze she herself criticized. Do her color and class allow her to colonize city space in exactly the way that men do in regard to women? In this passage does Virginia Woolf's fleeting passing as a man who gazes possessively on a woman reproduce in her own gaze at a black woman the unequal power she critiques in the male gaze at women, property, dogs, and racially other men? Since she knew so well what it was like to be reduced to an object by someone else's withering gaze, can we assume that we know why she seems to subject her "negress" to the same visual abuse?

Certainly in the spaces invoked in her text—the streets and quadrangles of Oxford and Cambridge—it is not very likely that Virginia Woolf or her narrator often passed negroes or negresses, or black people of any kind. There were few black Britons at the time, mostly, according to historians Peter Freyer and Paul B. Rich, small populations of sailors in ports like London, Bristol, and Liverpool.[9] It obviously never entered Woolf's mind that the "very fine negress" could be an Englishwoman. Indeed, Woolf's problem is still with us, as the definition of Englishness is contested in racial clashes, and violence erupts in Germany over a racial definition of national citizenship.[10] The rise of racism, neofascism, and "ethnic cleansing" in Europe today underscores the depth of political feeling on the role of race in national space and the failure of governments to resolve these issues successfully.

Woolf might not often have encountered Africans, Afro-Caribbeans, or African Americans in her daily walks in London or in Sussex in the 1920s. She might have encountered the wife of an African student at an English university, a member of the African Students Association, the elite training ground for future leaders of the colonies. Leonard Woolf told the Sri Lankan Shelton Fernando that he had entertained revolutionary leaders and their wives from Ceylon at home, where his wife admired the songs and dances they performed after dinner.[11] Yet it is not clear whether the black or Asian intellectuals, poets, and revolutionaries she may have encountered in the British Museum, or the guests of her husband's whom she entertained at dinner, would have fit the category "very fine negress."

Certainly Woolf's membership in the radical 1917 Club and her research and editing of her husband's position papers on imperialism placed her among the few white European intellectuals who were concerned about racial inequities in this period. Her youthful appearance in blackface in her brother's Dreadnought Hoax prank, imitating the Ethiopian ambassador's inspection party (and thus crossing both race and gender), may call her

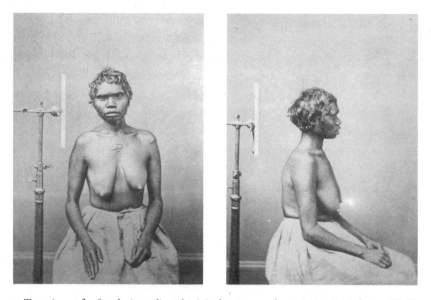

1. Two views of a South Australian aboriginal woman, taken in 1870 according to T. H. Huxley's "photometric instructions," of "Ellen," aged twenty-two, photographer unknown. Collection, Royal Anthropological Institute, London, 2116. From Elizabeth Edwards, ed., *Anthropology and Photography 1860–1920* (New Haven and London: Yale University Press, 1992) 101. Huxley specifically asked that the arm in female subjects be "so disposed as not to interfere with the contour of the breast which is very characteristic in some races" (100).

commitment into question. Yet in marrying Leonard Woolf and associating herself with radical ideas and ideals, Woolf shed many of the beliefs and prejudices of her family and class. That she falls into the racializing discourses of Victorian intellectuals like Matthew Arnold is to be expected. We know that she did a great deal of the fact gathering for Leonard Woolf's impressive anticolonial book *Empire and Commerce in Africa* (1917). Surprisingly radical in its Marxist economic analysis of imperialism, it documents the annexation of territory by the European powers: "the British State in a few years added 2,600,000 square miles to its territory in order to supply its citizens with free markets."[12] As publishers at the Hogarth Press, Leonard and Virginia Woolf produced many of the important British books on race and imperialism in both Africa and India.[13]

The words "very fine negress" are not, however, part of the discourse of political economy here. They exist in the visual vocabularies of anthropology and art history, produced by that possessive, measuring, and judging gaze from which Woolf herself suffered. Their racist ring also echoes the scientific discourse invoking the Victorian imperialist gaze of Mary Kingsley and the anthropologist-adventurers who photographed and measured the natives of Africa and Asia and their flora and fauna as they "explored" their continents, rivers, and mountains (fig. 1).

Woolf's passage recalls the invocation of the word *fine* to refer to a particularly good example of a type. The "negress" in this case might be a "very fine" specimen collected and displayed for observation. Woolf's words participate in an old and well-established discourse of rational specimen collection and exhibition, part of the Western scientific will to know and name and own, to categorize, judge for beauty and size and color, and place in museums or zoos or botanical gardens. This specimen-making gaze is deeply possessive and coldly judgmental. Steeped as she was as a child in the Elizabethan literature of exploration and adventure, Virginia Woolf simply absorbed the language of the master race. The phrase "a very fine negress" might figure on a label for an ethnographic photograph mounted in the Museum of Mankind or Musée de l'Homme or Museum of Natural History, or for a sketched or carved figure in some scientific or anthropological volume from Malinowski to Captain Cook or the *National Geographic*. Woolf's wording in this case would indicate an especially interesting example of a racial type, a model of physical health, or an example of extreme difference from Europeans. The further from the Englishwoman, presumably, the finer the negress.

It goes without saying that these figures were naked, often with prominent breasts. The eroticizing of the African woman's maternal qualities and the fetishizing of her breasts is a common feature of such ethnographic discourses, both written and photographic, from Michel Leiris to Margaret Mead.

The word *fine* also means pure, perfect, delicate and precious, or smartly dressed; the *Oxford English Dictionary* points out that it is often used ironically. But here Woolf seems to mean that the negress is an object of art of superior quality, an exquisite or rare piece of sculpture to be seen, admired, and acquired by the collector. The "woman" moves past the still figure of the negress, looking at her body as an aesthetic (and perhaps sexual) object. Is the negress she passes perhaps a version of the polished figurine (as in the famous Man Ray photograph), which the European

2. "Negro Sculpture," from the Collection Guillaume, Plate III in Roger Fry, *Vision and Design* (1920; rpt. Oxford: OUP, 1981).

viewer conflates with the African woman it resembles to emphasize the white woman's difference?

Dependent as European modernist art is on the forms of African sculpture and the theft or borrowing of African conceptions of the human figure in three-dimensional space for its creation of primitivism, it is obvious now that the colonial expansion into the space of Africa may have engendered what we call Spatial Modernism. Could it be that colonialism itself and its voyages out and back, its geographical greediness, was the origin of the artistic excesses of modernism in art, architecture, and writing? I would argue that the history of real black women has been obscured by the figure of *the very fine negress* that haunts the history of modernism.

When Roger Fry took Virginia Woolf to the Chelsea Book Club exhibition of Negro art in April 1915, she found it both "dismal and impressive," she wrote her sister Vanessa. After seeing the exhibition of sculptures, she wrote that she "dimly [saw] that something in their style might be written, and also that if I had one on the mantelpiece I should be a different sort of character—less adorable, as far as I can make out, but somebody you wouldn't forget in a hurry."[14] That she did not collect African art is no reason to suppose that she did not use the startling presence of these polished stylized forms as an impulse to writing and shaping her own fictional forms. What she wrote (*Room,* for example) is about Spatial Modernism. Roger Fry's claim was that the genius of African sculpture lay in its three-dimensionality.

Fry's essay in the *Athenaeum* championing Negro art collected in *Vision and Design* in 1920, wholeheartedly embraced African forms for their pure aesthetic qualities.[15] (Of course, it was only pure in the sense that Fry looked at these elegant plastic forms out of context, for they of course possessed cultural "meaning" in Africa.) At first Fry shocked the art world, but he began to change public attitudes by arguing that African sculpture was the closest thing there is to "pure art" without any romantic associations with real life or representation. His essay suggests that Woolf's negress may have been derived from a memory of the Yoruba figure that so captivated Fry, that her "fine" was an echo of his "pure" (fig. 2).

One could argue that Woolf has robbed her "very fine negress" of subjectivity in much the same way as men appropriated hers. The white female upper-middle-class gaze of the art collector or connoisseur reduces the black woman to a beautiful object to be "appreciated." When Roger Fry celebrated the African artist's aesthetic emphasis on the protuberant parts of the body, he must have been aware that metropolitan viewers would see savage sexuality where he saw vision and design. It was perhaps a struggle for someone like Virginia Woolf to use the word *fine* and the discourse of art appreciation to refer to a naked black female body. Britons' notions of themselves as the imperial race fostered a problematics of gendered social purity, setting the white woman against the native, which anticipated Roger Fry's artistic fascination with purity of forms. Helen Calloway argues, following Homi Bhabha, that the notion of purity emerged as a powerful signifier for the production of difference in the discourses of imperialism and English national identity, justifying repressive laws and "ruthless violence against incipient insurgencies."[16]

The "fragile boundaries," to use Louise Bogan's phrase, of Woolf's self-conscious role as *flaneuse,* her vacillation between safety and danger in looking at the black woman's body, and perhaps trying to erase difference by regarding the figure as an art object rather than a woman like herself, a sister subject to the same white male gaze that wants to possess "a fine woman," do not disappear. There is no bonding at the level of gender. Is it that under the Western woman's eye the negress becomes merely a racial subject and whiteness is not yet a racial category for Woolf herself? (It certainly becomes one in *The Waves.*)[17]

John MacKenzie has documented the British popular cult of spectacles of imperialism in pageantry and propaganda, film, photography, and theater.[18] Woolf's eye and that of her narrator may be indulging that European visual lust to see and categorize the other. As Ian Jeffrey argues, "the camera became a colonizer," a tool of ethnography that possesses the other. "Through photography Europe could provide itself with a visual representation of the remodelling of the world through economic and political control."[19] The power and widespread circulation of images of "savages" in a discourse of visual imperialism may have prevented the English public from seeing what Roger Fry could see in "a very fine negress," the beauty of pure form. But Virginia Woolf was perhaps more likely to pass a very fine negress in the flesh *outside* the confines of the exhibit at the Chelsea Book Club or the pages of Roger Fry or Clive Bell's theories of formal beauty.

As a standard feature, Victorian and modern exhibitions displayed "primitive" villages complete with living human villagers, and we know from her explosive essay imagining the destruction of the empire that Virginia Woolf was among the twenty-seven million people who went to the great exhibition at Wembley in 1924–25.[20] Images of the Indian pavillion also appear in *The Waves,* a novel that creates Indians as a medley of Africans, savages, cannibals with assegais in the imaginations of the white Londoners who are its characters. MacKenzie points out that the popular practice of bringing peoples from overseas began in 1867 in the Paris exhibition where exotic foods were served by exotic peoples in reproductions of the streets of Cairo complete with belly dancers and camel rides. And French "explorers" traveled around Europe with Senegalese and Dahomey villagers. Wembley's enormous spatial displays of imperial power (equivalent to today's air shows) in the colonies included an anthropological section whose official guide referred to "native customs" such as "human sacrifice and cannibalism," sensational propaganda that prompted "Students of Black Descent" to complain to the Colonial Office about the way Africans were "held up to public ridicule" in Wembley (110). The overwhelming spatial expansion and dominance of the exhibition grounds themselves, often requiring maps and guides and transportation for the crowds of viewers, themselves mimicked imperial expansion and enforced its naturalization as exploration and modernization (fig. 3).

If indeed Virginia Woolf or the narrator of *A Room of One's Own* passed a very fine negress in the context of such a colonial exhibition, it is understandable that she would have responded to the degradation and exoticizing of the other by protesting that as a woman she had nothing to do with the colonizing efforts of her compatriots or the imperialism that set before the eyes of metropolitan citizens the raw and naked "primitive" villages and people, which were the sources of their own material wealth and well-being.

Growing up as Leslie Stephen's daughter with little formal education, Virginia Woolf had been allowed to indulge a passion for the literature of English exploration and conquest from Hakluyt to Captain Cook. Reading for vicarious adventure and domination of land and sea runs as a powerful thread through all of her writing. Locked up in the Victorian house by the spatial limits set for a proper young lady, she had doubtless already seen more than one very fine negress in her imagination and in travelers' pictures. Her family on both sides, Stephens, Prinseps, and Pattles, had a long history of colonial work in India. Moreover, her grandfather James Stephen administered English territory in Africa and established colonial policy in the area. Reluctantly and against his own political views but having promised his father, an antislavery advocate and friend of Wilberforce, James Stephen wrote and shepherded through Parliament the bill that freed the slaves. It was a very mixed heritage that found in the same person the architect of the slaves' freedom and the framer of their imperial bondage.[21]

Perhaps some of the ambivalence we feel expressed in Woolf's spatialization of race, gender, the gaze, imperialism, and nationalism in this passage from *A Room of One's Own* has its source in the conflicts between her own upbringing and the Bloomsbury socialist and liberal anti-imperialist values she shared with her friends and her husband, if not with the negress she passed in the street. Certainly her very metropolitan "room of one's own" is a space where one can escape being the object of the gaze

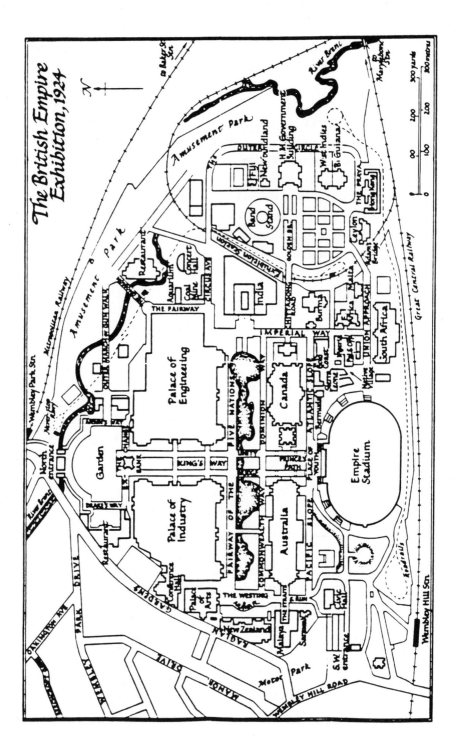

The British Empire Exhibition, 1924

3. (*Opposite page*) Map of Wembley stadium, built for the British Empire Exhibition which the Woolfs visited on 29 May 1924. Illustration for Virginia Woolf's essay "Thunder at Wembley," in Virginia Woolf, *The Crowded Dance of Modern Life: Selected Essays, Vol. II,* edited with introduction and notes by Rachel Bowlby (London: Penguin, 1993). Reprinted by permission of Julia Briggs, general editor of the series. Woolf's essay depicts nature's response (real thunder and lightning) to the artificial construct of "man-made moonlight" (the first floodlights) and loudspeakers to broadcast George V's inaugural speech, which boasted that the Wembley Empire Exhibition contained "the whole empire in little," 220 acres "of the architecture, art and industry of all the races which come under the British flag" (190). Woolf's essay is a brilliant and violent fantasy of the destruction of the British Empire.

of others, being judged by gender as fine or not so fine according to Victorian standards of womanliness, if not by race. But the freedom sought, the space imagined, is merely for privacy in confinement, to police one's own prison as it were, not to stretch into space without boundaries. The three-dimensional figures of African women that modernism admired and appropriated suggest a history and experience of physical freedom in immense spatial terms, far beyond the imagination of confined Western women.

Alibis

Woolf poses for us the problem that, as Mikhail Bakhtin writes, "One cannot understand understanding as emotional empathy, the placement of the self in the other's position (loss of one's own position). This is required only for peripheral acts of understanding. One cannot understand understanding as a translation from the other's language into one's own language."[22] The map of feminist theory often situates the woman as the quintessential outsider and assigns the critic the task of translation. Thus, in a passage much quoted by feminist critics, Luce Irigaray writes that woman "plays with mimesis" in order "to recover the place of her exploitation by language without allowing herself to be simply reduced to it." But "if women mime so well they are not simply reabsorbed in this function. They also remain elsewhere."[23] Irigaray's "elsewhereness" as an ethic would let us off the hook for the racist and colonialist mappings of history. But registering objections, or translating from the other's language into one's own, however important, cannot suffice. Abstinence is not enough. My task here is to attempt to understand the ethics of the woman writer's sense of her own elsewhereness. For elsewhere is not nowhere. It is a political place where the displaced are always seen and see themselves in relation to the "placed."[24]

Dis/placement and difference as categories of political and gender exile from writing, speaking, and acting circulate around notions of fixed positions in a substantial somewhere. A critic trying to map these moves is like a blind cartographer sticking pins into a territory called Lost Bearings, especially as the extraterritorial space around the edges of one's map, where the marginal cluster together with the noncanonical, threatens to destabilize placement and place altogether. One is "put in one's place" by the process of "putting her in her place," in that the gesture of placement reveals itself as authoritarian and academic, the naming and judging game played by the alternate rules of Who is most marginalized? rather than Who is central?

Our feminist mappings of women's culture are ghostly treadings on the dead bodies and songs of our ancestresses, the Judith Shakespeares of the past. Like the "dreaming-tracks" of Australian aboriginal peoples, the sacred secret knowledge of tribes and families passed on in rock, bark, and earth paintings (despite English claims that the land was *terra nullius, terra australis incognita*), we trace the "directions" plotted in women's songs across their own lost territory. Every rock and creek, desert and mountain on our cultural maps bears the (often erased and unmarked) footprint and song print of women's iliads and odysseys.

Nonetheless, the dominant culture continues to force the other to fit its own paradigms. In the Hayward Gallery show "ARATJARA: Art of the First Australians" (London, 1993) many paintings were marked boldly "Artist Unknown," even though the writers of the catalogue were aware that these works were produced as cultural and religious material in circumstances where the concept of the individual artist was not operative. Roger Fry's "appreciation" of African art early in the century was likewise obsessed with marking the artist as separate from the people and cultural practices from which she or he springs. This perspective allowed Fry to maintain his notions of Western superiority; it also constitutes part of the problem with the presentation of aboriginal "art" in Europe. For Fry, African sculpture was brilliant but came from a savage culture because it was unsigned. The attitude survives today.

What we need is a new compass for deciphering the legends of women's maps and the maps themselves. Disabled at the start, the critic balances one foot on the map and the other in the margins. Locating herself as she locates exiled writers, she learns of the cartographer-critic's power to falsify the map, to dissemble about the whereabouts of extraterritorial creatures. Some diasporas do not wish to be mapped or placed by the exiling agency itself. Such placement may indeed endanger their survival. Other exiled communities are confident that they take their culture with them into the promised land.

So the critic must engage the ethical question whether certain work lies "outside her jurisdiction." Perhaps that is just my alibi or excuse for taking a position outside of "elsewhereness," when it is obviously not possible to do so. If there is no outside for Virginia Woolf's Outsiders' Society, there is no outside from which I can critique her politics. I am inside and implicated in the culture that both of us occupy.

The Latin word for elsewhere is *alibi*. An alibi establishes one's innocence for not having been at the scene of a crime. But feminist criticism often romantically assumes that all women have equally plausible alibis for patriarchal crimes. For each historical case, we can measure the extent to which a woman's art is alibi. Feminist criticism has often acted as defense lawyer, constructing alibis for women writers. How will these alibis look to future generations? Are we merely registering our own objections? What do we think when white critics construct alibis for racism?

The method of this essay is to propose that we read the legends of exile and elsewhereness on women's maps not just metaphorically, but historically, contextually. A legend (or *fabula*) on a *mappa mundi* teaches us how to read, explaining the map's relation to the real world. We are just beginning to learn to read these legends. In charting the politics of women's exile we read the map's legend in that marginal space where legends traditionally appear. In the margin we may rewrite the scale in which distances are measured and values projected. This practice makes visible the difference between women's legends or stories and the legends about us. In invading this space we step on the territory of the canon, whose control of the scale in which women's work is measured has created a powerful illusion of scientific order. *A Room of One's Own* may expand to a continent. . . .

For me the classic figure of the woman exile is Emma Goldmann.

Legend has it that J. Edgar Hoover stood on the dock to make sure the dangerous anarchist was really on the ship returning her by force to the Russia she had left, and where she found herself as homeless an exile as she had been on entering the United States as a refugee. The contradictions of Emma Goldmann's exiles, forced and unforced, remind us that exile is a political condition of banishment from a threatened state. An exile is a stranger, whether or not she has chosen her condition.

Some, like Natalia Ginsburg, can write their way out of exile; making a story, she claims, was in effect building a home: "When I write stories I am like someone who is in her own country, walking along streets that she has known since she was a child, between walls and trees that are hers."[25] Some, like Ethel Smyth, find their identity in exile. Georgia O'Keeffe chose a Spanish exile in her own country, where not speaking the language appears to have been an impetus to creativity. Gertrude Stein's double displacement articulated in *Paris France* allowed her to work out from a third remove as a painterly problem in figure and ground why Paris stimulated her U.S. writing identity. Displacement by gender within the home culture alters the meaning of exile as it has traditionally been theorized. But it is a mistake to think that all female experience of difference is the same or all exiles equally victimized or empowered.

Furthermore, a woman exile is an uncanny figure, in Freud's formulation, for her very body means home and hearth, the womb/home of humankind. In exile the woman rejects her role as representation of home and the mother's body, and so she is a threat to patriarchy as well as to the state. The uncanniness of the woman exile's position lies precisely in the contradiction it poses in raising her from object to subject in regard to the state, as a person in her own right, not, as she so often was, an addition to a male passport who lost her nationality with marriage. In much of our culture woman is nation, and nation is woman, both sign and signified. Stepping outside this system, the self-conscious woman writer like Virginia Woolf claims that as a woman she has no country and wants no country, opting for the whole world as her country, equating exile by gender with the internationalism usually equated with Jews. But as we have seen, she does not extend her concept of gender to include a black woman or to imagine her as a fellow exile. Like other feminist rhetoricians of genius, she steals the tropes of slavery to mark the oppression of women, a category that does not include blacks. The figure of the negress is the difference, the ground against which the white woman claims whiteness (purity, Englishness).

As we debate these issues intellectually and privilege homelessness as impulse to art, let us remember that our recently dismembered world is full of the nonwriting homeless. As we analyze the discourse of displacement, refugees from political and racial oppression all over the world and at our very doorsteps are negotiating their own status as legal and illegal aliens (Turks, Palestinians, Kurds, Bosnians, Vietnamese, Haitians—the geography changes but the condition of exile appears to be a permanent political fact).

Border disputes between feminist critics and the establishment have largely been settled or become irrelevant. Feminist criticism itself is no longer beleaguered on the boundaries of academia or wandering in the wilderness, making mountains out of its marginality. Those mountains made very good platforms for preaching a radical message to inflexible institutions. But the academy has bent a bit, and in some quarters it is learning the language of an easily domesticated feminist criticism, and feminists of various persuasions have gained power within the academy.

Nonetheless we may continue to question notions of female diaspora, to sketch new maps of gender in exile, as new historical situations arise. We must continue to examine our own privileges, prejudices, and positions by raising issues of exclusionary critical practices bearing on canonicity, language, and genre. One issue that will continue to call for analysis is the intersection of exile and art with notions of race, class, individual genius, and collective culture. Another is the relation of women's art to the social text of domestic labor. Estrangement is not universally experienced, nor is it universally acknowledged. A negative ranking process obtains already as a subtext within the study of exile. It is in our interest to watch these mapping processes at work, to note who is calling whom "high" or "low," and to engage a debate on the meaning of these claims. Contested boundaries are part of the postmodern condition.

A 1948 story by Sylvia Townsend Warner called "The Mother Tongue" elicits these issues of exile, translation, and the voicing of self in or through the other. Warner explores the roots of cultural identity in geography, gender, and domestic labor in this story. She connects the problem of listening and speaking to power, also anticipating contemporary Chomskyan debates about the relation of language to thinking. As the hegemonic listener from the dominant culture, Miss Oliphant from the Acclimatisation and Training Centre for Displaced Persons decides that "her" refugees should retain some of their native Polish, for "the language in which one says one's prayers is one's native tongue." The two "clever" girls are sent to work in an orphanage in the town, and Magda becomes a servant on a farm. Miss Oliphant wants everything to be "nice," for them to meet on Sundays and speak Polish: "the Poles are natural-born linguists—think of Joseph Conrad."[26]

As a domestic laborer, Magda has no need for speech and soon loses both her English and her native Polish: "As a fish slides through the net and drops back into the water, Magda escaped from the mesh of words, vanished from conversations." She lives "unsignalized." "Behind not speaking lies the unspoken."

> But a language is a thing which can only be possessed by those who possess it in common. Language is a dozen voices clinging to the rope of a litany. Language is a hundred voices clattering against each other in the market place. Language is the lamentation of thousands crying out in terror and anguish. Language is the uproar of millions, a rustle of questions sprouting thick as corn all over Europe, saying *What now? When? Whither?* And presently language is a hundred voices clinging to the rope of a new speech, saying, *I-am-glad-to-see-you. Please-have-you-the-needle? Thank-you-very-much.* (136)

Magda finds speech again at the funeral of a farm laborer. As his coffin is lowered into the ground she begins to lament her own "innumerable dead . . . on the brink of a stranger's grave." She fills her mouth with earth— "Her outcry was of no language" (139)—and she stands at the graveside listening for a reply.

NOTES

My thanks to the Guggenheim Foundation for a fellowship that gave me the time to research and write this essay and to Clare Hall, Cambridge University, where a visiting fellowship gave me the space. Margaret Higonnet and Katharine Rodier edited and excerpted this essay from a longer version, and I thank them for the effort and for spirited discussions of the politics of these issues in several countries and across several frontiers of difficulties. I am indebted as ever to Angela Ingram's historical eye, to Claire Tylee for helpful suggestions, and to responses from audiences at the University of Bergen and Oslo University in Norway and Uppsala University, Sweden, in May 1994.

1. Christopher Hope, *The Hottentot Room* (New York: Farrar, Straus & Giroux, 1986) 37.

2. Louise Bogan, "Last Hill in a Vista," *The Faber Book of Twentieth Century Women's Poetry*, ed. Fleur Adcock (London: Faber & Faber, 1986).

3. This is also a territorial issue for the politics of feminist criticism. For some recent examples, see Jane Gallop's discussion of her dreams about a black feminist critic with Marianne Hirsch and Nancy K. Miller in "Criticizing Feminist Criticism" in Hirsch and Evelyn Fox Keller, *Conflicts in Feminism* (New York: Routledge, 1988) 349–369, and Elizabeth Abel's "Black Writing, White Reading: Race and the Politics of Feminist Interpretation," in *Critical Inquiry* 19 (1993): 470–498. Abel cites Gallop's insensitive remarks without comment as the initiation of a new critical discourse on the relation of white feminists to Afro-American literature and criticism, assuming that all current relations between U.S. black and white women intellectuals were determined by a particular feminism, an analysis that excludes recognition of any previous crossracial political bonding by women on the issues of the struggle for racial justice in the civil rights or the peace movement, or both. There is certainly a generation of white and black U.S. women, mostly but not exclusively of the Old and New Left(s), who came to feminism after or through civil rights or the antiwar movement, whose relations were not determined by this particular historical "feminism," though Abel like Gallop defines feminism as a discourse and not a political movement for social change. It could be argued that the feminist rhetoric of sisterhood springs directly from the black discourses in the struggle for racial justice. The work of Audre Lorde, Blanche Weisen Cook, Adrienne Rich, Tillie Olsen, Alice Walker, and Lillian Robinson comes to mind as examples. This is not to criticize those who come to study race through feminism, but to point out that histories of feminism that ignore such different political trajectories are often limited by the autobiographical projections of their authors (i.e., Toril Moi's *Sexual/Textual Politics* or Gallop's *Around 1981*). Feminist critic Nina Auerbach is a veteran of these struggles, for example, as are Susan Friedman, Nellie McKay, and Rachel DuPlessis, to name a few, and it would not be accurate to assume that racial issues entered their consciousness or their work after or as determined by this particular feminism.

4. Virginia Woolf, *A Room of One's Own* (1929; New York: Harcourt Brace, 1957) 52.

5. Virginia Woolf, *Three Guineas* (New York: Harcourt Brace, 1939).

6. See my *Virginia Woolf and the Languages of Patriarchy* (Bloomington: Indiana UP, 1987) for a discussion of Woolf's colonial heritage from her real aunts and uncles. Also "Britannia Rules *The Waves*," *Decolonizing Tradition: The Cultural Politics of Modern Literary Canons*, ed. Karen Lawrence (Urbana: U of Illinois P, 1991) 136–162.

7. Harriet A. Jacobs, *Incidents in the Life of a Slave Girl, Written by Herself*, ed. Jean Fagan Yellin (Cambridge: Harvard UP, 1987).

8. This phrase and the argument it makes are derived from Lisa Marcus, "A White Woman Is Being Beaten: The Rac(e)ing of Whiteness in Pauline Hopkins' *Contending Forces*," given at the American Literature Association Symposium of Women Writers, 3 October 1993, San Antonio.

9. See Peter Freyer, *Staying Power: The History of Black People in Britain* (London: Pluto, 1984), and Paul B. Rich, *Race and Empire in British Politics* (Cambridge: Cambridge UP, 1986, 1990), for attitudes toward both race and the presence of blacks in England. The

word *black* has a different meaning in Britain from its usage in the United States. As a political term it signifies British racist oppression. See also Beverley Bryan, Stella Dazie, and Suzanne Scafe, *The Heart of the Race: Black Women's Lives in Britain,* 2nd ed. (London: Virago, 1989). Though I find his essay problematic in its sensationalism, Sander L. Gilman's "Black Bodies, White Bodies: Toward an Iconography of Female Sexuality in Late Nineteenth-Century Art, Medicine, and Literature," in *Race, Writing and Difference,* ed. H. L. Gates, Jr. (Chicago: U of Chicago P, 1987), may be useful in understanding the historical context for Virginia Woolf's views on race, shaped as they must have been by her family's history in the colonies and her deep interest in the discourses of discovery and anthropology.

10. However legally determined the status of blacks as *English,* the election of Derek Beackon, British National Party "Rights for Whites" candidate in London's East End calling for deportation of all nonwhites, signals a problem (*International Herald Tribune,* 18–19 September 1993, 1).

11. See the Shelton Fernando correspondence in the Leonard Woolf Papers, University of Sussex Library. My thanks to librarian Elizabeth Inglis for her kind help with the archive.

12. Leonard Woolf, *Empire and Commerce in Africa: A Study in Economic Imperialism* (London: Labour Research Department and Allen & Unwin, 1917) 9. Wayne Chapman's paper at the 1992 Virginia Woolf Conference in New Haven indicated that Virginia Woolf's participation in the research and writing of this book was extensive.

13. J. H. Willis, Jr., *Leonard and Virginia Woolf as Publishers: The Hogarth Press, 1917–1941* (Charlottesville: UP of Virginia, 1992).

14. Virginia Woolf, *Letters,* ed. Nigel Nicolson and Joanne Trautmann, vol. 2 (London: Hogarth, 1977) 429.

15. Roger Fry, *Vision and Design* (London: Chatto & Windus, 1920). This aestheticism was also embraced by other primitivist modernists like Matisse and Picasso.

16. Helen Calloway, "Purity and Exotica in Legitimating the Empire: Cultural Constructions of Gender, Sexuality, and Race," *The Colonial State and the Pursuit of Legitimacy: Essays in Honor of A.H.M. Kirk-Greene,* ed. Terence Ranger and Olufemi Vaugh (Oxford: Oxford UP, 1993).

17. For a discussion of Woolf's interrogation of the idea of whiteness and her representation of the working of imperialism on a home culture, see Marcus, "Britannia Rules *The Waves*" 136–162.

18. John MacKenzie, *Propaganda and Empire: The Manipulation of British Public Opinion, 1880–1960* (Manchester: Manchester UP, 1984). See also *Anthropology and Photography, 1860–1920* (New Haven: Yale UP, 1993).

19. Ian Jeffrey, *Photography: A Concise History* (London, 1981) 63–64.

20. According to the annotation of Woolf's entry for 3 July 1924, the Woolfs went to the Empire Exhibition on 29 May. *Diary,* vol. 2 (London: Hogarth, 1977) note 2.

21. See my "Liberty, Sorority, Misogyny," *Virginia Woolf and the Languages of Patriarchy* (Bloomington: Indiana UP, 1987) 75–95.

22. Gary Saul Morson, ed., *Bakhtin: Essays and Dialogues on His Work* (Chicago: U of Chicago P, 1986) 180–181.

23. Luce Irigaray, *This Sex Which Is Not One,* trans. Catherine Porter (Ithaca: Cornell UP, 1985) 76.

24. Here, a portion of this essay is reprinted from my "Alibis and Legends: The Ethics of Elsewhereness, Gender and Estrangement," in *Women's Writing in Exile,* ed. Mary Lynn

Broe and Angela Ingram (Chapel Hill: U of North Carolina P, 1989) 270–275. Copyright 1989 by the University of North Carolina Press. Reprinted by permission of the publisher.

25. Natalia Ginsburg, *The Little Virtues* (New York: Seaver, 1986).

26. Sylvia Townsend Warner, "The Mother Tongue," *One Thing Leading to Another* (London: Women's, 1984) 135.

MARGARET R. HIGONNET

Mapping the Text:
Critical Metaphors

*One should perhaps clean up the metaphorical situation moment
by moment.*—Gayatri Chakravorty Spivak

Since Gaston Bachelard's almost mystical revery on the *Poétique de l'espace*
(1957), with his suggestive meditations on the "feminine" spaces of the
round tower, the closet, and the nest, the literary representation of space
has received widespread critical attention.[1] Studies have proliferated on
such topics as travelogues, utopian fiction, the city in modernism, and the
imaginative mapping of empire or nation. At the same time, growing
attention has been paid to connections between spatial motifs and gender
in distinctions such as those between private and public spaces, the "epistemology of the closet," and the line between battlefront and home front.
Settings have been linked to gender-marked genres such as the homoerotic
pastoral elegy, male and female versions of autobiography of the bildungsroman, and nineteenth-century novels of domestic realism.[2] As Daphne
Spain writes, "throughout history and across cultures, architectural and
geographic spatial arrangements have reinforced status differences between
women and men."[3] In the social domain, spatial distinctions weigh on
access to knowledge; they both mark status (of sex, class, and race) and help
reproduce it. In the domain of literature, the physical movement of narrative action and the metaphoric functioning of local description inscribe
and italicize gendered relationships of power. As a consequence, the representation of space in texts reinforces the gendered inflection of genres.

Less attention has been paid to the way critics themselves use spatial
metaphors to represent literary texts. The act of writing about writing

seems to invite critical (dis)placement. As Ruth Salvaggio reminds us, many theorists "explicitly define theoretical boundaries in terms of the concept of space."[4] Spatial metaphors accordingly are legion in literary criticism. These guiding metaphors recur at four different *horizons* (a term I borrow from phenomenology): the text, the corpus of an author, the amorphous extended field of literature, and the terrain and site of the critic. The image of the human body has been transferred to each of these conceptual horizons in order to evoke not only vitality but material amplitude, differentiated internal functions, and coherence—or the longing for limits and the fear of transgression. I could cite myriad examples, but one will do: Robert J. Clements thought that comparative literature could be tidily defined in terms of "juxtapositions of bodies of literature."[5]

Sexual metaphors have also energized literary theories since antiquity: Cicero and Quintilian contrasted a "taut," virile (*enervatus*) style to a "soft" (*mollis*) one. Rhetorical proprieties are frequently linked to virility or effeminacy: metaphor itself, along with other rhetorical figures, has often acquired a gender. The trope of *copia,* for example, served by metaphoric amplification and analogy, became associated with the garrulity of a "fat lady."[6] Even more tellingly, the ostensible impropriety of metaphoric displacements may be described homophobically as "painted rhetoric" or deceptive "dress" and linked misogynistically to wayward women.

By no means all attributions of femininity are negative in this kind of critical practice. In her analysis of French postmodernism and its postromantic oedipal struggle against phallogocentrism, Alice Jardine finds a positive "feminizing" of theory and of the centrifugal figure, the *mise en abîme.* As she points out, Derrida sexualizes his theory of deconstruction, drawing on such images as that of the "hymenal" gap or abyssal "invagination," and finding in woman herself a figure for the unrepresentability of truth and of the text.[7] Often, we find an oscillation between positive and negative connotations of the same gendered images. Gaston Bachelard, as I have argued elsewhere, encodes the transformative power of images as feminine, a power awakened by the male critic's poetic revery: "to reopen in words themselves their feminine depths." Yet metaphors also decompose and disimagine; like the image of woman, metaphors are caught between creativity and death.[8] As Patricia Parker and Alice Jardine suggest, the two figurative modes of thought, spatial and sexual, may become subtly blended. Often, contestatory theories of writers like Derrida or Lacan project "newly contoured fictional spaces, hypothetical and unmeasurable, space freely coded as feminine" (Jardine 69). Avant-garde and postmodern thinkers, in short, have often revalued critical metaphors of feminine space.

In the past history of such fusions, however, the feminine pole of a metaphor often held a relatively lower value. Thus Immanuel Kant and Edmund Burke distinguished esthetic modes according to size, surface, and sex, in definitions that operate by reciprocity: "All the other merits of a woman should unite solely to enhance the character of the beautiful, which is the proper reference point; and on the other hand, among the masculine qualities the sublime clearly stands out as the criterion of his kind," Kant wrote. And in Burke's view, "Sublime objects are vast in their dimension, beautiful ones comparatively small; beauty should be smooth and polished; the great, rugged and negligent." Burke goes on to note that "beauty, which is highest in the female sex, almost always carries with it an idea of weakness and imperfection. . . . Beauty in distress is much the most affecting beauty."[9] Even so brief a survey as that offered in this essay may suggest that the intersection of these two types of figures is never innocent of consequences. Metaphoric stress often implies someone's distress.

My first goal is a preliminary identification of the most conspicuous spatial metaphors that have been used to lay out a hierarchy of literary works in familiar critical discourses: metaphors of internality, centrality, and height. Although this vocabulary is not itself usually sexualized, its effects, as we shall see, may be implicitly sexist, as well as racist and classist. We find a "tenor" driving the metaphoric vehicle, not a soprano.

This frame is necessary for understanding the counterstrategies of recent feminist critics who, in their various efforts to revise our approaches to individual texts, genre classifications, or literary history, have likewise had recourse to gendered and transvalued images of literary space. Thus feminists have recirculated the image of margins, initiating a sustained discussion of its positive and negative implications. The other wide-ranging complex of images that I discuss here is that of narrative splits, subversive subsurface layers, and breaks, which can all be seen as forms of resistance to totalizing images of narrative wholeness and closure.

Although my main focus will be a range of feminist critical uses of metaphor, I will not, like Ruth Salvaggio, claim that "the spatial configurations fundamental to the production of theory [by men] are not at all the kinds of spaces occupied and described by women." In an important essay

Salvaggio maintains: "while theories produced by men take on certain gendered spatial contours, theories written by women . . . bring women's actual experience of space to discourse. Instead of shaping masculine space into something feminine, these women bring feminine space to life by writing from, through, and about the spaces women themselves have occupied" (261–262). Salvaggio thus boldly underscores the often painful actualities of human geography that may inflect feminist theories. But it would be dangerous to import a doctrine of separate spheres into an analysis of theory; stark contrasts between the "space" of writing inhabited by male and female theorists run the risk of reifying men and women, as well as "male theorist" and "feminist." That risk, I think, can be reduced by a recognition of the historical slippages, reversals, and evaluative inversions in metaphoric usage. In contrast to my epigraph from Gayatri Chakravorty Spivak, my goal here is not to "clean up" and purge our critical language of metaphors: these are not only inescapable traps but also powerful tools that enable us to release the energies of texts and mobilize institutional change. Instead, by exposing the latent organizational and evaluative functions of our critical vocabulary, I hope to defamiliarize it and to provoke greater awareness of its political implications.

The most obvious reason why spatial metaphors call for close examination is that some of our most familiar critical figures have distinguished between *legitimate* "intrinsic" and *illegitimate* "extrinsic" criticism, "central" and "marginal" genres, "core" and "remote" languages, or "high" and "low" forms of art. Such figures reinforce, however inadvertently, the status quo. They confirm the canonicity of texts by authors who in the majority have been white, European or North American, male, and on top. They divert critical attention from the literatures of countries such as the Netherlands, continents such as Africa, and narrative vehicles such as the diary or oral account. These spatial metaphors have a political, classist, and racial aura and impact.

Thus one of the most detailed and ecumenical overviews of literary theory ever written, *Theory of Literature,* by René Wellek and Austin Warren, has become identified in most readers' minds with a narrow New Critical (Kantian) aestheticism because of its division into two parts, one devoted to "intrinsic" criticism, the other to "extrinsic" features of the text. According to this sophisticated survey, the main stress of "intrinsic" criticism falls on formal conventions concerning such matters as style, metrics, rhetorical figures, genre, or narrative perspective. In today's terminology, we might say that such conventions are elaborated through the interplay of a text and its intertexts; they help us see the place of a text in strictly literary history. But knowledge of specific literary conventions might also be described as a territory defined and possessed by those trained in the classics. Knowledge as property is institutionally mediated, hence our commonsense use of terms such as *school* and *disciple* to describe literary relations among authors.

"Extrinsic" criticism, by contrast, attends primarily to what Wellek and Warren considered nonliterary factors: the social condition of the author, for example, or thematic elements (politics, psychology) studied with the help of other disciplines such as political science or anthropology. While they admit a certain exegetical value in such contextual study, they condemn any tendency to "causal explanation." In a radical passage on what they call "perspectivism," Wellek and Warren acknowledged the transformation of texts through their reception over time and their variable reception by different cultures.[10] Yet the readerly construction of value as well as meaning failed to win full recognition either in this volume or among most New Critics.

The line of exclusion between intrinsic and extrinsic analysis is one that comparatists and other critics have steadily worked to efface. In the intervening decades, critical movements such as discourse analysis, semiotics, cultural critique, and New Historicism have each in different ways eroded New Critical distinctions between literary and other discourses. Feminists have been among those critics drawn most dramatically to reject the line between intrinsic and extrinsic criticism. In light of feminist work on such genres as autobiography, one may query whether "a work of art forms a unity on a quite different plane, with a quite different relation to reality, than a book of memoirs, a diary, or a letter" (66). Until we reject the notion of a "different plane," women's texts will not be read on an even playing field.

The prescriptive implications of this binary classification scheme seemed clear to many readers of Wellek and Warren. Their stress on formalist criteria of analysis would preclude the study of works by women writers as such, since that would mean committing a biological, or sociological, or even sociointentional "fallacy of origins" (61). Such criticism would lie not "inside" but beyond the critical pale. To be sure, if "literary" traits can be discovered that distinguish the works of numerous women writers from other works, one may argue that there are "intrinsic" grounds for acknowledging a separate tradition; yet the very premise of such separatist research would be logically flawed, according to New Critical theory— as well as poststructural theory, which has declared the death of the author.

The problem is certainly not moot. Feminists of different allegiances still vehemently debate whether it makes sense to group together as a set all texts composed by women from around the world (or by women writers of color or by Chicana lesbians, as a colony within a colony). In today's version of this profound philosophic debate, the interpretation of texts in terms of cultural conditions that tacitly or overtly gender their authors face a challenge whenever they neglect historic and cultural variations or surrender to the determinism and ghettoization of identity politics. Whatever the conclusion of this debate, undoubtedly the classificatory norm for criticism that Wellek and Warren intended to be gender neutral had an immediate practical effect of resisting a women's studies approach to texts written by men or by women.

To a more striking degree, the ladder running from "high" to "low" art, now increasingly kicked aside, overlapped with overt political and economic privilege. "High" art has often coincided with monumental art, works commissioned by the monarch or state or works ratified by public institutions such as a Salon or prize committee. "Low" art has included art for the lower classes, penny dreadfuls, children's literature, ethnic literature, especially that written in minority sociolects, literature about the domestic world, and stories in "women's magazines."[11] Many of these distinctions draw an ostensibly formal line between "high" and "low" genres. Yet embedded in such genre classification, as Alastair Fowler has pointed out, is a covert class distinction between an elite, narrow audience and broad, mass readership, between those in the first tier of the literary theater and those in the pit.

While the class accent of this contrast speaks loudly, its gender accent is more muffled. Nina Baym notes that women writers of fiction in the nineteenth century often justified their labors (in defiance of aesthetic censorship) as an economic necessity. From Harriet Wilson to Louisa May Alcott, they let us know that they wrote not to compete overtly for the laurels reserved for the men who wrote in elect forms, but to support their families (whether they were married, widowed, or single). They therefore strove to reach a sufficiently broad market. Indirectly, then, the class line between "high" and "low" literature came to overlap with a gender line.

The definitions at stake in this stratification are often circular: esthetic inferiority may be attributed to intertextuality whose points of reference are oral, commercial, domestic, or "low," as opposed to the ostensibly more resonant references to established "high" art, regardless of structural similarities in the ways in which such references function. At an art history conference not long ago, a renowned Harvard Marxist rejected Linda Nochlin's suggestion that a superior work by a French impressionist woman should have greater critical value than an inferior Monet. When he explained that a Cassatt would have "less resonance and depth," he might as well have argued (as Anthony Burgess did about Jane Austen) that it would have less "thrust." Spivak tellingly asks, "What, then, must a woman do with the reactionary sexual ideology of high art? It is not enough to substitute 'low' for 'high,' and perpetrate an ideology of complacent rejectionism."[12] This dispute over height measurements has been adequately adjudicated in the literary courts by advocates of institutional change such as Spivak and Gerald Graff, and we need not linger over it.

More preoccupying for feminists has been the broad reliance of literary histories on a topographic vocabulary of centers and margins to naturalize their criteria for inclusion and exclusion. "Centrality" marks a text's, genre's, or author's position in the literary tradition that has been ratified by the test of time so dear to neoclassical critics such as Samuel Johnson. It is now widely recognized, however, that the image of "centrality," like that of high art, veils institutional selections made over many centuries according to criteria that have specific historic biases: the choices of publishing houses, the curriculum in (boys') schools, the fraternal or totemic marking of texts with allusions to predecessor texts already accepted as central.[13]

A discourse of centers and margins, of course, can be used to discredit or trivialize literatures on stylistic, generic, or historic grounds. Thus a German literary history centered on Goethe discounts the experimental, fragmented novels of the autodidact Jean Paul Richter; a Western literary tradition centered on the Bible may discount the Sumerian epic *Inanna*. Likewise, the notion of the discipline's "natural fief" (a term used by Pichois and Rousseau to designate Western and European literature) has led comparative literature departments to neglect African and most Asian literatures.[14] But location on the margin has been of particular concern to feminist critics, because women, as we have seen, historically have gravitated often to "low," private genres such as autobiography and letters.

From a "central" perspective defined by the a priori selection of such magisterial writers as Goethe or Tolstoy, women who write in other genres and styles may seem "marginal." A gendered canon, of course, problematizes the handbooks and anthologies of comparative literature, where one may count oneself lucky to find a few snippets of Akhmatova or Colette. Marginality is produced by particular critical codes that in turn reproduce themselves institutionally through anthologies and examinations for degrees.[15]

As Gerald Graff has argued, a variant on what we might call centralized instruction is that of "field-coverage," which subliminally implies that our field of study can be bounded by a disciplinary fence against materials or approaches that lie beyond the legitimate fold. In practice the field-coverage model often avoided ideological clashes by superficially permitting the peripheral addition of such "disruptive novelties as contemporary literature, black studies, feminism," or Marxism. Yet the field-coverage model also relied on a methodological "grid of literary periods, genres, and themes" whose very disconnection inhibited self-interrogation. "The cultural text"—including such cultural texts as Blackness or Woman—"tends to fall into the cracks separating periods, genres, and fields."[16] The same problem obtains for older studies of the interrelations of literature with other disciplines: the interdisciplinary goal is undercut by the binary pairing of forms of study perceived as separate.[17] Grids, field boundaries, and focusing terms of centrality are ultimately mechanisms of disciplinary self-definition through exclusion.

By a sleight of hand (or eye), the thematics of centrality conceals one of the most important concepts of literary space: the inquiry into the site of the critic responsible for selecting and identifying the object of study. Within what frame is a text perceived as being central? As any amateur photographer knows, objects of representation do not float automatically into central focus, like roast pigeons into our critical mouths. Questions triggered by the theories of Louis Althusser and Michel Foucault have led feminist critics like Gayatri Spivak to argue that the notion of the individual subject is an illusion that conceals the multiple "subject positions" we occupy. Yet the question of the site of the critic is precisely one that New Criticism effectively silenced by cultivating the ideal of objective, transcendent reading—an illusory ideal that was made more alluring by the stylistic brilliance and structural insights of many New Critical close readings.

One of the most telling strategies to decenter the canon and destabilize dominant norms has been the device of consciously multiplying the approaches of the critic. Jane Marcus, for example, has proposed a critical "triologue" or quotational polyphony that would correspond homeologically to the plurivocality of texts themselves.[18] Likewise, Spivak, as a Marxist-feminist-deconstructive critic, hyphenates herself and attempts to occupy different sites in order to "interrupt" the narrative logic produced from a single angle of critical vision. The teacher "re-constellates" the text by "circulating" among similar and different critical "operations." Such "interruptions" enable further questions about the relative status of the critical subject and the subject of study. In her famous formula, "there has to be a simultaneous other focus: not merely who am I? but who is the other woman? How am I naming her? How does she name me?" (150).

Here we may find a model that eludes definitional constraints. While Spivak at times casts herself as a woman of color, and thus on the margin—in spite of avowed privileges of caste, academic status, or mobility—she also casts doubt on the project of recuperating the margin: "By pointing attention to a feminist marginality, I have been attempting, not to win the center for ourselves, but to point at the irreducibility of the margin in all explanations. . . . The deconstructivist can use herself (assuming one is at one's own disposal) as a shuttle between the center (inside) and the margin (outside)." This restless movement of the cartographer herself strives to disorient the imperialist centering of the literary map on canonical texts, to resist the "continued subalternization of so-called 'third-world' literatures" (107, 241).

The obvious politics of center and margin does not, however, exhaust the complexity of this metaphoric cluster as it has been engaged by feminists. Marginality, in turn, can be exploited as a lever that empowers the critic. To be on the margin implies critical distance and objectivity. The shifting evaluative connotations of the margin in a broad range of feminist criticism deserve our closer analysis.

A great number of critical texts not only assume a separation between masculine and feminine literary territory but imply that the woman writer enters Herland as if she were forced into exile. Virginia Woolf's texts are a rich mine for such metaphors of exclusion. In *A Room of One's Own,* she depicts the segregated spaces of learning at Oxbridge and gives anecdotal shape to the exclusion of women from libraries as well as lawns. Partly in response, Woolf defended women's need for a separate productive sphere ("a room of one's own") and called for a society of outsiders.

Many critics of the 1960s and 1970s implicitly accepted this (defensive) concept of a separate literary Herland, making the plausible assumption that literary differences mirror a divided, uneven social terrain. Elaine Showalter, for example, has adapted the anthropological notion of a "muted" or "wild zone" of women's culture.[19] This hypothetical feminine linguistic zone unacknowledged by male-dominated institutions, she argues, in turn justifies an exclusively feminist critical terrain, "gynocriticism." The accomplishments of such critical "herstory" can hardly be denied: aided by anthologies such as the *Norton Anthology of Literature by Women,* the *Longman Anthology of World Literature by Women,* and the two-volume *Women Writing in India, 600 B.C. to the Present,* gynocritics have given a "voice" back to writers like Alice Dunbar-Nelson, Rebecca Harding Davis, Gertrudis de Avellaneda, Hedwig Dohm, and Svarnakumari Devi, who shared a common oblivion, if not the same literary or social sphere.

Gynocriticism, however, has been contested as the creation, in Lillian Robinson's phrase, of a "women's literature ghetto" that would simply reify the alternative canon of feminists without altering the critical institutions that produce such ghettos. In the eighties, further political contestation has in fact arisen over the (non)representation of minority voices within anthologies that themselves claim to speak from the margins. The recent sharper focus on subaltern and minority women has cast light on connections between the experience of social marginalization, often quite concrete geographically (in ghettos cordoned off by highways or "highrise" projects, in experiences of deportation or emigration), and the literary exploration of borderlines and boundary-traversing poetic strategies.

These recent critical texts re-center (if that is the right word) the "borderlands." In the process a creative terminology has arisen that strives to define the tools for "remapping" the world of literature, setting the texts produced by certain ethnic groups or in "Third World" portions of the globe at the center of the analysis, both for their own sake and for the insights they may generate into the literary theory and critical methodologies derived from work on the "First World."

Gloria Anzaldúa's meditations on what it means to be a Chicana lesbian poet constitute one of the most influential and lyrical of these recent studies. Geographically, of course, the culture of the Chicana or Chicano literally straddles national boundaries and moves back and forth across unmarked state boundaries within the outline of a nation that usurped the lands and languages of mixed-bloods, mestizo, Hispanic Indians. Anzaldúa accordingly starts from the negative connotation of the border: "A borderland is a vague and undetermined place created by the emotional residue of an unnatural boundary. It is in a constant state of transition. The prohibited and forbidden are its inhabitants. *Los atravesados* live here: the squint-eyed, the perverse, the queer, the troublesome, the mongrel, the mulatto, the half-breed, the half dead; in short, those who cross over, pass over, or go through the confines of the 'normal.' "[20]

Although the borderland originates as a negative site of exclusion, it can also become a site of self-performance where the intersection of allegiances or exclusions enables a creative distance from oppressive ideologies. The border territory is linguistic as well as geographic, racial, economic, and political: the Chicana switches codes, inviting the reader to abandon purist notions that "macaronic" verbal products are vulgar and unesthetic. As a lesbian Chicana, furthermore, Anzaldúa writes from another kind of exile. Like a turtle, she must carry home with her. But as a voluntary exile, she has chosen her sexual condition if not her racial and political heritage: "*I made the choice to be queer.*" Being "both male and female," she gains "an entry into both worlds" (19). She can also *make* a literary space: "I will have to stand and claim my space, making a new culture—*una cultura mestiza*—with my own lumber, my own bricks and mortar and my own feminist architecture" (22). Anzaldúa's literary *métissage,* in which she braids together not only language codes but genres, mixing autobiography, history, poetry, and poetics, makes an asset out of its site on the borderlands/frontera.

Warning voices can also be heard. Gayatri Spivak in particular has spoken out about the discomfort of being a token representative of marginality: "I find the demand on me to be marginal always amusing. And as I have said, I'm tired of dining out on being an exile."[21] Jane Marcus, too, exposes the hazards of exile as metaphor. Marcus in this volume pinpoints the use of "otherness" as "alibi" in a feminist criticism that often neglects its own "others." One of the risks run by those who attempt to critique repressive systems of knowledge is the implied premise that the position of the critic is protected from such critique: a location "elsewhere as innocence. . . . Border disputes between feminist critics and the establishment have largely been settled or become irrelevant. Feminist criticism itself is no longer beleaguered on the boundaries of academia or wandering in the wilderness, making mountains out of its marginality." Yet feminists still seek critical methods and strategies to avoid the authoritarian gestures of labeling and displacement that they risk when invoking marginality. By calling our attention to the "legends" or codes through which we locate ourselves and others, as Marcus puts it, she unsettles the very distinction between center and margin that has been so central to feminist theory.

Perhaps because changes in time are commonly represented through movement in space (the most obvious example being the movement of hands on a clock face), the temporal aspect of narrative in particular has provoked a critical vocabulary of space. In a somewhat flattened variant on the organic metaphor, Joseph Frank proposed in 1945 the concept of "spatial form" to describe "non-linear" narratives. Such spatialized narratives "fragment" the narrative "line" or "juxtapose" multiple narrative lines; their ultimate coherence or "closure" must be achieved by the reader's imaginative mapping of an interconnected whole.[22] Frank's landmark essay, which was still being debated in *Critical Inquiry* in the late 1970s, may have fostered the reception of later feminist studies of "writing beyond the ending." Yet there is a significant difference: feminist critics, especially those influenced by poststructuralism, have sought to find critical devices and metaphors that will enable them to subvert (if not entirely evade) the concept of closure itself.

A number of the most suggestive feminist applications of these spatialized theories of literary form connect narrative form to social distribution of space and status. Most start from the premise that female authorship and poetic authority do not coincide, as a result of social prohibitions such as the limits on women's education, their confinement to "proper" places at "proper" times of day, and the taboos on their use of certain language (whether to describe men's bodies or sacred rituals). Thus the texts the critics wish to describe present the poetic results of a contradictory situation of production.

One way that contradiction inscribes itself is in forms of literary irony. A widely used term for such irony is Sandra Gilbert's and Susan Gubar's *palimpsest,* a paleographic image that distinguishes a masculine surface text, derived from received norms and directed at conventional reception, from a feminine, subversive subtext (73). The metaphor of the ironic, cross-written palimpsest, derived from the page of medieval writing itself, fosters analysis of the way a marginalized writer may subversively participate in literary tradition. Each literary tradition, of course, will encode different formal features as masculine or feminine, conventional or unconventional, and therefore will provoke different modes of subversion.

In similar fashion, Sigrid Weigel's "schielender Blick" (*schielend* may be translated as double, wall-eyed, or askance) points to a female writer's split narrative persona. Women whose "femininity" is threatened by entry into a "masculine" profession, she holds, fall into divided narrative attitudes. She thus connects the social situation of the woman writer to the technical question of women's access to the narrative "threshold," which some women writers resolve by creating a "double" or "slant" narrative pattern. The split gaze, she suggests, can be further linked to the traditional association of women with the doubling of mirrors and masks. The dramatic increase in the number of women who pick up a pen at the end of the eighteenth century she attributes, in turn, to a shift in theoretical norms that made such self-reflexivity acceptable and that dissolved the "closed" text into fragments.[23] Thus the revolt against neoclassicism made it possible for violations of formal unity, long attributed to women writers of letters and fiction on the grounds that they were less erudite or skilled than men, to be reconceived as deliberate deviations.

From Friedrich Schlegel to Virginia Woolf to our own time, indeed, critics have seen fragmentation as the technical means of subversion most typical of women's writings. In a famous chapter of *A Room of One's Own,* which remains one of our boldest essays on aesthetics and sexual politics, Woolf identified contemporary women's writing with "breaks" in the sentence, in the sequence, and in the tradition (whether defined by Samuel Johnson or by Jane Austen). Her fictive author, Mary Carmichael, "interrupts" the "smooth gliding" of sentences, tersely heaping up her materials and violating social convention governing lesbian representation. "First she broke the sentence; now she has broken the sequence."[24] Woolf's suggestive hypothesis has been applied in more detail to twentieth-century women's writing by Rachel Blau DuPlessis, who maps alternate quest structures and different ways of framing literary space ("liminal endings"). She argues that gender ideology lies coiled within narrative structure; the "site" of literary form grounds social practices.[25]

Woolf's French heir, Claudine Herrmann, links social oppression in the past to the formal practice of a "break" with previous conceptions of stylistic or structural unity. In *Les Voleuses de langue* Hermann starts from the premise that "Woman" is "colonised" culturally, placed both within and without, split in relationship to social law, and alienated not only from her context but from herself. Although a woman may recognize the distance or "margin" between the lived and the expressed, she has no choice but to learn a colonized knowledge and a falsified tongue. Herrmann claims that current relationships of power between men and women express themselves spatially, a thesis she supports by exemplary comparative analyses. In women's travel literature, for example, she finds multiplied perspectives, by contrast to monologic travelogues by men. To recover a lost capacity for innovative discontinuity (usurped by "Man"), woman should "bring a different cutting-pattern (*découpage*) to time and space, refuse their continuity, fragment them."[26] The woman artist turns each fragment into an archipelago that points to the unknown.

Just as Hermann starts from an implicitly negative view of writing by women as "colonized," Xavière Gauthier holds that women have internalized conventional aspects of institutional literature. Likewise she suggests that for women to disrupt their own history, they must follow the example of Monique Wittig in *Les Guérillères*. They must invent a literature made of "blank pages, gaps, borders, spaces and silence, [and] holes in discourse."[27]

The idea of a break dominates much theorizing of women's writing today, even among writers who do not qualify themselves explicitly as feminists. Thus to define women's writing, a number of critics such as Teresa de Lauretis and Hélène Cixous have recourse to images of the break, cut, and gap. These are not, however, simply abstract images of rupture; many of them are embedded in playful representations of the female body as fissured, split, or castrated. A focus on the female body and liquidity, according to Ruth Salvaggio, has enabled recent theory by women to transform the structures of discourse (273). In order to understand the historic role that body images—along with gaps or breaks—have played in contemporary feminist theory (as written by both men and women), it is helpful to recall one of the most influential metaphors in twentieth-century literary criticism, a metaphor that we could even say gave birth to modern critical practice in the hands of Coleridge and the Schlegel brothers: that of "organic" literary form.

The concept of a text as resembling a physical organ entailed the productive premise that a text is a bounded entity, an "organic unity," and at the same time *in process*. The text is understood to differentiate itself from whatever may surround it, therefore to be "closed," but also dynamically to "fuse" heterogeneous internal elements in ways that may shift or at the very least be continuously reinterpreted. Organic unity, of course, is a metaphoric projection onto a text of certain critical intentions and performances, such as the search for unity or the rejection of evaluation by excerpt. Its defining opposite term is *mechanical form*—initially associated by romantic writers with their neoclassical predecessors, both writers and critics, in an (oedipal) rebellion against conservative rigidity of form and esthetic value.

Yet the gender associations of any such metaphor are tellingly arbitrary. The contrast between mechanical and organic soon became associated with a distinction between effeminate, passive genius or fancy on the one hand and virile, active genius on the other. Thus Jean Paul Richter's *Vorschule der Aesthetik* distinguishes between the feminine *weibliche Phantasie* and the presumably more masculine *Phantasie* of artistic genius. Twentieth-century critics, as Celeste Schenck has shown, go even further in identifying mechanical creativity with the "feminine": "poetesses," it has been suggested, write "straight-jacket, rhymed verse" that mutilates the organic beauty of the poem-in-process.[28]

Even such images of castration or of female castration can be turned around and revalued. Hélène Cixous's essay on "Decapitation" offers a Lacanian explanation for her theory of women's subversive literary production. Because woman lies "outside the Symbolic" for Freud and Lacan, these thinkers also postulate that woman's entry into language is organized by her "lack." Indeed, woman is "ever caught in her chain of metaphors." Cixous locates the reemergence of the repressed feminine psyche in a challenge to masculinist dualisms or hierarchies. A "feminine textual body," she writes, will be "without ending" or closure; it allows "breaks, 'parts,' partings, separations."[29] The metaphor of a "feminine textual body" animates and gives genital, procreative force to Cixous's concept of narrative breaks and openings. Elsewhere she turns to images grounded in maternal production, comparing experimental, "feminine" writing to inscription in "white ink."[30]

French feminists have relied extensively on body images to ground their theories of sexual difference and lend poetic force to their theories. In order to distinguish between a monological, masculinist theory of the textual body, and a dialogical, feminist theory, Luce Irigaray has recourse to images of female genitalia. For her, the key body image is that of the "two lips" that are not lips.[31] Julia Kristeva likewise uses a language of the body that draws on Gestalt theory in order to project modes of innovation. These will "break with the . . . specular relations ruling the coherence, the identification, of the individual" by creating a voice closer to the "flesh" of language, more tactile, indeed at the threshold not only of "feeling" but of the involuntary, allied to menstrual flow and vomiting.[32] In a metalanguage that itself violates taboos, she exhorts an artistic innovation that will necessarily cross such barriers.

As Naomi Schor has pointed out, the project of rooting feminist theory in images of the female body is a "risky enterprise," for it implicitly valorizes the essential and biologically unique aspects of femininity; specific images such as the vagina or clitoris lead to preoccupation with specific forms, such as metaphor or synecdoche.[33] Schor and Kristeva help us see what is problematical in these theories. Not only is the syntactical existence of a "women's language" dubious, but the creative model offered up by this approach has two shortcomings. First, the identification of women's writing with formal subversion collapses distinctions between the conditions of production experienced by women and by other minority groups and simply identifies women's writing with the avant-garde. Second, Kristeva suspects that attacks against language and sign as the ultimate supports of phallocratic power may be self-defeating and "phantasmic" or illusory, insofar as they operate in the name of "a semi-aphonic corporality whose truth can only be found in that which is 'gestural' or 'tonal' " (32).

Another difficulty would be the implicit devaluing of actual experience by the deliberate exploitation of shocking bodily images to describe critical practices. How should we respond when Spivak uses the image of rape to condemn Western critics who engage in "information retrieval" and thus exploit the work of Third World writers and critics to obtain cost-free, token evidence of multiculturalism or diversity? Rape and the sale of women and children into the sex trade are a literal product of economic imbalances and discrimination; their distribution on an urban and international map coincides with political upheavals, poverty, race, and sex. The pain and social costs of rape can be erased by identifying it with the visual "rape" that occurs when a reader assumes the ethically dubious position of voyeur.[34]

The cultural variety of women's experiences and forms of literary production invites a multiplicity of critical approaches and metaphors. It was logical for "gynocritics" who focused on writing by women to turn to metaphors of the female body in order to break the hold of masculinist models of literary production; but such feminocentric models should not gain exclusive or defining force. Rather, if we multiply the schemes through which we frame our literary analyses, it may be possible to escape the confinement of binaries that regulate most of our systems of value. The images on which we build our criticism are made of shifting sands; by exploring the site of our critical self-production, we can more quickly recognize the covert, treacherous biases of class, race, and gender.

It is important also not to reify male and female critics, but rather to identify common rhetorical strategies deployed by a range of contemporary critics, as well as their differences. The gender of critical metaphors has been readily reversible in the past: logical organization and tight rhyme schemes may be virile in the eighteenth century, but effeminate in the early twentieth. Ornament may be masculine for Cicero, but feminine for Bachelard. Once we recognize the arbitrariness of those gender assignments, we can become attuned to the ways that our metaphors limit or liberate our critical vision.

Because critical metaphors presume prior maps of reading but also become signposts to artists, they are two-way streets. Our notions of a text that is open or closed, smooth or rough, high or low depend upon conventional expectations that channel their own violation. Those expectations, we should remember, take shape within specific literary cultures that bear the imprint of economic and political structures of power—structures that may dictate what access women have to education, what rules of linguistic propriety they face, and what entries they find to the marketplace of ideas. Thus the social geography of gender weighs heavily on our formulation of critical metaphors, with their valences of value.

NOTES

1. Gaston Bachelard, *The Poetics of Space* (New York: Orion, 1964) 24, 96. Bachelard's relish for "intimate" spaces, however, blurs gender attributions.

2. See Paul Fussell, *The Great War and Modern Memory* (London: Oxford UP, 1975), chapter 7; Bella Brodzki and Celeste Schenck, eds., *Life/Lines: Theorizing Women's Auto-*

biography (Ithaca: Cornell UP, 1988); Eve Kosofsky Sedgwick, *The Epistemology of the Closet* (Berkeley: U of California P, 1990); Elizabeth Abel, Marianne Hirsch, and Elizabeth Langland, eds., *The Voyage In: Fictions of Female Development* (Hanover: UP of New England, 1983); Nancy Armstrong, *Desire and Domestic Fiction: A Political History of the Novel* (New York: Oxford UP, 1987).

3. Daphne Spain, *Gendered Spaces* (Chapel Hill: U of North Carolina P, 1992) 3.

4. Ruth Salvaggio, "Theory and Space, Space and Women," *Tulsa Studies in Women's Literature* 7 (1988): 261.

5. Robert J. Clements, *Comparative Literature as Academic Discipline: A Statement of Principles, Praxis, Standards* (New York: Modern Language Association, 1978) 21.

6. Patricia Parker, *Literary Fat Ladies: Rhetoric, Gender, Property* (London: Methuen, 1987), especially chapters 2, 3, and 6.

7. See Alice Jardine, *Gynesis: Configurations of Woman and Modernity* (Ithaca: Cornell UP, 1985) 178–207; Jacques Derrida, *Disseminations,* trans. Barbara Johnson (Chicago: U of Chicago P, 1981) 209–215.

8. Gaston Bachelard, *La poétique de la rêverie* (Paris: Presses Universitaires de Frances, 1965) 17. See Margaret Higonnet, "Métaphores mortelles: *L'Eau et les rêves,*" *Cahiers internationaux de symbolisme* 53–55 (1986): 47–48.

9. Immanuel Kant, *Observations on the Feeling of the Beautiful and Sublime,* trans. John Goldthwait (Berkeley: U of California P, 1960) 76–77; Edmund Burke, *A Philosophical Enquiry into the Origin of Our Ideas of the Sublime and Beautiful* (London: Routledge and Kegan Paul, 1967) 124, 110.

10. René Wellek and Austin Warren, *Theory of Literature* (New York: Harcourt Brace & World, 1956) 61, 244.

11. Deborah McDowell points out that experimental African American texts that record patterns of regional speech have been treated as subliterary.

12. Gayatri Chakravorty Spivak, *In Other Worlds: Essays in Cultural Politics* (New York: Routledge, 1988) 26.

13. Sandra Gilbert and Susan Gubar have exposed the mechanisms of exclusion in a theory of literary influence such as that of Harold Bloom in their landmark volume *The Madwoman in the Attic: The Woman Writer and the Nineteenth-Century Literary Imagination* (New Haven: Yale UP, 1979), chapter 1, *passim.*

14. Claude Pichois and A.-M. Rousseau, *La littérature comparée* (Paris: Colin, 1974).

15. It should be noted that these institutions are changing. Mary Ann Caws and Christopher Prendergast have edited a new, more truly multicultural comparative literature reader: the *Harper-Collins World Literature Reader* (New York: Harper-Collins, 1993), and older anthologies are under revision.

16. Gerald Graff, *Professing Literature: An Institutional History* (Chicago: U of Chicago P, 1987) 7, 10.

17. For all its sophistication in identifying a multiplicity of approaches that draw on two disciplines, the MLA volume devoted to this topic continues to be governed by such binarisms. Jean-Pierre Barricelli and Joseph Gibaldi, *Interrelations of Literature* (New York: Modern Language Association, 1982).

18. Jane Marcus, "Registering Objections: Grounding Feminist Alibis," in this volume.

19. Elaine Showalter, "Feminist Criticism in the Wilderness," *The New Feminist Criticism: Essays on Women, Literature, and Theory,* ed. Showalter (New York: Pantheon, 1985) 261–263.

20. Gloria Anzaldúa, *Borderlands/La Frontera: The New Mestiza* (San Francisco: Spinsters/Aunt Lute, 1987) 3.

21. Gayatri Chakravorty Spivak, *The Post-colonial Critic: Interviews, Strategies, Dialogues* (New York: Routledge, 1990) 40.

22. Joseph Frank, *The Idea of Spatial Form* (New Brunswick: Rutgers UP, 1991). This volume includes his later essays from *Critical Inquiry*.

23. Sigrid Weigel, "Double Focus: On the History of Women's Writing," *Feminist Aesthetics*, ed. Gisela Ecker (London: Women's, 1985) 71, 67. See also Weigel's *Topographien der Geschlechter: Kulturgeschichtliche Studien zur Literatur* (Reinbek/Hamburg: Rowohlt, 1990). Salvaggio points to other related images, such as Teresa de Lauretis's use of the term *space-off* from film theory to describe an implied but unrepresented space alongside the camera, whose image the spectator reconstructs (273).

24. Virginia Woolf, *A Room of One's Own* (New York: Harcourt Brace Jovanovich, 1981) 85, 95.

25. Rachel Blau DuPlessis, *Writing beyond the Ending: Narrative Strategies of Twentieth-Century Women Writers* (Bloomington: Indiana UP, 1985).

26. Claudine Herrmann, *Les Voleuses de langue* (Paris: des femmes, 1976) 161.

27. Xavière Gauthier, "Surrealism and Sexuality," *New French Feminisms,* ed. Elaine Marks and Isabelle de Courtivron (Amherst: U of Massachusetts P, 1980) 164.

28. Celeste Schenck, "Exiled by Genre: Modernism, Canonicity, and the Politics of Exclusion," *Women's Writing in Exile*, ed. Mary Lynn Broe and Angela Ingram (Chapel Hill: U of North Carolina P, 1989) 226–229.

29. Hélène Cixous, "Castration or Decapitation," trans. Annette Kuhn, *Signs* 7 (1981): 44, 53.

30. Hélène Cixous, "The Laugh of the Medusa," *New French Feminisms* 251.

31. Luce Irigaray, *This Sex Which Is Not One,* trans. Catherine Porter (Ithaca: Cornell UP, 1985) 24.

32. Julia Kristeva, "Women's Time," *Signs* 7 (1981): 24–25.

33. Naomi Schor, "Female Paranoia: The Case for Psychoanalytic Feminist Criticism," *Yale French Studies* 62 (1981): 214.

34. See Rajeswari Sunder Rajan, "Life after Rape: Narrative, Theory, and Feminism," *Borderwork: Feminist Engagements with Comparative Literature,* ed. Margaret R. Higonnet (Ithaca: Cornell UP, forthcoming).